Joy Packer was born and brought up in South Africa and, on her husband's retirement, they decided to build a house and settle in the Cape Peninsula. 'What will you write about now?' she was asked. 'There won't be all those exciting travels anymore.'

In *Home From Sea*, the fourth volume in her autobiography, she describes how she first began to write fiction – fiction with a background of fact. She tells how her first novel *Valley of the Vines* was a fantastic success and how her second novel, *Nor the Moon by Night*, was filmed in a valley in Zululand. She learns about wine-growing at the Cape, meets the rangers of the wild-life sanctuaries in the Transvaal and Natal and the whalemen who go down to the ice.

She shares, too, her own hopes and anxieties, comedies and tragedies, and the simple philosophy that is the outcome of a wide experience of living . . .

Also by Joy Packer

Fiction
THE HIGH ROOF
NOR THE MOON BY NIGHT
THE GLASS BARRIER

Non-Fiction
PACK AND FOLLOW
THE GREY MISTRESS
APES AND IVORY

and published by Corgi Books

Joy Packer

Home from Sea

Home is the sailor, home from sea,
And the hunter home from the hill.

ROBERT LOUIS STEVENSON,

Requiem

CORGI BOOKS
A DIVISION OF TRANSWORLD PUBLISHERS LTD

HOME FROM SEA

A CORGI BOOK 0 552 09558 3

Originally published in Great Britain
by Eyre & Spottiswoode (Publishers) Ltd.

PRINTING HISTORY
Eyre & Spottiswoode edition published 1963
Eyre & Spottiswoode edition second impression 1963
Eyre & Spottiswoode edition third impression 1964
Corgi edition published 1974

Corgi Books are published by
Transworld Publishers Ltd.,
Cavendish House, 57–59 Uxbridge Road,
Ealing, London W.5.
Made and printed in Great Britain by
Cox & Wyman Ltd., London, Reading and Fakenham

Contents

FOREWORD

HOME FROM SEA was completed, after an interruption, early in 1963. It covers not only personal events and experiences – happy, sad, and sometimes frightening – but a mounting crisis in my own country (South Africa). This period is reflected with the immediacy of my close involvement with its every stage at many human levels. I reported it from day to day in my "scribble book" with an insight less objectively academic than that of a visiting reporter, for I am an eleventh generation South African of Huguenot, Dutch, Danish, German and English-Irish extraction. These blood-ingredients descended from various migrations from Europe to Africa, cannot help but result in a deeper understanding of the explosive situations arising from the conflicts inherent in my country's history.

Now, re-reading HOME FROM SEA for the first time since I passed the proofs over ten years ago, I can honestly state that I do not wish to retract one single opinion – or warning – expressed in this book written during a thought-provoking and often alarming period of the utmost significance to South Africa.

Joy Packer.

Cape of Good Hope. 1973.

CHAPTER ONE

AN END AND A BEGINNING

OUR little Chelsea flat was in a turmoil of excitement.

My husband was getting ready to go to Buckingham Palace to be received in audience by the Queen. He had recently returned from South Africa, where he had flown his flag as Commander-in-Chief of the South Atlantic Station, and it is customary for the Queen to talk to her admirals after the termination of such commands.

Our daily help, Mrs. Elton, had removed the flimsy strips of orange paper that protected the broad gold rings on his sleeves and brushed every speck of fluff from his navy blue uniform. I pinned the long bar of medals across his chest, and the K.C.B. star beneath it, and tied the ribbon of the C.B.E. order under his collar. He fastened his sword belt and turned to me for inspection.

'You'll do,' I said.

It was noon on a spring morning in 1953. The sun shone, the pigeons wheeled round the spire of the bombed church outside our windows and sparrows twittered in some newly-planted trees. A few gulls planed in from the river, white-winged and nostalgic, mewing of seas and oceans the wide world over. I will never see the flight of a gull without the ghosts of grey warships rising to haunt me.

Our great friend, Hillie Longstaff, came to lunch. Her taxi crossed with my husband's in the courtyard, and she waved. She laughed as she greeted me.

'So there he goes, in all his glory! Aren't you envious?'

'Not today. This is his own particular naval occasion.'

An hour later he was back and Hillie scratched her cheek on that impressive row of medals as she welcomed him.

'Darling, you look like a man in love! What did she wear?'

He unbuckled his sword-belt as he answered her question.

'A nice blue dress,' I repeated. 'I'm glad it was nice.'

'An *ice*-blue dress! I knew you'd want to know. It was a lovely ice-blue dress. Her hair was lovely too – soft and natural. So was everything about her.'

I poured him a seamanlike pink gin.

'I don't need it,' he said.

But he raised his glass to 'The Queen – God bless her!'

We made him tell us all about it. There were no delays – just a few minutes in an ante-room talking to a very pleasant Equerry – a Group Captain in the Royal Air Force. Good-looking too in a tense, fine-drawn way. And brave. His name was Peter Townsend. Townsend had ushered him into a small room, where the Queen stood alone.

As she sat down she made a sign to her visitor to do the same.

She was poised and relaxed, deeply interested in South Africa, and showed considerable knowledge and understanding of that most difficult of her great Dominions. But she was personal too. She knew that this Admiral had been at Dartmouth with her father, and she spoke of the late King George VI with simple daughterly affection.

My husband said: 'I was in the Royal Navy before I was thirteen. I served your great-grandfather, King Edward VII, your grandfather, your father ... and now you, Ma'am.'

She looked at him with sympathetic eyes – this young lovely Queen he was so proud to serve – and remarked gently that it would be very hard for him to say good-bye to the Royal Navy. She asked him what he planned to do when he retired.

'I am going to settle in South Africa.'

Yes, she knew that his wife was South African, and it was a beautiful country – with a perfect climate. She smiled as she wished him luck and happiness.

That day he packed away his uniform. He had worn it for the last time.

That same spring I finished *Apes and Ivory*, the third of my naval travel autobiographies. They'd brought me round full circle, those three volumes, *Pack and Follow* with its light-hearted beginnings in the land of my birth, a youthful marriage, a little son and the world my oyster as I chased round the globe in the wake of my naval officer husband and his grey warships: *Grey Mistress* when the shadow of the war years fell upon us: and now this more mature account of two years in an official position, journeying around and across the vast African continent, by sea, air and land, visiting States and Dependencies in various stages of evolution and 'emergence', and trying to see the future pattern of newly awakened Black Africa.

The book was several weeks overdue, and it was with a sigh of relief that I finally wrapped up the typescript and prepared to take it to my publisher. Mrs. Elton looked at the litter of papers on the table in our dining-alcove.

'What about this lot?'

'Into the wastebasket.'

'That poor wastebasket – always bulging with your throw-out papers! But now it's really finished – your book?'

She had children and grandchildren to keep her young, and she understood 'hobbies'. My writing was to her a rather extreme form of hobby, one to be treated with respect. She would come in of a morning, 'run through the flat', as she put it, give me a 'cuppa' and say, 'Now I'll shut you in,' after which she'd do my marketing and prepare the lunch.

'Yes, at last it's really finished. I'm going to take it to the publishers right now.'

Like the Queen, Mrs. Elton recognized a moment of transition.

'When the Admiral retires and you're living in South Africa there won't be all those travels to write about, will there?'

'Not in the same way. We're going to put down roots.'

The raw material I had used so lavishly in my writing would be gone. But, after all, life itself was raw material, never mind the travel and adventures in far away lands.

'There's fiction,' I said.

She turned the word over in her mind.

'Fiction. Stories, you mean?'

'Novels.'

'That's love and crime.'

It was my turn to reflect. 'Why, yes. Boil it down, and there you have it. Love and crime, that's life.'

She had pretty daughters, and a policeman in the family. 'It certainly is!' she agreed. 'You'd better hurry, hadn't you?'

I took my parcel and caught the Number Eleven bus from the King's Road to the Strand and rejoiced in the familiar enchantment of springtime London. The plane trees were always the first to show their flags of green; blossom nodded in squares and crescents; regiments of tulips paraded in the parks; window-boxes glowed with colour, and doors and railings were painted bright frivolous reds, blues and primrose or mustard yellow. Yellow was popular that year.

I walked up from the Strand towards Covent Garden with its echoes of grand opera and its emanations of the vegetable market all mixed up with the dingy exciting smell of newsprint. Here were the unpretentious offices of publishers and literary agents, the premises of printers and those dark little cafés where aspiring authors go for a cup of hot coffee and a bun to allay the nervous emptiness which assails them as they wait to hear a verdict on the work which has, for months or years, been the focal point of all their hopes and fears.

I climbed the steep narrow staircase to the book-lined lair of the editor-in-chief.

She was sitting at her desk in front of the window and she turned round on her swivel-chair as I entered. The desk was littered with manuscripts, printer's proofs, jacket designs, advance copies of catalogues and new publications, and a wire basket crammed with correspondence. Undismayed, she made room for my bulky type-script and swept a pile of books from the only other chair in the room to allow me to sit down. Her unhurried manner and deep lazy voice contradicted the evidence on the desk and suggested that she had all the time in the world for discussion with her authors.

'Where do you go from here?' she asked, when we'd settled the outstanding matters concerning *Apes and Ivory*.

'There you've got me. I'd like to have a shot at fiction. But a journalist may not be a novelist. I did try – once. The effort finished in the wastebasket.'

'First novels almost always do. The so-called first novel is usually the third. In any case, you shouldn't find it difficult to master a new technique, or to harness your interest in human nature to fiction. You make fact read like fiction, so why not make fiction read like fact?'

She knew the quick depressions and elations of creative authors and was encouraging wherever possible.

'I don't even know what should come first,' I said. 'The characters or the plot.'

'There's no rule. The place might come first. Think of somewhere you want to write about. The people and the situations – call it the plot, if you like – will follow. But don't try to force the pace. The idea has to take root in your mind. It has to grow there and work on you.'

When I left her it was with the feeling that it would be tremendously exciting to break out in a new direction.

We arrived in Cape Town by the mailship early on a November morning. Gaunt old Table Mountain, facing out to sea like a fortress rampart between her watch-towers, Devil's Peak and Lion's Head, was in one of her ethereal summer moods, veiled in a lavender heat-haze, while the city at her feet shimmered among palms and flowering shrubs.

We had taken a small flat to tide us over the few months during which we would be building our first and last home together.

We knew what we wanted. All our married lives we had lived in other people's houses. Some had been fun and others dreary. The dreary ones had been 'digs' in home ports and a semi-basement flat in London. The fun included various Moorish flat-roofed houses in Malta with stone floors and narrow gardens looking down upon the historic battlements of the Knights and grey warships in sparkling creeks. In the clear Mediterranean air bugle calls from the ships had floated up the many-tiered steps and terraces to mingle with the music of goat-bells and the melodious chiming of the angelus. There'd been blissful summers too in the tiny North China island of Wei-Hai-Wei off the mountainous coast of Shantung, where the war-lords were always fighting each other while pirates seized merchant vessels and bandits kidnapped anybody they reckoned worth a ransom. An arrogant North Chinese 'Number One', aided by a flock of 'makee-learn' coolies, had run our flimsy bungalow and I was constantly entranced by our little 'washee-washee-sew-sew' *amah* who had a bird voice and tiny bound feet like the hooves of a fawn.

But the Greek villa on the shores of the Aegean, a few

miles out of Athens, had been as near our dream house as it would be possible to find.

My husband had been a Captain then, Naval Attaché to Greece, Turkey and Yugoslavia with headquarters in Athens. His pay, by our naval standards, was lavish for, in that appointment, he was paid on the Foreign Office scale and enjoyed all the financial as well as social perquisites of the privileged Diplomatic Corps. So we were able to spread ourselves and take a charming villa belonging to a young Athenian film starlet whose career had wafted her away to London. The villa had a summery spaciousness. A decorative staircase curved down into the living-room, which was part of the dining-room, although on a lower level to give it loftiness. Both led on to a wide terrace and a casual garden which was tended erratically by a handsome lad who wore a scarlet flower behind his ear and sang a great deal.

This villa on the shores of Homer's 'wine dark sea' was the inspiration for our South African home. We too put in wide landscape windows to allow us to enjoy our view to the full. And what a wonderful view it is! Often, when I should be scribbling diligently, I am sitting tapping my teeth with the rubber end of my pencil, gazing across the wooded Kirstenbosch valley to the mighty southern bastions of Devil's Peak and Table Mountain, or across the distant Flats spreading north to the jagged amethyst ranges between us and the vast hinterland of Africa.

Before the year was out a bulldozer was growling back and forth over the building site at the summit of our steep two acre plot on its high ridge.

'Those silvers in the top corner – whatever happens please don't harm them!' I implored the young man who drove the juggernaut. 'Nor the tall stone pines.'

He did his best, but a silver took a nudge that set it at an angle of forty-five degrees for life. It's the one I love most. In Spring it seems to lean forward and hold its flowers out for inspection so that we may see them growing in the shining saucers of protective leaves. First the flower is no more than a tiny reel of pale grey silk, then it shows a yellow heart like a baby chicken which develops into a furry cone about the size of a golf ball. When the cones fell to the ground my grandsons would collect them to scatter in their own garden so that they too might have silver-trees. But silvers hug their mountain slopes, living in beauty and dying, like human beings, suddenly of unexpected diseases. If you plant them where they aren't happy they wither slowly because they are homesick and there is nothing to be done for that sickness.

We decided to call our home 'Cressage' after my husband's birthplace, and we planted an oak to remind us of 'Christ's Oak' from which the Shropshire village of Cressage derives its name. In his native village you can still see the riven shell of that ancient Shropshire gospel oak under which the early missionaries used to preach, but now it has a strong new young oak growing up through the hollow trunk and overtopping it. Our South African oak – a pin-oak – is tall already and spreads a lacey green umbrella over a rose bed where Peace and Queen Elizabeth bloom side by side.

The adventure of building was a big thrill for us and we haunted the site. Bantu, Coloureds and Malays were all employed, the Bantu doing the heavy unskilled tasks such as unloading and heaving bricks, which they threw to one another with a rhythmic movement and a Xhosa chant, so that it was like part of a modern builder's ballet. The Coloureds and Malays did most of the skilled and semi-skilled work.

Quite often we'd go to 'Cressage' in the evening after the builder's lorry had fetched the team. Only Thomas, the watchman, would be left.

Thomas was a lanky cheerful fellow with Bantu features slightly modified by the Coloured blood of his mother. He was the cross-breed now becoming increasingly common at the Cape where once the tribesmen and the Cape-Coloureds would never have deigned to mix, each sure of their superiority over the others. The Coloureds have always set great store by their White blood and the Bantu prided themselves on racial purity. The Malays and the Coloureds, too, inter-marry more and more frequently, and almost every such marriage is a gain to the Moslem faith.

Thomas, squatting over his little fire, greeted us by touching his hand to the fanciful emerald-green 'jellybag' that covered his frizzy head, and which had most likely been knitted for him by the dark lady who kept him nightly company when his work-mates had gone their way.

'Now, who's that broody old vulture?'

Bertie glanced in the direction of an aged Coloured man

crouched on a mound of earth thrown up by the bulldozer at some time during its performance.

'He's been here before,' I said. 'He lurks around.'

The old man rose and descended from his perch to introduce himself. The moment had come, it seemed, when we would be well advised to employ him and his henchmen. There were many things that needed doing before the winter rains washed our neighbour's garden into our backyard and carried our soil away into the Liesbeek River. He would build us a wall of mountain stone to shore up our back border, he would turf our lower banks, and clear our wilderness of wattle and noxious weeds where the juggernaut had not been permitted to make a dust-bowl of the bush. He would build us rockeries and lay the crazy-paving of our terrace.

'How do you propose to set about all this?' asked my husband.

'I got three men working with me. Master pay us each week as we go along. I get the stone and the slate and Master give cash for it.'

'Where will I find samples of your work?'

He made an extensive gesture. His work was all over the estate. He told us the names of houses and their owners where we could see and judge for ourselves.

Bertie took his little diary from his pocket.

'What is your address? I'll write it down.'

But the old man shook his head. 'No need.' He indicated the Kirstenbosch valley. 'I live down there by the willage in the hollow. Yus' ask for Mr. Bent. Anyone will know where to find me.'

He tipped his battered felt hat and ambled away down the earth track that would later be our drive.

We stayed awhile, realizing that the old man was right. Turf and stone were certainly needed if we were to keep our soil on this steep slope. We could picture a garden that was already forming its own natural shape in front of the house.

We left Thomas singing to himself by his little fire in the bloom of the autumn dusk, and we knew that, when we had gone, the plump dark shadow of his woman would materialize out of the pinewood to join him for his evening meal.

Next day we drove round the estate and saw the walls and rockeries that were monuments to the skill and industry of

Mr. Bent. The walls were works of art, rough-hewn mosaics of rosy mountain-stone. Big grey 'monkey-face' boulders sustained rockeries where weird aloes and succulents adapted their Karoo and desert habits to this well-watered mountainside. We headed down into 'the willage in the hollow' to hunt out our craftsman.

There were scores of merry dark-skinned children in that village, the woods their playground; and the washing that hung on the lines in sunny glades fluttered like the bright-hued banners of a gay people.

'It's got the feel of a West Indian village,' Bertie said. 'Even unto the palms and pawpaw trees, dogs, cats, fowls and babies and lots of life and music.'

The music was its breath of life. On summer nights it floats up to the ridge. There is a trumpeter too – maybe a lad from the Boys' Brigade – and the old traditional calls come sweetly from the hollow. On 5th November the children swarm on to the affluent estate, carrying their Guy on an old stool like a sedan chair, or in a soap-box cart. Their faces are clownishly daubed; some sport skittish little tails while others play their mouth-organs and home-made bamboo flutes or perhaps a guitar or a mandolin, and they sing and dance with tremendous verve. '*Got* no farder, *got* no mudder, *penny* for de poor ole guy!' Coins flash into their palms as they romp off to the next fine house for further contributions. Then, when night falls, we can hear the fire-crackers and laughter and see the rockets leap up into the stars and fall in showers of golden rain. On Christmas Eve they come in their good clothes and sing carols, sweet and clear, and there is no buffoonery.

We stopped the car to ask where we could find Mr. Bent. A party of jostling children swarmed into it. He was out working, but they would show us where to go.

They directed us in a roundabout fashion, for the fun of the drive, and we wound up at last on the highest point of the estate, where the old man and his trio were rounding off their labours by planting out banks of agapanthus lilies.

My husband and Mr. Bent soon came to a satisfactory financial arrangement; a day was fixed for work to begin at 'Cressage', and we returned our giggling guides to the 'willage in the hollow'.

A new entrancing phase of our lives had begun. The seeds

of a garden had been scattered in our imagination. Green thoughts were sinking in and taking root. From the outset the garden was Bertie's. It was his care and responsibility, but I contributed ideas when I liked, and to both of us it was always a continual joy.

By the late autumn the shell of our home was complete.

I was particularly in love with the open corner fireplace in the living-room. The master builder had personally seen that the yellow mountain stone was left as rough and chunky as I wished, with two comfortable stone hobs on either side, 'So that you can practically sit in the fireplace if you want to,' I explained.

'The hearth is the heart of the home,' he said. 'You must have it as you want it.'

One evening, when we happened to pass near our future home, I said to my husband, 'Let's go to "Cressage". It's not out of our way and it's only half past seven.'

'It's pitch dark,' he said. 'We won't see much.'

But he turned into our road and up the track to the house. The window panes were in already, smeared with big crosses to remind the workmen to take care. A flag flew from the highest point of the roof and, lo and behold, smoke curled out of the chimney. It was cold and clear with the first nip of winter in the air.

'Thomas must be trying out the fireplace,' said Bertie, as we got out of the car and went round the terrace-to-be. 'I don't think it's fair to disturb him.'

But women are less sensitive and more inquisitive than men, and I couldn't resist peeping through the glass. Silently I took my husband's hand and drew him forward so that he could share a simple domestic tableau.

A wood-fire blazed merrily in the open hearth. A bottle of red wine stood before it. On one hob sat Thomas, smoking his little carved pipe with the filigree cap, on the other sat the dark lady of the woods, her knitting in her hands. They were laughing and extremely at home. It was a picture I shall never forget.

'They even mull their wine!' I whispered, as we tiptoed stealthily away.

Yet we didn't really feel intruders, for that glimpse of contentment at our own future fireside had warmed us both. It was surely a good omen.

CHAPTER TWO

A BEGINNING AND AN END

WHILE all this was going on – the planning and building of our first real home together and the renewing of old friendships – both my husband and I were being drawn into the particular interests that were to keep us busy and occupied during the years of retirement ahead. Among many other activities he became Federal President of the Navy League of South Africa, a nation-wide association encouraging a love and understanding of the sea in the youth of this country which depends for her existence upon her searoutes and their protection. Meanwhile, I was already deep in my first serious attempt to graduate from travel-autobiography into the creative sphere of novel-writing.

Up to now I had interpreted places, people and events in a purely personal way. But, apart from a new technique, a novelist would need a more intimate brand of insight into character, and a wide objective viewpoint, especially a South African novelist. And I fully intended to write about my own controversial country because it is, to me, the most beautiful and interesting in the world with its immense scenic and climatic variety, and its human beings of many races trying to get along together, sometimes failing and often succeeding.

I decided to set my scene in the beautiful Constantia Valley only a stone's throw from our new home. We were on the Table Bay side of the ridge and Constantia is on the False Bay side with the wide sweep of its vineyards lying between the purple spine of mountains and the sparkling sea.

From childhood the valley had enthralled me.

We had often spent Sundays there at 'Bel Ombre', the home of my mother's brother, Uncle Piet Marais, and his wife, Aunt Ethel, and their children. The Marais' and Aunt Ethel's Rathfelder relations owned many morgen in the valley, and most of the families round about were connected by blood or marriage and divided by immortal but half forgotten vendettas.

The true core and glory of this gradually shrinking greenbelt is, of course, the beautiful homestead of Groote Constantia, which once belonged to the Cloete Family and is now part of the Government Wine Farm. (Its decorative gable and a bunch of purple grapes are pictured on the 2½ cent stamps of the new South African Republic.) The Cloetes still battle on at historic Alphen, growing grapes and making Constantia wine as their ancestors have done for generations, but under increasing difficulties. With the suburban tentacles of Cape Town extending into the vineyards and putting up the price of land and labour it is no longer an economic proposition to farm in a big way near the city. However, few of these financial considerations made much impact on my youthful imagination. It was Aunt Ethel's personality that impressed me most, and her spirit that symbolized the lovely quarrelsome valley of the vines.

She was a bundle of contradictions. Kittenish and kind, yet autocratic where 'Bel Ombre' was concerned. My Uncle Piet died in early middle age and from then on the farm was her care and her love, shared jealously with her children. She regarded her land with a fierce combination of adoration and avarice and knew its worth down to the last pebble and grape-pip. She was capable of loyal friendships and lasting feuds, which was very much in tune with the valley where road and water rights roused passions to fever heat and took their place in the foreground of many a complex web of love and crime.

Some years after my uncle's death, Aunt Ethel married a widower whose family had grown up with her own children. But she refused to leave 'Bel Ombre', so her new husband sold his magnificent farm and joined her in the part of the valley she so dearly loved.

I have pleasant recollections of old 'Pam' Cloete, my Uncle Piet's successor. He called Aunt Ethel 'Wifey' and had courtly manners and the Cloete good looks. When he grew venerable he took to wearing a woollen skull-cap or jaunty yellow beret because the top of his head was always cold, and this little eccentricity added an individual touch to his habitual air of distinction. He loathed motor-cars and petrol fumes and his tall figure on horseback was a familiar and respected sight in the district.

When she was over seventy Aunt Ethel fell downstairs and sustained an injury to her leg that eventually necessitated the amputation of the limb. She expressed herself 'thankful to be rid of the darn thing'. Her courage was remarkable and she soon learned to use her wheel-chair with great aplomb. When she could not negotiate it herself over uneven or terraced ground she summoned her young Coloured attendant in his starched white uniform. Her Golden Labradors never left her side, and with them at her wheels she continued to inspect every inch of her vineyards, orchards and packing-sheds and issue her orders with the same asperity as before. If she required one of her retainers she blew a shrill blast on the police-whistle hanging round her neck on a black velvet cord.

Her children and their families lived round about, and this part of the valley is still called 'Les Marais', though 'Bel Ombre' has changed hands and is now known as the 'Barn Theatre' which brings interesting plays to country audiences.

'When I was a kid,' I said to Bertie, 'the whole of Constantia was green, with just a few big homes among all those wonderful oaks and orchards and vineyards. In spring the blue lupins were like a ground-mist under the young vines, with guinea-fowl running between them. Now, whenever one of the old folk dies, the heirs cut up the property. It's being urbanized with horrid new houses biting into the green-belt like sharks' teeth.'

'Your theme,' he suggested. 'The conflict between old and new – the valley as it was and as it is becoming.'

Very soon I came up against a major snag – my own ignorance. It was not enough to be able to visualize the valley and its people in all their moods. I must learn about their work – the growing of grapes and making of wine, the disasters that could befall a crop, and the problems that make every season a new hazard for the farmer and his labour.

Soon after our arrival in Cape Town our friends, Dudley and Beryl Kiernander, came to the rescue. They at that time owned 'Natte Valleij' ('Wet Valley'), an historic wine farm near Klapmuts, less than an hour's drive from Cape Town. I was given 'the freedom of the farm' at all seasons and time and again enjoyed the hospitality of my helpful hosts.

Bertie left me to it. He encouraged and criticized, but took no part in my work.

The homestead, with its central Dutch gable, was one of the earliest in the district. The original title deeds of 1705, yellowed and mottled with age, were written in a copperplate Nederlands script and included permission for the owner to shoot 'a load of hippopotamus or eland meat' when he required it for his household or his slaves.

The house, shaded by ancient oaks, is characteristic of the original Cape architecture. Single-storeyed with a deep thatched roof cradled by two side gables; a teak front door surmounted by a carved fanlight and single graceful gable; a high stoep with a stone *bankie* at either end and teak shutters hooked back against white walls dappled by the fluid shadow of oak leaves. A spacious *voorkamer* – or entrance hall – leads into the *agterkamer* which is the true living-room of the house. Inside everything is dim and cool and lofty with yellowwood floors and rafters and heavy old Dutch furniture with silver fittings wrought by the hands of long dead Malay craftsmen. There are many such homes in the leafy valleys of the Cape.

I spent a few days there with my friends at the beginning of February during the picking and crushing season.

All day long men, women and children worked in the vineyards, gathering the harvest into the great wicker baskets. The picking was done by the Coloureds, whose ancestors were tending the vines of Good Hope three centuries ago. Even now, many of the descendants of slaves identify themselves with farms that bred their forebears and with families whose fluctuating fortunes moulded their own. But it is important to remember that the Dutch East India Company, which first colonized the Cape, permitted none of the indigenous population to be enslaved, and 'black ivory' was only imported because the idle, feckless Hottentots had an inborn aversion to any form of work. In the course of years many bloods have mingled to evolve our Coloured people, who are gay, moody, God-fearing, no more reliable than most of us, and possessed of wit as quick and penetrating in its own way as that of the London Cockney. They have, in the towns, developed a solid, respectable, well-educated middle class; they have a number of highly intellectual and sadly frustrated leaders and various gifted and enthusiastic cultural groups, but a sense of inferiority is forced upon them by the laws of *apartheid* and a new bitter twist has found its way into their songs and jokes and budding literature.

In the gabled cellar, adjacent to the house, and looking like a humbler twin to it, the harvest was being tipped into the crusher, and soon the juice – 'must' as it is called – was bubbling merrily in the great fermenting tanks. I remembered the vintage in Greece, and the smiling peasants standing in the doorways of their little white houses, their bare feet stained from crushing the grapes in the old pagan fashion just as the slaves of the Cape had once danced round in the great vats, the soles of their merry feet pulping the harvest that would one day find its way to Europe and the tables of kings and connoisseurs as the wine of Good Hope.

I stood with my friends in the cool sour-smelling cellar watching the must heave and swirl as it approached the 'stormy period' of fermentation. The white wine was made in closed tanks without the 'doppies' – the skins – but the red, in its open cement tanks, bubbled and agonized, throwing up waves of sickly-smelling spume.

'If you fell in there you'd be dead in a few seconds,' said Beryl, who has a keen sense of theatre. 'The fumes are lethal.'

Betty Frith, who was responsible for the book-keeping and innumerable other duties, laughed.

'Makes you think, doesn't it? When it calms down it's pumped into the casks where it goes on muttering to itself. The whole cellar mutters.'

The rows of enormous oak casks, that could take from five to fourteen hundred gallons, were in a different part of the cellar. Many were empty, waiting to receive the must.

'How do you clean them?' I asked.

'A man goes in,' said Dudley. 'For the little casks a boy does the job – a *klonkie*.'

'Surely a man could never get through that small trap?'

Dudley is tall, lean and supple, and in a second he had flung an arm up, and, in that position, with one shoulder out of the way, he had dived into the empty cask.

'I hate you doing that!' said Beryl, as he emerged once more. 'I'm terrified of these casks.'

23

Her husband smiled. 'It's all right so long as the fumes have evaporated.'

She turned to me. 'We have a ghost. In the days of slavery a *klonkie* was put into one of the little casks too soon – before the fumes had evaporated – and he died instantly. He haunts the cellar.'

'Have you seen this ghost?'

Beryl is psychic and has published occult works. 'Of course. *And* heard him sob, poor little fellow. Unfortunately he doesn't always stick to his cellar. He gets around. The Coloureds think it's an evil portent when he walks. The cats have seen it too, and the dogs. They bristle.'

There was a score of cats – half Persian stoep cats and common kitchen cats, who seldom encroached on each others' territory – and several dogs, to say nothing of Algernon, a tame seagull. But Algernon, it seemed, was impervious to spectral manifestations. He alone did not bristle when the *spook* was out haunting.

We looked into the wine-maker's den, which, with its glass retorts, chemical contrivances and tasting glasses, was a real necromancer's lair. Like most wine-makers this one was a German from the Rhineland, and well versed in the delicate arts of making, blending and preserving wine. So important are these specialists that during the war many of them were released from internment as enemy aliens to resume their occupation during the vital crushing season. He was a fair quiet man with a gentle smile.

'The must is a patient now. Every two hours, day and night, we take its temperature.'

Dudley took me into the cellar that night to watch the process. The moment I got back to my room I scribbled my impressions in the writer's notebook that had now taken the place of the diaries I had kept sporadically during our travelling years.

Midnight. Feb. 1954. THE CELLAR.

A few naked bulbs hang from the ceiling. The must – a porridgy sour-smelling mass – squirms and froths in the tanks. Two Natives stand on the rim of this devil's punch-bowl and stir the brew with a long wooden oar. They look immensely tall, featureless in the gloom as black men are, their long shadows weaving to and fro, drawing together and apart, as they paddle their motionless Bacchanalian craft in the stygian gloom of the cellar.

One is aware of life and death in a weird elemental form – the ferocious life-after-death of the grape and the deadly gases it exudes. Dudley plunged a gigantic thermometer into the writhing mass, withdrew it and nodded to the wine-maker. So far, so good. If the temperature had been too low more yeast would have been added; if too high the must would have been pumped through the coolers.

When we went out into the starlit night I breathed deeply of its purity. I felt that what I had seen and smelt – and heard – was evil, breeding germs of lunacy and death. Man's corruption of the sweet natural delicacy of the grape.

In the summer-garden it is a night for young lovers.

After the vintage the farm celebrates.

I was there at 'pay parade' on the Friday evening, when Dudley dispensed the wages as the foreman called the names. He spoke to every hand, for these were his people. He lent them money, kept their savings for them, and knew their needs. The women waited outside the office to grab their share of their husband's pay packet before it could be put to a less worthy cause. The children played and butted at each other with their heads like young rams.

Later there was a *braaivleis* (barbecue). Wood and sticks were collected by the children and piled out of doors near the cow-shed. Sheep had been killed and cut up and the meat grilled on the great wire trays over the flames. Again I made my notes that night.

VOLKIES' BRAAIVLEIS. *The Compound by the Cowshed.*

The *volkies*' (farm-labourers') feast. There are generous tots of wine and a bottle per head for the band. Then they dance and that is really a sight. The men wear their threadbare patchwork trousers, gaudy shirts and any sort of headgear or none. Boots, sandals, shoes or bare feet. The 'ladies' in flowered cotton dresses, some with *doeks* tied round their heads. Shoes optional. Little children and small babies sleep in the arms of friends round the fire, or in empty stalls or mangers in the cow-shed.

There are Natives as well as Coloureds. Better dressed. They are the new élite and the girls fall for them. They are flashy, gay, and those who work in the house earn more money. Two Coloured floosies came along and were thrown out by Dudley. They are known to be dagga-pedlars (marijuana). Betty says it's common here. 'You can tell – especially if a man has smoked and had a tot as well. He gets a frightening animal expression.' Betty had been a v.A.D. and is in charge of all first aid whether it's a broken head from a fight or a case of snake-bite.

The band-leader is blind – works at the basket factory – and is very much in demand as leading violin. The others are guitarists. They play calypso-fashion, picking up the theme of a *liedjie* and repeating it again and again. Instruments like babies' rattles keep the beat. The jitter-bugging gets more frenzied. Anybody dances with anybody or anything. If no partner is available a baby is seized and carried aloft in a crazy jig. The babies adore it. Dan, the shepherd, very tall and supple, danced with his crook, and the cowman performed with his milk-pails, making a comic turn on their own whenever the dusty compound was reasonably clear.

Smell of embers and burnt meat, of poultry, cattle and hot human bodies. Six huge dark turkeys roosted asleep and undisturbed on the wire farm-gate with a white hen beside them. Others roosted in the trees.

When the band stopped for a drink you could hear the crickets shrilling in the hot night.

By the time I returned to the flat my Writer's Notebook was bulging with facts and fancies and I told my husband that now I was 'all set'.

'I'll lift that farm out of the Klapmuts area and put it into the Constantia setting. I've got my characters taped. I know just what I'm going to make them do, and where and why and when.'

The hot month of February had drawn to its close. I was elated. It seemed to me that the two important enterprises of our retirement were well underway. Our home was growing steadily and the novel was launched. I had the title: *Valley of the Vines*.

In Constantia too the grapes had been harvested, and the vineyards rested. The first touch of autumn tinged the valley with red and gold, and the young wine matured in the casks of Groote Constantia and Alphen. The winds of March lashed the poplars and scattered the papery oak-leaves.

Up on our property Mr. Bent and his team were chipping the mellow mountain stone to make our supporting garden walls. We had chosen saplings from the Government Forestry Department at Newlands, and the forester had told us that we must wait to plant them till the first winter rains had soaked the thirsty earth.

Meanwhile I had established the working routine which has since become habitual. The first draft is in long-hand, then typing which includes revising, then very often another retype and revise, after which the final draft is professionally typed. All this takes many months, even years. But my working hours are consistent as far as is humanly possible. Eight-thirty to twelve-thirty in the morning, a short rest after lunch, then back to work till I'm too cross-eyed to go on or until some engagement catches up with me. No lunch parties. And no work after dark because my eyes rebel against artificial light.

One afternoon in March – which my mother was always convinced was a disastrous month for all her family – my husband returned to our flat from a game of golf.

I had been very busy.

He looked from my face to the wastebasket stuffed with torn typescript. He shook his head.

'No! It isn't possible? Not at this stage!'

I was proud of my destructive achievement. It had taken a good deal of determination to make such a clean sweep.

'It's there – every bit of it. Thirty thousand words. One third of a novel. What's more, that's where it belongs.'

'When did you decide to be so drastic?'

'It's been in the back of my mind for ages. And suddenly, this afternoon, I faced it. My characters have been sending me to Coventry. When I want to make friends with them they refuse to play. It's like trying to horn in near the fireside on a winter's night in an English residential hotel.

27

Everybody has his or her special chair in the warm circle and nobody welcomes the newcomer. The valley's no better. They've turned their backs on me – the whole darn lot of them!'

'No survivors? Not a page or a paragraph or a person?'

'Not one word. I'm not a novelist and never will be, and that's that!'

CHAPTER THREE

MY TWO WORLDS

THROUGHOUT the sparkling month of April I didn't so much as open a scribble book. I turned my attention to our home.

The interior was assuming its real personality. An open-work wrought-iron bannister with a scroll design curved down into the living-room. Parquet floors were laid. Dome-headed doors of Philippine mahogany were hung, electricians veined the walls with essential wiring and at last the painters arrived with their long ladders and dust-sheets.

The shape of the garden was wandering its own sweet way. We put down a lawn but left most of our two acres wild and wooded. Then my husband said: 'Here, by the lawn in the lee of our special oak, we must have a little rose-garden.'

'Let's get our roses from "Old Nectar".'

I was swayed as much by sentiment as by the excellence of General van der Spuy's roses, for 'Nectar', some forty miles from Cape Town in the Jonker's Hoek Valley, is one of the traditional Cape homesteads and was, for many generations, the home of my mother's family, the Huguenot descended Marais clan.

After the Abolition of Slavery, however, the Cape farmers faced ruin, and in the middle of the nineteenth century my grandfather, then scarcely more than a schoolboy, rode away to seek his fortune in the hinterland being opened up by the Boer *voortrekkers*. His father gave him a saddle horse and five golden sovereigns as a parting gift. Nearly forty years later 'Long Piet Marais' returned to end his days at the Cape.

With luck and enterprise he had made a fortune on the gold-bearing Rand. During his absence 'Old Nectar', the home of his childhood, had changed hands and he bought a property near Cape Town on the Liesbeek River. It was named 'Wheatfield' and the huge rambling house was always over-flowing with his children and grandchildren. Today it is a nursing-home, and 'Old Nectar' is a rose-farm and nursery owned by General van der Spuy and his wife, Una, who are both well-known horticulturalists and landscape gardeners.

So one fine day we drove to Jonker's Hoek through the lazy autumn scene of fallow farmlands and golden vineyards.

The elegant French gable of 'Nectar', dappled with leaf shadow and backed by tall peaks, seems to symbolize the gracious living of those early Dutch and Huguenot land-owners who had tamed the wilderness and made their per-manent homes in the land they cultivated. The gardens straggle charmingly down to a trout stream and, even at this ragged season, they led from one enchantment to another. If ghosts haunt them they are the ghosts of my ancestors.

Here, in the middle of the nineteenth century, my great-grandmother had noted in the family bible the departure of her son, Petrus Johannes Marais, to Graaff-Reinet, the springboard for the new Boer Republic north of the Vaal. The inscription was in Nederlands, the language of the Marais home, for French had long since been obliterated as a matter of policy by the Dutch East India Company, which had no intention of allowing its Huguenot refugee colonists to become an alien minority and Afrikaans, as it is spoken today, had not yet been developed. The old leather-bound bible – now in the possession of my uncle, Wilfred Marais, weighs eleven pounds and is printed on thick paper in the Nederlands of eighteenth-century Holland. It is lavishly illustrated with blood-thirsty action pictures and must have been a delight to many generations of readers, young and old.

My grandfather found his bride, Sarah Belfield, in the little English garrison town of Grahamstown. She bore him twelve children, eight sons and four daughters.

Religious and racial tolerance were the guiding lights of their household, and this was understandable, for my grand-father's ancestry was Huguenot and Calvinistic Dutch – an aggressively Protestant combination – whereas the wife he adored was a Roman Catholic of English and Irish origin.

In those days it was evidently not unusual for the sons of such a marriage to be brought up in their father's religion and their daughters in that of their mothers. Thus my uncles were educated at Anglican colleges and my mother and her sisters attended the convent schools in whatever place the roving Marais' chanced to find themselves. The Marais girls ate fish on Fridays and enjoyed the psychiatry of the confessional, while the boys helped themselves to meat if they wished and kept their sins to themselves.

Whether a compromise which splits a household into two religious camps is a good thing is open to argument, but the cardinal principle in my grandfather's home was that each camp should respect the doctrines of the other.

When my Catholic mother married my Anglican father it was agreed between them – surprisingly, I think – that any children of the marriage should be brought up in what was then the State religion, Church of England. Since then the wheel has spun full circle and the State religion is once more Dutch Reformed. My father, a third generation South African, was of Danish and German extraction, a man much loved for his kindliness and humour. He warned us never to let politics or religion interfere with our friendships, and went so far as to practise what he preached. He was never anti anything, except inhumanity.

We were quiet on the way home from 'Nectar'. Bertie was no doubt thinking about the roses we had chosen, while I was aware of a quickening in my dormant imagination. 'Nectar', with its old family associations, had resuscitated the theme of *Valley of the Vines*, and during the next few days I was prey to the mood of abstraction that is a sure prelude to writing. The characters I had so recently thrown overboard returned to haunt me. They came at night in the phantom interval between wakefulness and falling asleep and began to whisper their secrets. So that was the truth of it? I'd find myself thinking. No wonder you all hated my pushing you around! I was terrified of losing them again. Then, suddenly, with a burst of insight, I knew that I could keep them only by listening to them and letting *them* tell *me* their story instead of dictating to them.

Quite recently someone asked me if, when I wrote a novel, I knew exactly what would happen next. I answered emphatically.

'Oh, no! If I knew that I'd be bored before I started.'

At the very beginning of a novel my characters may be strongly reminiscent of people I have known, but very quickly they assume their own personalities. They introduce friends and relatives, bring along their pets, and astonish me with their inconsistencies. If I remain passive they will, with only a hint from me, fulfil their own destinies according to their stars.

Once more I settled down to work. Routine morning hours, insulation from the telephone and restriction of social engagements. But now I no longer used my pen like a ringmaster's whip in the lion cage. It was I who had been licked into shape.

As the weeks passed I became more and more absorbed in this fictional world. It was like living two lives – my own and that of my characters. I used to say to my husband, 'Now I'm going into my other world.' It was an Alice Through the Looking Glass experience, and sometimes I found it difficult to snap back into everyday reality.

We moved into 'Cressage' on 28th August, 1954. My mother was superstitiously delighted, for 28th August was the anniversary of her wedding day, and therefore, in her opinion, a fortunate and auspicious date for embarking upon any new family enterprise.

It was hard to believe. Our own home after nearly thirty years of roving. Although my father had died before the outbreak of World War II, my mother, now in her eighties, still lived in 'Tees Lodge', my childhood's home in Cape Town, where she was cared for and cherished by the faithful domestics who had been in our family for decades. Our surgeon son, Piet, his wife, Glendyr, and their little boys, Ronnie and Chris, were down the hill from us. Tony and Willie were added to the family later.

Our domestic staff was average for our circumstances; a Coloured woman cook and housemaid who lived in, and a Bantu gardener who came daily from the Bantu township of Langa, week-ends and public holidays excluded. If he elected to work on a Saturday or a public holiday, for us or anybody else, he was welcome to do so and thus supplement his wages.

The standard of living, for both White and Black, is higher in South Africa than anywhere else on the African Continent, but even so it varies considerably. Some of our friends managed with a daily 'girl' while others ran lavish establishments staffed by a butler and his minions in glamorous white suits and vivid sashes. The experienced Bantu butler in private service has a great sense of hospitality and identifies himself closely with his master. The guest, greeted on the threshold by such a trusty, can gauge by the width of a smile his own personal standing in that particular household.

The White woman in South Africa is a member of a tribe doomed to extinction, but tribal custom still smiles on girls' gossip over tea and scones or coffee and cakes at eleven and the talk is more often than not of servants. These conversations can be illuminating, for the uninhibited private lives of their subjects are usually dramatic in the extreme and orgies of dark love and crime frequently spill over from the kitchen quarters into the more limited experience of the master and mistress of the house.

It is often said that the master-servant relationship is the only one which a South African can contemplate with a person of colour, and, although this attitude is changing, there is still a great deal of truth in the accusation. The official government policy vigorously discourages any contact across the colour line and to establish a genuine friendship with a non-European *in South Africa* on a basis of equality, even with an intellectual, requires great determination and tenacity. In any case one side fears to patronize, the other is touchy, and the law has deliberately devised a system of embargoes and embarrassments calculated to sabotage all human bridges between the races.

At the Cape the Coloured people are more privileged than the Bantu labour force which has thoroughly infiltrated industry and agriculture during the past thirty years. The tribesmen do the heavy work for which they are better suited than the Coloured people who, in any case, have progressed on to more skilled rungs of the economic ladder. Even so, the rule of 'job reservation' imposes ceilings intolerable to any ambitious human being. The Bantu is debarred from this or that job because his competition would create a threat to the Coloured worker, and the Coloured in turn dare not be employed in occupations reserved for Whites. For the White, of course, the sky's the limit.

It always amazes me how good-tempered the average non-European continues to remain in spite of the innumerable official restrictions on his life and liberty. In the hills around our home the Bantu milkman rides or pushes his bicycle with its huge wicker carrier loaded with milk-bottles. He wears a bright knitted cap and his little carved pipe is always between his teeth whether it is lit or not. Newspapers are delivered by another cyclist, also with a jaunty cap and pipe. His round is a big one, uphill and downdale, and his papers weigh heavily, but he is a merry fellow, and at Christmas time his gift-book is well written up with generous donations.

In the lunch hour the Bantu gardeners loll on the grassy verge of the road outside the gates, and often some coy Xhosa maid from roundabout finds that she is free about that time and they relax in little groups and laugh and joke as if they hadn't a care in the world. Yet they live in danger of being sent back to the native territories which cannot support them, for the Government policy is to reduce the number of Bantu in the Cape to the bare minimum.

On the principle of a place for everybody and everybody in his place, the Western Cape has been designated as the 'natural ethnic homeland' of the Cape Coloureds whose mixed blood relegates them to a social no-man's-land somewhere between the 'poor White' and the pure bred Bantu. The fact that migrant Bantu labour is necessary to agriculture, and that the flourishing industries of the Cape are built upon the assumption that this vigorous labour force has come to stay, leaves the Government theorists cold. So does the reluctance of the feckless and physically feebler Coloured folk to undertake the heavy work they have long regarded as being fit only for 'Kaffirs'. Be that as it may, the reversal of the Bantu tide cannot be accomplished overnight and in the meantime many thousands continue to dwell in the locations of Langa and Nyanga (the Sun and the Moon) that have gradually expanded to replace the squatter settlements of ramshackle *pondokkies* made out of old packing-cases and biscuit-tins.

Parts of Langa and Nyanga are pleasant and well-established, with churches, schools, clinics, shopping centres and

33

playgrounds, but others are sandy wastes. The most fertile breeding ground for the trouble-maker is the gaunt grim barracks known as the 'Bachelors' Quarters'. Here the agitator is no stranger, and the intimidation of Bantu by Bantu is more commonplace than sporadic police raids. Here a man may be murdered by his own people because he refuses to pay twenty-five cents to join a banned political society and in this community only a fool would seek justice or compassion. Yet mirth and a genuine camaraderie are to be found among the tenants of the Bachelors' Quarters, for the Bantu is by nature a sunny fellow as ready to be amused as to be roused.

When our Shangaan gardener, Sombani, was not working in our garden on the wooded ridge he dwelt in Langa Bachelors' Quarters in company with other Bantu of various tribes.

I have a clear picture of the day my husband hired Sombani. Our house was not yet finished, but Mr. Bent and his team were already working in the wilderness that would one day be a garden. The tall Bantu stood diffidently outside our glass and wrought-iron front door. Pale sunshine fell on his matt blue-black skin, slightly prominent eyes and small well-fitting ears – an attribute of his people. His shabby suit covered a wiry warrior-frame and he held a stained felt hat limply in his right hand. They have beautiful hands, these Bantu, long and narrow with pale palms and almond nails. In repose they hang supine, but when they spring into action they show astonishing strength and dexterity, and they can tell a tale. Sombani has the hands and gestures of the born story-teller. In everything the Bantu have their own pace; it is a countryman's pace, slow and steady, and it is wrong to hurry them because the life-rhythm of a city is feverish, with buses and trains to be caught or missed and policemen with revolvers at their belts looking suspiciously at 'loiterers'.

'Master wants a gardener.'

It was not a question but a statement, made without urgency. He was not asking for a situation but offering his services where they were clearly required.

His gaze wandered over the ravages left by the recently departed juggernaut, across bush waiting to be selectively cleared by hand, and over the wooded Kirstenbosch valley to the southern ravines of Table Mountain and Devil's Peak where the waterfalls were already foaming.

'Soon there will be too much rain,' he added. Later we learned that 'too much' meant 'a great deal of'.

'What is your name? Where do you come from? And why do you want to work for me?' asked my husband.

Sombani smiled. Because it is dangerous for a Bantu to change his place of work and risk a period of unemployment which may result in enforced repatriation it is important for him to find a good master at the outset. There is, in consequence, a grapevine information service on the merits and demerits of possible employers, whether in industry or private homes.

'Sombani is my name. My country is far.' He indicated the snow-capped barrier range to the north, beyond the Flats and the townships of Langa and Nyanga. 'I am of the Shangaan nation. But I have work for Sir Alfred Beit up here in Primrose Avenue. He have sell his house; he will go to England.'

'Is your reference book in order?'

'Yes, master. But if I do not get a job soon the police will send me home.'

He drew the grubby reference book from his pocket and handed it to my husband with distaste. If he were found without it he could be picked up by the police and put in gaol as a lost dog is caught and put in the pound. It was his friend and his foe, and he hated it as much as my mother hated her hearing-aid, the 'darned contrivance' that cheated and tormented her but without which she was lost.

Bertie studied the pass-book with equal dislike, and returned it to its owner.

'Come back tomorrow, and I will give you my answer.'

We knew that we would be meeting Sir Alfred Beit that evening at a party – and quite possibly Sombani knew it too, for such is the grapevine. When Bertie asked about the Shangaan who wished to work for him, Sir Alfred said:

'Oh yes, he was one of my gardeners. Rather a sweet chap. Gentle with plants.'

This charming reference was all my husband wanted.

That the 'sweet chap' was vulnerable to many forms of disaster we had yet to discover.

We acquired a puppy and reckoned that at last we had really settled down. I lived contentedly in my two worlds, 'Cressage' and *Valley of the Vines*.

The last winter storm lashed our young trees and whipped the poplars on our neighbours' boundary till they groaned and threw themselves about as if they were tall lamenting women wailing at a wake. The garden was left drenched, battered and exhausted. Next day it was spring. The blades of the silvers shone sharp as the spears of young knights going forth to conquer evil; the long-tailed sugar-birds swooped among the proteas crying *tsk-tsk-tsk*, the doves discovered tiny leaves unfurling in the oak and the elm, and the squirrels flew from branch to branch in the pine woods as though they too were winged.

At my desk by the window commanding all this glory of young green growth I typed the last words of *Valley of the Vines* and burst into tears.

Bertie found me there.

'It's finished ... I've written my first real novel!'

I was quite convinced that, like *Valley of the Vines*, I too was finished – written out to the very last word.

CHAPTER FOUR

ANIMALS AND AUTHORS

OUR little dog, Snowy, was a stray puppy our grandsons, Ronnie and Chris, had picked up in the Malay quarter of Claremont. He resembled one of my novels in that there was no knowing how he would turn out.

He was roughly terrier-shaped with the lively gentle black eyes of a Sealyham, a Pomeranian black button nose, pricked fly-away ears and a plume of a tail jauntily curled left-about over his rump. He was long-haired and took a good deal of explaining away. Occasionally he was mistaken for a Maltese terrier. He soon showed a remarkable fervour for hunting, and sometimes catching, moles. He was a great burrower and burier. One afternoon, when a visitor came to tea, she rose from her armchair after a while with an expression of distaste and said, 'I'm sorry, but really I think there's *something* here . . .'

She lifted the seat cushion, and we were dismayed to discover a small mole in the early stages of decomposition. When my husband had removed it to the compost heap, he came back with the explanation.

'We have to expect it,' he said. 'Our little dog is a Shropshire terrier – a very rare breed, almost extinct. They are trained to hunt moles. So useful in the garden!'

'In the garden,' she agreed pointedly, and took her departure.

But a good many of our gardening friends were interested in our Shropshire terrier and urged us to breed from him.

'A dog any day rather than a snake,' said one acquaintance. 'Even your Shropshire terrier!'

There'd been some bother about snakes recently. A well-known bowling club was having trouble with the turf. Out-size moles were making sand-castles all over it. The club had bought mole-snakes by the yard to deal with the situation. Unfortunately, the snakes were lethargic and fled when the moles showed their teeth. This made news. 'MOLES EAT SNAKES.' The serpent-vendor was incensed and pointed out that the club had seen fit to paint its initials on the snakes, which had clogged their pores and upset their morale.

There was a very old kennel in the back yard of 'Tees Lodge,' my mother's home. It had once belonged to Piet's dog, Gyppie, defunct these many years. I asked Mother if I might have it for Snowy. To my surprise she demurred.

'Ask Arend,' she said.

The old Coloured chauffeur-gardener flung up his hands in horror at the idea of parting with this ancient kennel.

'It is our *shrikmaker*, Miss Yoy! If people sees the kennel they's frightened for the dog.'

There was no dog any more, but Arend had long ago printed a sign, 'Beware of the dog' and attached it to the front gate, which made everybody feel nice and safe.

'But I will make a new kennel yus' as good,' he promised. He was an enthusiastic carpenter.

By the time the kennel arrived at 'Cressage' we had yet another addition to the family. Beryl Kiernander had come to lunch from Natte Valleij bearing a basket containing two of her best half-Persian kittens, one black and one white. Snowy was introduced and became temperamental but not violently antagonistic, and the kittens, who were accustomed to dogs, ignored his excitement. Unfortunately, the black kitten, who was an exploring type, fell into the kitchen sink one afternoon when Mary, the cook, was washing up. It shot out of the window above the sink and was never seen again, though we searched the surrounding woods for days. I like to think that some child found it and took it home where it lived happily ever after.

Snowy and the white kitten then formed a devoted relationship.

The puppy carried the kitten round in his mouth like a mother cat, and the kitten, used to such treatment in infancy, was unperturbed though often soaked with canine saliva. At first Snowy and Kittie occupied the kennel together and then they decided that they were not 'yard animals' and settled for sleeping on the porch, and once again an Arend-constructed kennel was consigned to the position of *skrikmaker*, but I think it lacked the efficacy of the original, which had housed the dynamic Gyppie for over thirteen years.

Snowy soon declared noisy war on the squirrels who inhabited the pines and ate the doves' eggs and our young lettuces and tomatoes. The squirrels swore back at him, 'chitter-chitter-chitter, ghrrr!' The bolder ones came to drink from the bird-bath scooped out of one of the two squat rough-hewn pillars at the top of our terrace steps. In the hollow of the other was bird-seed.

One evening we were enraptured to see, in a patch of sunlight on the tallest pine, a snow white squirrel.

'It's the kitten!' said Bertie. Then it fled up the trunk and almost flew from bough to bough – undoubtedly a white squirrel. Later, my brother, Norman, told us that there used to be a small colony of these albinos in the woods nearer Kirstenbosch. Ours was unique, very shy and vulnerable, deprived by nature of his protective colouring, and he never ventured on to our low stone wall like his grey relations. But Sombani often reported his tomato raids in the vegetable garden.

The low wall between our terrace and the grass banks and lawns had been built by Mr. Bent out of the mountain stone that matched the plumage of the laughing-doves. They brooded on it, or walked along on dainty pink claws, as if they knew that the sunset-rose and soft-blue-grey sheen of their feathers was set off to perfection. Flocks of Cape turtle-doves came too, larger than the laughing-doves, pearl-grey with black velvet neck-bands. They were all equally quarrelsome, greedy and amorous, but their presence delighted my mother when she came to see us, and she spent happy hours idly watching their quarrels and their courting.

Orange-breasted thrushes and robins were attracted by the lawns, a smart black and white butcher-bird perched on the masthead of our little cypress tree, and sometimes a pair of glorious green plush bokmakieries, wearing sulphur yellow waistcoats and black bibs, looked in on us with their ringing calls and responses. When the crimson bougainvillea was in bloom and the violet-blue petria nodded over the porch, tiny jewelled sunbirds hovered among the sprays of flowers, and, down in the protea bushes, the sugar-birds flitted in towards dusk and filled the air with their high scissor-cries. Waves of tiny green *witoogies* – white-eyes – vibrated in our lemon tree in company with huge black and yellow butterflies.

'We should attach bamboo tubes to the tails of the doves,' I said to Bertie. 'Like Chinese pigeons.'

He smiled. 'You try it!'

I never did. But often the rushing sound of their wings reminded me of Peking and pigeons flying over the green and gold pavilions of the Forbidden City with the sound of aeolian harps.

At the end of February we went to Plettenberg Bay for a fortnight's holiday.

It is an easy day's run from Cape Town across mountains and undulating grainlands to the Indian Ocean seaboard. Green cliffs, matted with tropical foliage, tower above the coast where the scalloped rollers cream in on to shining beaches, curved like scimitars and bounded by the blue rocks that are the fisherman's heaven.

We stayed on Beacon Island, and found, to our pleasure, that Stuart Cloete and his American wife, Rehna (Tiny), were there too, relaxing after their epic African safari which was to result in Stuart's important survey *The African Giant.*

and Tiny's light-hearted version of the same journey, en-titled *Nylon Safari*. Stuart's book was illustrated with her startling photographs, themselves a feat of lavid journalism, and her own volume was adorned with her witty skittish line drawings. She was overjoyed at having broken into her husband's field, and was busy on a 'follow up'.

'I'm calling it *To Catch a Man*,' she said, with a proud adoring glance at the magnificent man she had so cleverly caught.

Stuart smiled at her benignly. He was in one of his bearded phases at that time, impersonating a pioneer-hunter. Tiny was just herself, an extremely sophisticated feather-weight with a scintillating sense of humour. Stuart said of her, 'I can never trade her in for a younger blonde just like her. There isn't one. They don't make these models twice.'

She gave a little yelp of laughter, and turned to me.

'Have you tried fiction yet? We advised you to.'

'I've just finished my first novel, *Valley of the Vines*.'

'Is it good?' asked Stuart.

Bertie grinned, 'Constantia folk'll pin-point the charac-ters.'

'We knew you could write fiction,' said Tiny. 'Remember? At Libris.'

We remembered very well. A few years ago Stuart had owned a farm in a coastal valley planted with exotic trees he had brought from all over the world. The little old farm-house was simple and attractive and was always overflowing with dogs and cats. Wild birds darted in and out of the *voorkamer* over the open top of the front door, which was a 'stable door' in two halves. Swallows nested against the rafters and outside were white peacocks with their wives and babies. The peacock families used to fly over the roof at dawn with unearthly screeches. Stuart's book-lined study was a menagerie where no live thing was ever destroyed. Woe betide anyone who brushed a cobweb from the ceiling, thereby 'upsetting the balance of nature'. It was there, at Libris, that they had put the idea of trying to write fiction into my head. Stuart had been most encouraging.

The evening after our arrival at Beacon Island there was a film showing in the ballroom of the hotel. It was *The Cruel Sea*, and, to our amazement, the author and his lovely South African wife were present.

We had not seen Nicholas and Philippa Monsarrat since he had been transferred from his post as Director of United Kingdom Information in Johannesburg to Ottawa. While in Canada they had acquired a baby son and another was on the way. They had brought the baby to visit his maternal grandfather, Mr. Jim Crosby, who lived in Plettenberg Bay.

Goodness knows how many times they had sat through the film of *The Cruel Sea*, but I believe they really enjoyed it, because, as far as any film about the Royal Navy can produce the illusion of authenticity, this one did. Of all Monsarrat's books, gripping as they invariably are, only *The Cruel Sea* is illumined by that indefinable plus quality which shines through the work of a first-class author who has given his heart to a book as well as his brain.

We had dinner with them the next night and feasted on a steenbras superbly presented by Mr. Crosby's Bantu cook.

Nicholas had caught the fish himself. He was crazy about fishing that summer and used to get up at four in the morning to go out with a dark hawk-faced gillie who had Highland blood in his veins. But, by way of a profitable diversion, he was also writing a tense thriller serial set in Plettenberg Bay.

Nicholas Monsarrat and Stuart Cloete are about as unlike as two very masculine and uncompromising best-selling novelists could possibly be.

Monsarrat is saturnine and sword-sharp. Stuart is ruthless but a lush descriptive writer. Monsarrat is a nocturnal writer, while Stuart finds that many of his literary problems 'sort themselves out' in his sleep. As soon as he wakes in the morning he springs at his typewriter and begins work without so much as shaving or brushing his teeth.

That was a good year for the Monsarrats. They were happy and successful. Since then their marriage has crashed. Nicholas has remarried, and old Mr. Crosby has died. But the rollers still break on the blue rocks round Beacon Island with a noise like thunder, the gulls wade as they've always done in the opalescent shallows between the shore and the dense green bush, and Nicholas continues to write enthralling best sellers.

We returned to 'Cressage' on a Sunday evening. Our first home-coming. On top of the pile of letters waiting for us was an orange envelope.

'You open it,' I said to Bertie. Since the war I have never opened a telegram without anxiety.

He did so and I saw the smile break on his face. It was from my literary agent in London. *Valley of the Vines* had not only been accepted for publication in the United States, it had also been selected as their book of the month by the Literary Guild of America.

I rang Stuart in Plettenberg Bay and read him the cable.

'I've never been published in America and I know nothing about the Literary Guild. What does it mean?'

'Congratulations,' said Stuart. 'You've hit the jackpot first shot. Open champagne!'

Pack and Follow, *Grey Mistress* and *Apes and Ivory* had all been best sellers throughout the Commonwealth, but only *Apes and Ivory* had been translated into a foreign language – Swedish – and now, suddenly, with this first novel I had so feared and longed to tackle, a new pattern of literary good fortune was shaping.

J. P. Lippincott were publishing the American edition, to say nothing of the special Literary Guild edition which ran into hundreds of thousands of copies and tens of thousands of dollars advance for me. Other book club editions followed in the Commonwealth, so did paper backs and digests. The book was serialized by an English women's magazine with a weekly circulation of several million. Then along came the foreign translations. *Who's Who* in America and Britain wrote to ask for my *curriculum vitae*. It was all very thrilling and incredible.

My friends began to say, 'Have you started another book?'

The suggestion alarmed me. Unlike Tiny Cloete, I had no 'follow up' on the stocks. One day I knew that I would open a clean scribble-book, tap a pencil against my teeth, gaze over to the far mountains and wait for the first words of a new story to float into my mind from some unknown dimension in space. But not yet.

Writing a book, to me, is like having a baby. From the first roughly jotted note to the last typed word of the final draft it is a nine-month commitment with outside entertainment and activities gradually reduced to a bare minimum in the final stages. But my literary 'family' is spaced. Between one birth and the next conception there is a substantial interval, with two phases. Void and receptive. During the receptive period some paragraph in a newspaper, or some incident, sparks off the idea for a story which develops in my mind till it is ready to touch paper, and after that come the false starts. I am, by now, accustomed to at least one 'miscarriage' before a novel is really on its way, so my output is never more than one book every two years, which is feeble by most standards.

I am often amazed at the dash and confidence with which other authors attack their work. Many of them, like Stuart Cloete, can write two books at a time, to say nothing of a few short stories!

Ursula Bloom, the popular novelist and journalist, occupied the flat opposite ours in Chelsea, and, when the weather was warm and the windows all open, I could hear her typewriter hammering busily at all hours of the day and night. She is industrious and prolific, and, so varied is her scope, that she writes under several pen-names as well as her own. She keeps a notebook of plots and, when she needs one, there it is. Her will-power and vitality ride rough-shod over her health, but her husband, Commander Robinson, helps her both in her career and in the home. When I used to go out to buy vegetables I often met this tall retired Naval officer with the Scottie and Dachshund at his heels, and we'd pass the time of day, choose our fruit and greens, and he'd tell me what article, book or story his wife was working on at the time. It might be anything from the love-life of Hitler and Eva Braun to her own experience of cosmetic surgery. That was one of the lessons I learned from her. Everything, good or bad, pleasant or painful, that happens to a natural writer is stored away to become part of his or her equipment. No suffering, emotion, impression, or aspect of living or dying is ever wasted.

When the time came to plant parsley or sweetpeas in our garden Bertie got the little packets out of a deep drawer in his desk and gave them to Sombani to soak.

'I will let them sleep in the water all night,' Sombani would say, and next day they'd go into the ground.

A writer's mind is like that drawer. The seed of experience may lie there, dry and forgotten, until, in its season, it will be brought out 'to sleep in the water all night' where it will swell and soften in preparation for rebirth.

CHAPTER FIVE

DOMESTIC DRAMAS

MARY, our cook, and her niece, Sybil, our maid, had been born and bred in a tiny picturesque hamlet among the mountains of the beautiful Villiersdorp farming district, but, like so many country folk, they were glad to exchange their rural existence for a more lucrative life on the fringe of Cape Town. They had a number of young relatives who had likewise migrated to Cape Town, and of these, the one who came most often to 'Cressage' was Mary's niece, Moira, always accompanied by her two children, Olivia, aged three, and Karen, a lovely child of eighteen months. I'd see the little girls sitting at the kitchen table, dainty as dolls in their frilly frocks and bonnets. But the doll-look was deceptive. They were both brimful of life, and Karen, who still spent most of her time on all fours, was as inquisitive as the next member of her sex and applied the usual baby test to everything. How does it taste?

One afternoon, when I came back from the hairdresser, Mary met me in the hall with Karen in her arms. The child was limp and drowsy, her skin bloodless and her pretty dress stained with some dark sticky substance like toffee. I could hear Moira wailing loudly in the kitchen accompanied in a higher key by her daughter, Olivia. Mary was agitated and breathless.

'We put ant-poison down in the yard this morning by the bins . . . I never thought any more about it, but, while we were having tea and talking, Karen must have crawled into the yard. Sybil found her by the bins, her hands and face covered with ant-poison. I gave her hot salt-water to make her sick . . . but we must find a doctor . . . She looks bad to me.'

She looked bad to me also.

'When did this happen?'

'About half an hour ago.'

'We'll take her to the hospital at once. Moira better come.'

'No, my lady. Moira just cries and makes it worse. I'll come.'

So we left Sybil to console Karen's weeping mother and sister and within seconds we were on our way to Wynberg Hospital.

The Out Patients department was, as usual, overflowing. People spilled on to the long narrow stoep with their children and their aged, or sat in the sun near the entrance with the under-privileged sick who know that they may have to wait for hours. Many of them chatted as if they were already well acquainted and some had brought food with them.

I went straight into the waiting-room with its crowded benches and found the sister in charge. Mary followed me, carrying Karen.

'The mother of the child must get a card up at the office window,' said the sister, who was about to hurry away to another emergency.

'Wait!' I said urgently. 'This child has swallowed ant-poison – quite a lot of it – more than half an hour ago!'

She turned sharply and took Karen from Mary at once.

'You go through the formalities at the office,' she said to her. 'Then come back here.'

A few seconds later the little one was undergoing ordeal by stomach-pump. When Mary returned to the ante-room, where I was waiting, we could hear Karen crying.

'That's music in our ears,' I said.

Mary nodded, her eyes full of tears. After what seemed an eternity – perhaps ten minutes, perhaps twenty – the sister showed us a very subdued tot wrapped in a blanket in a wooden cot. But at least the child's sleepy eyes were open.

'You can leave her here till tomorrow,' she said. 'She'll be all right, but we must keep her under observation. And do please be careful where you put that sticky ant-poison! Children love it.'

Next morning I took Moira to collect her little daughter who was as chirpy as a cricket, but very disgruntled when she found that our yard had been swept and washed, leaving no trace of the delicious 'melted toffee' she had licked up so happily the previous day.

But before the month of April was out, with its sun and rain all mixed up to make 'a monkey's wedding', another domestic crisis arose.

Sombani vanished off the face of the earth.

The beginning of the week was often 'blue Monday' for him, or rather 'red Monday', when his fiery eyes told their own tale, so, when Monday came and no Sombani, we didn't disturb ourselves. But Tuesday and Wednesday brought no sign of him and we became worried.

'He's probably on an imperial blind, or in gaol,' suggested my husband.

'Or he's been murdered!'

'I'll telephone Langa Administration.'

Langa Administration knew nothing about him. He had not checked out of his room in the Bachelors' Quarters, and they ascertained that he was not in gaol. The police were informed and would let us know if anything came to light. Piet, who was on the staff of the great teaching hospital of Groote Schuur, checked with Casualties, but Sombani had not been brought there, although every week-end had its harvest of non-European calamities. We telephoned all the likely hospitals, including Wynberg, and were told that no one of his name or number had been brought in during the past few days.

On the morning of the fifth day we received our first clue.

Sir Alfred Beit's house, further up the ridge, where Sombani had worked before coming to us, was now in the possession of friends of ours. Their butler, an imposing Shangaan of considerable standing since he was also a parson, happened to be Sombani's uncle and was generally known among his people as 'the Big Old man up the Hill'. I suspect it was through the agency of the Big Old Man that we heard news of our missing gardener.

When my husband and I returned home from a game of golf, we found a young Bantu waiting outside the garage. Bertie asked him what he wanted.

'I have a message from a man who has returned to our country near Louis Trichardt by the train that is now gone.'

He waved in the general direction of Cape Town and the north. 'This man says I must tell master that Sombani is in the hospital.'

'Which hospital?'

'I think perhaps Wynberg.'

'He is not there. We have asked.'

'I think perhaps master will find him there.'

'What is his sickness?'

'He was cut up.'

'Who cut him up? And when?'

'I really don't know.'

'Where did it take place – this cutting up?'

'I really don't know.'

'This man who has gone by the train – is he a friend of yours?'

'He is man of our nation.'

'What do you know of this affair?'

'I know nothing.'

Whatever he may have known, our informant had said his say and there was nothing more to be got out of him. He had imparted what we needed to know and we could be relied upon to take the next step.

Bertie checked on his own record of Sombani's full name and his number at Langa, and we got back into our car and went down to Wynberg Hospital, where last I had driven at such high speed with the life of a poisoned child at stake.

But there it seemed that we had drawn a blank. As we had already been informed over the telephone, no one of Sombani's name or number had been admitted during the past few days, or, in fact, at any time.

'We have been assured by one of his friends that he is here,' said my husband.

We were allowed to go through the non-European male wards in search of him.

Sure enough, we found him in the surgical ward.

His face was soot-black against the clean white pillow-case. As many tubes and appliances were attached to his anatomy, from nostrils down, as you might expect to find protruding from an ape about to be rocketed into space. An attractive young European nurse stood beside him, her hand on his pulse. He opened his eyes and smiled sheepishly as we came to his bedside. He was clearly not surprised to see us.

We were needed and we were there. The mysterious grape-vine had done its duty.

'Nicholas has been very ill,' said the nurse. 'But he will get better.'

'Nicholas?'

'That is the name we know him by.'

Sombani managed to look bashful.

A young Jewish house surgeon joined us. 'It was touch and go,' he said. 'When you've spoken to him come and see me in my office and I'll tell you what I can.'

'He's worried about his family,' explained the nurse, which, of course, was our cue.

My husband arranged to send money to his wife addressed to the Indian store-keeper near Louis Trichardt, some fifteen hundred miles from Cape Town. The store-keeper, it appeared, acted as scribe and go-between for the illiterate women-folk of the Bantu absent from this area to earn money in the cities. As time passed we came to know his writing, and once I said to Bertie, 'It's too bad. Sombani never gets a letter that isn't asking for something.' Later, when, at intervals of two years, our gardener was in his distant country, we, too, were the recipients of letters written on his behalf by this talented Indian with a rare gift for the phrase best calculated to extract a dividend.

'My passbook has been stolen,' said Sombani, 'and my room at Langa ... if I do not pay for it I will lose it.'

My husband promised to attend to these matters also, and left him feeling reassured and free of at least some part of his anxiety.

We sought out the house surgeon who told us what he knew.

'He was picked up for dead in a ditch at three o'clock on Monday morning by a police patrol. There was another casualty who identified him as Nicholas. His own papers were missing. He'd been stabbed over the kidneys and the knife had been rotated to inflict the maximum injury – we often see the results of that little trick! – and he was too drunk to take an anaesthetic for several hours. I operated at eight that morning.'

The operation had been long and difficult. 'But they're tough!' said the doctor, with admiration. 'I don't think he has the least idea what really happened. Just one of those brawls that blow up for no reason. Senseless. Motiveless. The result of shebeen liquor and dagga.'

We thanked him and took our leave. We knew that Sombani's assailant would probably never be brought to book. I doubt if even the victim would have recognized him, since these week-end crimes are mostly the result of *skokiaan* or the wild hemp known to us as *dagga*, to America as *marihuana*, and to India as *hashish*, the infuriator from which the word 'assassin' is derived.

When he was dismissed from hospital he was sent to a Bantu convalescent home until he was pronounced well enough to do light work about the garden once more. Although we do not at present have National Health in South Africa, the Coloured and Bantu receive virtually free hospitalization and medical care, though, if they are able to, they pay a token sum for the drugs they take home with them. Like everywhere else in the world, however, there are never enough beds or doctors to meet the continual need for medical attention.

Although Sombani seemed happy enough working at the Cape, he was a very homesick person, and I think he was constantly haunted by the longing for his own territory and his family. Once, when we were sorting out old A.A. routes in the garage, he asked if he might have a tattered map which I was about to throw away. His long index finger traced the mountainous area in the northern Transvaal watered by great rivers where the hippos and crocodiles abound.

'This is my country,' he said simply. 'My father is a Chief here.'

His father could make 'strong medicine' and knew much magic, and owned many cattle and several wives, including a youngest 'little wife', to whom, I suspect, Sombani was much attracted, for, during the peak of his ordeal in hospital, sinister menacing apparitions of his father appeared to him in this context.

Much later, when he told me of his dream – only to him it was not a dream but a spiritual revelation – I was aware of the white hand of modern western science clasping the black hand of ancient African superstition across the unconscious form on the operating table.

It was a discussion on the medicinal properties of certain

roots and herbs that sparked off his confidence. His father, it seemed, was very wise in such matters. As we stood in our vegetable garden he leaned on the handle of his long rake, and his voice took on the mystic quality of the true story-teller.

'My father, he knows strange things. That time when I was littie bittie dead he came to me. Sometimes he change himself.'

I knew that Sombani believed in the transformation of men into animals at certain times, and I wanted to hear more. Yet I feared to break a spell by putting a question. He continued of his own accord.

'I slept. Then the Great Wind carried me up and up ...' His hand made a spiralling gesture and I saw the red 'dust devils' that rise here and there on the parched veld, each one an individual whirling column dancing its separate *pas seul* doing its own curious rope trick into the blue sky. 'And I came to the Place of the Ice Cold ...' Shudders passed over my skin as he too shivered in the sun. 'That was bad! I was a long time in the Ice Cold before I went to the Place of the Shop with the Big Window. Inside the Shop was a table with a white sheet—'

'Sheep?'

'No. A sheet like on a bed, but it was on a table and round the table were three men dressed like Romans in church, but their faces were covered too.'

Sombani is only 'littie bittie Christian' but he had evidently associated the white gowns of the doctors with the vestments and incense and ritual of a Roman Catholic church. 'The Shop' must surely have been the operating theatre, and somewhere in this 'Shop' was his father, the Chief. One of the white-robed 'Romans' took a handful of red soil and threw it at Sombani, saying, 'You have been talking bad things with your father's little wife.' But Sombani did not reply, nor did he touch the soil with his hands or try to pick it up. He closed his eyes and felt himself pass once more through the Place of the Ice Cold and into the Whirlwind, and when he opened them again the Romans were waiting for him.

They led him to a blazing furnace, before which his father crouched, 'big as a car'.

'A cow?' I asked, thinking in pastoral terms, but here the

city had encroached upon his vision. He looked at me gently over the handle of the rake.

'A motor-car. My father was a motor-car waiting to kill me.'

Now the second Roman threw red soil at him, and again he made no move. Then the third did likewise, but still he remained immobile. It was the Test.

'If I picked up the soil my father would be right to kill me because he would know I had talked bad things with his little wife. But I did not pick it up, so he was not cross. After that they brought me from the Place of the Great Fire to the bed in the hospital.'

As he told me these things in his voice of mystery my hair prickled on the nape of my neck and the goose-pimples rose on my arms, for I knew that this man had felt the chill touch of Death himself, that he had heard the Voice in the Whirlwind that is the Voice of Final Judgement, and that he had looked into the Inferno and been singed by Satan's breath.

By the time our gardener was fully recovered we were well into winter. Our little 'Christ's Oak' was stripped of its pretty leaves, the young elm was naked, and fierce rain storms raged violently round our house.

Then one day the postman brought a parcel of books bearing the label of my literary agent. I tore the wrapper off in wild excitement. My advance copies of *Valley of the Vines* had arrived from America and England, and suddenly I realized that this book meant something different to me. Not only because it had been lucky, but because there was no taint of journalism about it. It was my own creation, born of my imagination. I had no wish to re-read so much as a paragraph – I have never re-read any of my books after the proof stage – but it was an oddity, the cuckoo in my literary nest.

My cousin's daughter, Gillian Boyd, who was then living in the valley, had designed the English jacket, which faithfully and charmingly reflected an old homestead among the Constantia vineyards and mountains, but the American jacket was abstract, a pattern of rich greens. Later, all the foreign translations arrived, each in a different dust-cover. The finest productions were the German and the Finnish. I looked at them in awe and pride. If my simple novel had

51

been a great classic it could not have been more elegantly presented! Later, when I had occasion to talk to the wife of the Finnish Consul General, I told her how impressed I was, and she smiled.

'We make paper. It is one of our major industries. It is the best paper in the world.'

'It isn't only that,' I said. 'It's the cover, the binding, everything. I'm very thrilled with my Finnish translation.'

These foreign editions of my Cape Peninsula story gave me the illusion of having gone out into the world to make new friends for myself, and perhaps for my country.

This, I think, was the essence of my own personal vintage from *Valley of the Vines*.

CHAPTER SIX

THE BORDER

IN November we set off on a journey to the Eastern Province. This part of South Africa, between Port Elizabeth and the Transkei, is still known as 'the border', for only a century ago it was frontier territory dividing the old Cape Colony from Kaffraria and was the scene of endless Kaffir Wars between the settlers and the tribesmen.

The area was originally colonized by nomadic Boer cattle-men and their families whose numbers were later reinforced by the British immigrants of 1820.

These new colonists arrived under a scheme evolved by the Governor, Lord Charles Somerset, who aimed to create a wall of flesh and blood to bolster up his meagre military patrols along the turbulent border. England, then in the throes of her Industrial Revolution, offered little opportunity to her own enterprising young men, and pamphlets, as alluring as they were misleading, attracted prospective settlers with promises of grants and assistance in the 'ideal farming country of the sunny Cape'. No mention was made of drought or hostile stock-thieving Kaffirs, or burned out farmhouses and dense bush, where stolen cattle were concealed, elephants roamed and assegais flew from dark hidden hands. The Governor reckoned that by the time the immigrants were wise to these matters they'd be too far from home to change their minds, and – knowing his countrymen – too proud also.

The story of their cruel disillusionment and bitter hardships, of their simple border farms serving as fortresses against marauding Kaffirs, of wives and mothers who held these isolated outposts while their menfolk rode out with the patrols to recapture stolen stock, is a saga as moving to the English-speaking South African as the Great Trek is to his Afrikaner counterpart. When the Boers trekked north into the unknown hinterland the British colonists saw them go with heavy hearts. Their departure left the border sadly depleted and the settlers had little reason to trust the Cape Town administration.

But they made good. Like the pioneering Boers their courage was crowned with achievement. Churches, schools, hamlets and towns sprang up in the bush. The first merino sheep were introduced. The line of military forts and hilltop look-out towers along the wagon-trail from the coast became the blue-print for the speedway that today serves a thriving agricultural and industrial area. Lord Charles Somerset had been right. His people had proved bold, hardy and tenacious in adversity.

In the mid-nineteenth century there were various infusions of new blood, notably from the German Legionaries whose origin is commemorated in town names like Berlin and Stutterheim. Some of these warriors were already blessed with wives and children, and, for the rest, a shipload of brave young brides was transported from Ireland. What an enterprise! Imagine crossing the ocean to make a home in a new wild land as the wife of an unknown foreigner! Yet the history of the colonies includes the story of many such adventurous women.

Queenstown, the centre of the prosperous wool and dairy farming district, is famed for its two fine schools. Queen's College with over seven hundred boys, and the Girls' High School with about five hundred and fifty pupils. My husband and I had been invited to the prize-givings of these two colleges as the guests of honour.

We always enjoy touring in South Africa and we decided

to take the coastal Garden Route and then up through the Winterbergen, breaking our journey at George to stay with friends and again at Uitenhage for a night.

After crossing the first mountain range above Gordon's Bay we struck inland towards Swellendam and the undulating plateau which is one of the Cape's finest granaries. The pastel tapestry unfolded before us – the burnt umber of contour-ploughed earth, blue-green onion-lands, ripe wheat and biscuit-pale barley alive with a plague of finches and ready for the reapers.

On the uplands we passed the combined harvesters on their way to the wheatfields, and the suntanned young drivers waved us a greeting. Their hair was bleached light as the barley and their eyes were blue as the sky. They might have been the godlike Aryans of Hitler's dreams, and were certainly fine examples of the Afrikaner ideal of racial purity. Very good to look upon; gay and laughing because the harvest was a bumper one. But I found myself thinking of the Golden Age in Ancient Greece and the tall fair Achaeans who had come from the north, bringing their complex Olympian mythology with them, an intelligent heroic race. Yet, in the fullness of time, they had been absorbed by the small swarthy Pelasgians of the coast and even their gods had assumed an earthier character. Their immortal culture has remained, and their conception of democracy, but the people have changed. The blond hero is no more and the modern Greek is cast in the olive-skinned, dark-eyed Mediterranean mould so much better suited to the climate of his country. Here too, in this sundrenched land, the Nordic type may eventually become a survival.

There is an intense quality about the Afrikaner's love of his country which sets it apart from conventional patriotism and which must not be underestimated. It is rooted in his nature and his history.

Boer means farmer, but the Boers of South Africa were farmers with a difference. They were pioneers, nomadic cattle, men and hunters, pushing the frontiers of the old Cape Colony north as they extended their pasturage. They lived by the Bible, took the law into their own hands, and were already establishing outlying republics, such as Swellendam, in the days of the Dutch East India Company, for they liked the rule of 'Jan Kompanie' no better than they did the British régime which followed it when the Cape peacefully became a British possession after the Napoleonic Wars. It was the *method* of the emancipation of the Cape slaves which finally precipitated the Great Trek. Compensation for slaves could only be collected in London. This was manifestly impossible for frontier farmers, so the Boers sold their farms and claims for the price of wagon wheels, and, with their families, their flocks, herds and servants, the *voortrekkers* – those who go before – began their exodus into the unknown, pledging themselves never to enslave any man.

Many *trekkies* set off, some parties going one way, others blazing a different trail. Some found the Promised Land across the Orange River, others across the Vaal, and numbers of families were massacred by warlike tribes. In the mighty Drakensbergen – the Dragon Mountains – the Boers moving north and the Bantu warriors moving south came into inevitable conflict. But the twin Boer Republics of the Orange Free State and Transvaal were born, albeit with blood and tears. It was only the discovery of diamonds and gold that brought Imperial Britain back into the picture. By the chicanery of Cecil John Rhodes she acquired the Kimberley diamond-fields, and by a long bitter war, with little right on its side, she brought the Transvaal to its knees and a pastoral people saw their new young country disembowelled by the *uitlanders* – the foreign fortune hunters.

The true Afrikaner nationalism is born of the epic of the Great Trek and nourished by a century of accumulated wrongs culminating in the prolonged anguish of the Second Boer War. It is dedicated, emotional and militant, and what it has it intends to hold at any price. We at the Cape, with our older and less belligerent history, have been politically invaded by this vigorous northern spirit. Our destiny is being shaped by it, and, although we may dislike, resent and fear it, we are compelled to respect its fanatical determination. Meanwhile, Black African Nationalism thrives on the same dangerous food – a growing diet of grievances constantly stimulated both at home and abroad.

Near Swellendam we stopped to picnic on the banks of the Breede River and found that the migrant European swallows were there before us, scores of little navy-blue pearl-breasted birds, darting and twittering or resting and flexing their wings after the long flight from breeding-grounds perhaps as far away as Russia.

By tea-time we had run down to the coast to meet the Indian Ocean swell of Mossel Bay broken by rocky islands where the seals and sea-birds basked. Soon the Outeniquas – the Honey Mountains of the Hottentots – rose against a sky that was no longer burning cobalt but soft and pearly, a Lake Country sky filtering its sunlight through billowing clouds touched with evening gold.

Forests and heatherlands surround the pretty open town of George where a number of retired British military and colonial officers have settled, tempted by the low cost of living, a mild climate, beautiful surroundings, and the excellent country golf course. They refer to George affectionately as 'the burial ground of ancient Britons'.

Our host, Captain Gerald Hoare-Smith, R.N., retired, was a not very 'ancient' Briton who had fallen in love with this enchanting enclave. He and my husband were term-mates. They had entered the Navy at the same time, at the age of twelve, had fought in both world wars, had served on the Cape and China stations together, and shared the same selfless devotion to the Service which had given them their best and worst years. I had known Gerald since I was eighteen, but his striking brunette American wife, Frances, had only come into our lives after the war, for theirs was a brief wartime courtship when Gerald was already a senior Captain in command of an armed merchant cruiser refitting in America. It was he who said to me, after Bertie retired: 'You never lose the Navy. It's with you in your dreams. Night after night you take ships into battle or safely into harbour. Or not so safely!' He had grinned, with his mouth down at the corners and his eyes melting, for he was never able to speak of the Navy without emotion. He was a big man with teddy-bear coloured hair and eyes, who concealed a tender heart and a sentimental soul beneath a somewhat truculent exterior.

Gerald and Frances lived near the golf course, which is set in majestic scenery, and, when we stayed with them, golf and bridge were our recreations. Their house was single-storeyed, like most of those round about, with a delightful garden, a green lawn and shady clumps of giant snow-drops, violets and lilies-of-the-valley. Round the side were strawberry and asparagus beds and all sorts of delectable vegetables. From the stoep you looked across thick dark forests to the rugged slopes of George Mountain. But, once inside their home, the personality of our hostess took charge. Everything was comfortable and homely, yet highly original, from the ikon in the hall – almost a shrine – to the illuminated scrolls in our bedroom.

'Gerald's step-father did those. Exquisite, aren't they? He must have been a reincarnated monk!'

She used colours in a dashing way in her decoration, but formal portraits of her ancestors hung in the dining-room. Outside it the enclosed sun-stoep had an oriental flavour, with Gerald's Peking rugs on the floor, his wrought iron silhouette pictures on the primrose yellow walls, and the jade goddess of mercy, Kwan Yin, on a lacquer stand, her gentle slant eyes benevolently fixed on the cage of Chumley, the canary. Chumley was extremely vocal and never lonely, for, apart from enjoying the company of Kwan Yin, his rhapsodies attracted wild birds to the open windows by his cage, and we were often regaled with choirs of trilling birdsong.

That evening, when we had eaten a delicious dinner, Frances and I left our husbands navigating the Yangtse Rapids and reefs of the fog-bound China Sea, where the pirates wait to loot wrecked ships and kidnap wealthy voyagers.

'I'll take their coffee to them in the dining-room,' she said, 'and leave them in peace – or, rather, at war!' Her deep voice made the strong black coffee sound like some dark draught thick with the lees of memory.

We put out the card table for our family game of bridge, well knowing we'd have some time to wait for our partners.

She took a book from a shelf stocked with a considerable variety of literature, including naval histories, fiction, travel, biographies and a set of rare elaborately bound books that had come from Gerald's old home like the Staffordshire china on the mantelshelf under a portrait of her father.

'Your *Valley of the Vines*,' she said. 'Here's a pen for you to autograph it.'

A good deal of the *Valley of the Vines* had been written in this hospitable home. I signed it and she glanced at the inscription and smiled as she put it back on the shelf.

'You haven't asked me what I thought of this book.'

'I was afraid you'd tell me.'

She laughed. 'The American critics called it the plantation novel of South Africa. You certainly gave the reader the works.'

'Too much?'

'It read to me as if you were scared you'd never write another novel as long as you lived. All heaven, hell and high water had to go into this one.'

The doors in her house were left open in summer, and I watched her go along the covered stoep and put a cloth over Chumley's cage.

'Even echoes of China,' I said. 'The Chinese love birds. You often see a Chinaman flapping along in his grey gown with a cage swinging from his hand, just as we might take a dog out on a leash.'

She half turned. 'Yes, they tie wild birds together at each end of a long string and throw them into the air for the fun of seeing them go crazy when they feel the jerk of the string. The strong one drags the weaker or they get tangled up in a tree. Usually, one is destroyed. See, I remember your analogy – that marriage can be like that, a partnership without freedom. Individualists pulling two ways, tormenting themselves and each other in the process. As you say, even China found its way into your picture of the Constantia valley.'

'I was five years in China, off and on. It's in me, so it's bound to creep into my books. Most of one's experience does, one way and another, I suppose.'

Our husbands joined us. The dachshund, a sexy animal, snaked off into the summer night with the air of one who has important business on hand, the big black Labrador sprawled by his master's chair, whipping round with a grunt every now and again to bite at a flea or a tick.

The grandmother clock struck ten in a peremptory fashion, as if to say, 'Bedtime in the country! Away with the cards!' Up on George Mountain the nightly train puffed its way towards Oudtshoorn and the ostriches, uttering a shrill whistle as it reached the tunnel through the pass. Gerald poured out nightcaps.

'You're right,' I said to Frances. 'I *did* put too much into

Valley. Maybe a first novel is a bit like a first love affair. One feels it's the first, the last, and the only one.'

'And then one learns better. Where d'you go for honey now?'

'I don't know yet. But I'm on my way. The urge to begin is prickling in my nerves.'

'Good,' she said. 'This place seems to inspire you.'

Next morning we woke to a serenade from Chumley and his friends, to the scent of roses and the soft mizzle that keeps George grass so green. It can rain there any day of the year, torrentially in winter and gently in the driest summer, which is, I believe, what makes the 'ancient Britons' feel so very much at home.

The day's run from George to Uitenhage is a scenic delight.

The excellent road winds along a superb coastline, threads a shining chain of lakes and lagoons, and crosses mountain passes where the arum lilies stand waist high in shadowy fern-carpeted ravines. Primeval bush alternates with impressive timber plantations, and, in the Tsitsikama jungle-forests the giant yellowwood trees reach for the sun, their soaring arms festooned with liana monkey-ropes and orchid-aceous creepers, while fever-trees strain upwards in their tatters of weird parasitic growth. Here the last of the monster Knysna elephants still roam the verdant hills and vales and the awesome silence, broken only by bird-calls, makes one dream of Eden before the creation of man.

Towards evening we arrived at Uitenhage.

The leafless jacarandas, in the fullness of their blue-mauve glory, stood in pools of fallen petals, their pure remote beauty off-set by the silver-oaks with their heavy clusters of amber flowers. Now we were really in the Eastern Province.

Early next morning we sped along the old military line of forts to the one-time garrison base of Grahamstown that is now a provincial town full of intimate charm and academic dignity. The 'redcoats' of last century have been replaced by the gowns of the professors and graduates of Rhodes University which sponsors the not far distant Bantu University of Fort Hare. Unfortunately, Fort Hare today is a sullen seat of learning where angry young African intellectuals fret and fume against a White government which controls their destiny and strives to 'keep them in their place'.

The sun was high when we reached the grazing lands, citrus farms and pineapple groves in the lush foothills of the Winterbergen, and then we began the long dramatic ascent of the Katberg Pass.

At the summit, over five thousand feet up, we stood, small and humbled by the infinity of Africa. Down in the blue haze, darkened here and there by slowly moving cloud shadows, were human habitations sparsely scattered and scarcely visible. The keen air was fresh with the cool elusive scent of waterfalls and the sweet fragrance of mimosa: the solitude, intensified by every sound, was absolute.

Queenstown, on the edge of Bantu territory, is the heart of a prosperous wool, dairy and grain-farming district. It is on the banks of the Great Kei River and its fine open streets ray off a Hexagon with gardens and fountains that was once the defence core of a frontier town. Groups of 'red Natives' in ochre blankets, with ochre-painted faces and copper bangles, add their exotic pagan touch to a pleasant citadel of modern South African youth. On every side we saw the black and orange blazers and straw boaters of Queen's College and the dark skirts, white blouses and scarlet-bordered blazers of the Girls' High School. The mascots of the town were a pair of royal swans sent from the Thames to populate this distant reach of water with the cygnets of the Queen.

During our short stay we were the guests of Dr. P. J. Davies, the Principal of Queen's College, who was not only a distinguished scholar but an international athlete. His wife made us feel at home immediately with her serene air of nothing being any bother. And, while we were having sundowners after our day's journey, their eight-year-old daughter Rhonnda, looking just like Alice in Wonderland with a snood on her soft dark hair, appeared proudly wheeling a doll's pram in which sat an alert beaming piccaninny belonging to the Tembu cook.

On our last evening, before the Girls' prize-giving, we were entertained to a buffet supper by Mr. and Mrs. Green. Mr. Green was Chairman of the Girls' High School and the whole family was closely connected with Queenstown's two famous colleges. We were all much saddened, however, when, during supper, Miss Dankwerts, the Head Mistress, was urgently called away. Instead of being present at the prize-giving – the culmination of a year's hard and successful work – she was driving through the night along the lonely road to Port Elizabeth to the deathbed of her mother.

We left Queenstown next day with many regrets and a picnic basket sumptuously replenished by our kind and thoughtful hostess. We returned to Cape Town by way of the Karoo.

At midday we took time off for our lunch-hour break in a dry river-bed where thorn-trees offered the luxury of shade. Far off a sunlit cloud of dust told us that a flock of sheep was on the move, while nearer at hand cattle huddled under willows fringing a dam. An eagle left its makeshift nest at the top of a telegraph pole and planed gently overhead in search of a victim. A meerkat scuttled across the road and sat up on the verge, tiny paws upraised in gratitude for a safe crossing. A lizard sunned himself on a flat stone, a few large black ants interested themselves in our crumbs and birds cheeped among branches guarded by strong stiletto thorns pale as bleached bones. The shimmering skyline was broken by lavender sugar-loaf koppies and flat sliced mountains floating, ark-like, in swamps of mirage.

Bertie spread a canvas dust-sheet on the parched earth and flung down a couple of cushions and I unpacked the feast provided by Mrs. Davies. A newspaper, dated two days back, covered the contents of the basket. As I put it aside a paragraph caught my eye. 'Girl Flies to Wed Pen Pal, Changes Mind'.

After our meal, while Bertie dozed, I read the story. A young Swedish woman had flown to Rhodesia to marry her tobacco farmer pen pal, but the romance had not survived so much as one day in his company. She had flown home by the next plane.

The situation intrigued me. Would a pen and ink love affair ever be likely to materialize in a flesh and blood marriage without one single meeting or any normal courtship? There was an inset photograph of the Swedish girl. She was pretty enough. Surely she could have found someone in her own country to make her happy. Perhaps her home environment bored her and she felt the need to do something spectacular and improbable. Her case was very different from the bride cargoes imported for the early colonists. They were committed. There was no quick flight back if they didn't fancy their draw from the lucky bag. In the days of Van

Riebeeck, three hundred years ago, a number of unendowed orphans from Rotterdam had risked the long perilous Cape passage to marry eligible servants of the Dutch East India Company; and even the Irish girls chosen for the German Legionaries last century had probably been influenced by clever propaganda and dire poverty in their own country. In any case, they were a group, catching excitement and optimism from one another, even if these sentiments were, at times, spiced with panic.

'You're very quiet,' said Bertie.

'You were snoozing. Actually, I was thinking about girls who come to a strange country to marry men they've never set eyes on. Like the Greek fruiterer near Tees Lodge who married a girl sent to him by his relatives in Athens. And, as far as one could tell, it was a success.'

'The families knew each other. The arranged marriage is a tried institution and can work out all right. The Malays often marry girls they've never seen before the wedding service. If the horoscopes are propitious and the parents are satisfied that's enough for them. You should know that, you've lived in China. Moreover, a good African tribe likes to choose the wife for its Chief.'

'The Malays and Chinese are Eastern people. They have a different outlook. But a modern European woman – a Western individualist – surely she must do her own choosing! Now, a pen-pal romance, could that really light the physical flame?'

'It could discover interests in common – stimulate the mind. The rest might follow, I suppose.'

I began to repack the picnic basket, covering it once more with the folded sheet of newsprint. I had torn out the paragraph about the girl who had flown to 'wed pen pal' – and left him flat! But I wasn't really interested in her any more. She was a stupid looking blonde with a petulant mouth.

The first exciting twinges of creative inspiration were already gripping me, and already I could see a dark intense young woman of fierce passions inhibited by self-discipline. She was in love with Africa, but duty held her bound in England. Correspondence with an unknown South African was her channel of escape, giving her life a deeper meaning. Free her and see what happened! Africa and a certain type of man could be strong pressure-cookers for the pent-up emotions of such a girl.

I took a deep breath of the warm Karoo air. It smelt of sunbaked earth and dry desert winds.

Soon we were on our way, slowing down to pass the jostling sheep in their gold dust cloud with the Bantu shepherds and the dogs to harry them. This was the tame aspect of my land of infinite variety. Here men struggled to protect the sheep from the jackals and the leopards, yet further afield there were great well-watered sanctuaries where such killers had their own *lebensraum*, where man existed on sufferance and fire and poachers were the only enemies.

Thus it was that Mrs. Davies, in covering our cold collation with a folded newspaper to keep out the dust, inadvertently provided me with the inspiration for my second novel.

Although the idea for *Nor the Moon by Night* took fire that day in the Karoo I had to live with it for weeks before I could begin working on it. Since my hero insisted on being a game warden, I had to read up wild life and its conservation from a new angle. Instead of seeing our sanctuaries with the eyes of a tourist I had to try to put myself in the place of the rangers and the wild creatures. My heroine refused to be anything except a fully trained hospital nurse, and luckily I had learned something about her vocation a few years earlier in London when I had been commissioned to write a series of articles on medical subjects for a glossy magazine. These included the training of student nurses and a pen portrait of the young modern-minded matron of St. George's Hospital.

This attractive matron was a wary animal to track down and reluctant to be featured, but when she did consent to 'come to hand' she proved to be one of the most stimulating and helpful personalities I have ever met. She was also photogenic, and my colleague, a penetrating Austrian Jewish photographer, brought out the sincerity and lively humour in the face of this slim dark woman whose humanity was unblunted by a routine involving continual familiarity with suffering.

St. George's has various offshoots, for its many departments could not all be contained within the limited space at Hyde Park Corner, and one evening, after we had visited the Children's wards in Chelsea, the matron came back to our flat with me and met my husband.

She was frankly envious when she heard that we were soon going to South Africa to settle down for good.

'I've always longed to go to Africa,' she said. 'I even went so far as to learn Swahili with the intention of working in East Africa.'

'What stopped you?'

'It just wasn't possible in the end. I was needed here in England.'

I wondered about the nature of the duty that had held her chained and guessed it to be personal. When she left, looking rather dashing at the wheel of her little car with her outdoor cape over her shoulders, she said:

'If ever you're in trouble and I can help, let me know. I mean it.'

I smiled and waved, but her words sank into my mind and remained there, to be recalled years later in an hour of need.

CHAPTER SEVEN

EAST-ABOUT AFRICA

Soon after the Christmas and New Year holidays we let 'Cressage' to the Netherlands Ambassador for the parliamentary session. Pretoria is the administrative capital of South Africa but Parliament sits in Cape Town during the summer, so the diplomats have their official residence in Pretoria and, with a few exceptions, have the inconvenience of hiring houses at the Cape during the session. The same applies to the majority of civil servants and politicians. Our dual capital is an expensive luxury all round.

Jan van den Berg, then the doyen of the Diplomatic Corps, and his wife, Erica, are much loved in South Africa. Both are generous and large-hearted and they never forget that the greater part of our countrymen came to this land from – or by way of – the Netherlands. Erica is one of those exuberant personalities who simply sweeps difficulties aside with a gesture and the words, 'It will arrange itself, you'll see.'

'Your cat and dog, Joy? Just let them stay. Snowy is sweet, so cheeky! He'll adore our dogs as they are both females. Kitty'll be all right. Don't worry about Kitty.'

We didn't bother with an inventory. It was all very un-business-like and easy-going. Our cook, Mary, took a temporary job, and our little maid, Sybil, returned to her village near Villiersdorp to study for her confirmation in the Dutch Reformed Chruch. In the next few months she learned the Bible almost by heart. To learn to be a true Christian, of course, takes a whole lifetime and is a much more painful process. Even the best churchman don't always make the grade, and, as for the rest of us, we are usually, as Sombani would put it, 'only littie bittie Christian'. Sombani remained on at 'Cressage' during our absence to tend the garden to the best of his ability.

Our reason for letting our home was to enable us to go back to England and see our friends and relations. We had decided to go by the East Coast, and sailed from Cape Town early in February, 1956, in a one-class ship crammed with passengers doing the round trip from England. Many of them were retired north country business men with their wives, keen to see the 'twenty sunny ports' advertised by the Shipping Company. Others were elderly folk dodging the tail-end of the European winter, and there were various families and young people going out to East Africa. The most interesting passengers, however, were five Cape Malay pilgrims making the long journey to Mecca, two married couples and a widow. The ladies were plump and veiled and the men wore European suits. The leader of the party was slight and fair-complexioned, with gold-rimmed glasses, and, of course, a fez. All were middle-aged, for the Malays work all their lives to save enough money for the pilgrimage, and often their children contribute to help them. When they have been to Mecca they can live and die in peace.

The south-easter had raged all day, but by nightfall, when we sailed, the wind had dropped, the cloud had lifted from the mountain and the myriad shimmering lights of my home-town were blinking up at the stars. All the children on board clutched paper streamers attached to hands ashore, and the pilgrims leaned over the rail to call 'totsiens' to an enormous and decorative crowd of Malay well-wishers who had come to see them off.

The ship drew away from the wharf, the paper streamers snapped and floated away on the dark water, our jaunty tugs whooped and whistled farewells that echoed round the bay, and there was the familiar creak and groan of a liner under way that has been so much a part of my life.

We soon settled down; and the pilgrims found themselves a secluded nook in the stern under the awning that covered the kennel housing two Alsatian police-dogs on their way from London to Mombasa. At Port Elizabeth and East London we were met by friends, while the pilgrims were welcomed by large groups of fellow Moslems.

At Durban we spent a lovely day with Ian and Nan Bassett. Bertie and Ian played golf on a delightful course where little grey monkeys with sapphire behinds swung out of the trees to steal golf balls, but Nan and I, too lazy for golf, stayed at home to swim in their pool which was set in a corner of the terraced garden among exotic trees alive with birds and butterflies. When our husbands rejoined us they were exhausted by the heat, dehydrated and crying out for iced drinks.

'This is like being in the desert again,' said Ian, who had been one of the many thousand South Africans taken prisoner at Tobruk in World War II. 'Ah, this shandy was the sort of thing that haunted our dreams!'

Ian and Nan had made the East Coast trip in an Italian liner some years after the war. It had been as much a pilgrimage for them as our own voyage was for our Mecca-bound Malays. They had taken blankets and tinned food to the peasants who had sheltered Ian and two of his fellow prisoners when they had escaped from their Italian prison camp after the collapse of Italy.

'The poverty of those peasants was heart-rending,' Nan said. 'Yet they had shared what little they had, and they'd risked death and torture to help our men. When we went back there to that tiny mountain village, the old man, Mario, who had hidden and looked after Ian, just couldn't believe his eyes. He put out his arms and said, "My son, you have come back!" and they walked towards each other like that, arms outstretched, and both were weeping . . .'

While Ian was in the wild mountains of the Abruzzi, making his difficult way back to freedom, I, too, had been in

Italy, working in the Anglo-American Psychological War-fare Branch of the Allied Forces. My section of this unit was a news and information service and, throughout the Italian campaign, we followed the allied armies up the boot of Italy to Trieste, opening information centres in the various cities as they were liberated. But there was another section which operated closely with the Partisans, supplying them with their needs for purposes of sabotage and the assistance of escaping Allied prisoners. Thus bold young Partisans often came into our offices in Florence or Milan, shabby but dashing in their dark green uniforms and Robin Hood hats. Their work was dangerous and secret, constantly jeopardized by treachery among their own people, and, if they were caught, their families were made to suffer. They were tough and wiry, and I have never forgotten a certain look in their eyes – the alert wariness of men who were hunters and hunted. So it interested me to encourage Ian to talk about his adventures as a prisoner and a fugitive, and I soon realized that to him that period was the most significant in his life, a time in which he had learned the worst and the best in human nature.

It is extraordinary how a novelist collects human material and stores it away in the attic of the mind, just in case it might come in useful some time or another. Echoes of Ian's experiences found their way into my fourth novel years later.

After Durban we said good-bye to South Africa and sailed into steamy equatorial heat. I was working hard by then, setting aside several hours a day for writing, even though I dripped all over the pages of my scribble-book.

The most popular place in the ship was the little swimming-bath on deck. It was always as crowded as a London night-club dance floor – no room to do anything except tread water. We were now in the safari zone and the purser would broadcast plans for 'this vessel' before arrival at every port. Passengers could arrange to leave the ship at one East African port and rejoin it later, having rushed up the coast in safari cars in the meantime. They came back on board with exciting tales of the animals they had seen and photographed. I listened avidly. It was all in line with my new wild life attitude of mind.

Unfortunately, Bertie felt the heat even more than I did,

and was often afflicted by headaches. None of the cabins were air-conditioned; the children became fretful and some were foolish enough to tease the Alsatians, but the fiercer of the two took a steak out of a small boy's rump and that taught the rest a sharp lesson. The young contingent lived in bikinis and the briefest briefs and played deck games thus attired. The pilgrims averted their eyes from the sight. In the purser's broadcasts he implored 'the young ladies of this vessel not to go ashore improperly clad as this would give grave offence to Moslem susceptibilities'. Our pilgrims, their susceptibilities pulverized daily, remained unruffled. One felt that they were armoured in spiritual contentment, immune to the outrageous ways of western youth.

In all my travels I have never seen an isle of greater charm than Zanzibar.* Our vessel anchored in the harbour early one morning, and was instantly invaded by the inevitable Indian merchants with their families and their wares consisting of the usual Indian and Japanese kimonos and slippers, carved African elephants and Native heads, basketwork, amber, ivory and filigree beads, and bizarre shirts stamped with eastern symbols. After the usual bargaining I bought three little cotton dressing-gowns for my grandsons, embroidered with fearsome dragons, and tried them on a small Indian boy who sniggered and swaggered, clearly feeling ridiculous. Not the sort of thing *he'd* be seen dead in! My grandchildren were in complete agreement with him, and gave the gowns to three dear little girls of their acquaintance within an hour of receiving them.

An ancient and unreliable ferry-boat, run by a very old Swahili in a grubby nightshirt and little round cap, conveyed us to the fragrant spice island where dazzling white Moorish houses gleamed among palms and flame-trees.

Waiting for us on the jetty was Mr. Tommy Dyer-Melville, to whom we had been given an introduction by our friend Gordon Taylor, the South African artist, who often spent a painting holiday in Zanzibar. Mr. Dyer-Melville, a much travelled man, who had lived in the island on and off since 1911, was Engineer to the Clove Growers' Association. He had recently returned from Nairobi, where he had undergone a cataract operation for both eyes.

'It's given me a new lease of life,' he said. 'For years I've

* Now part of Tanzania.

lived in a fog. Now everything has an outline again and I can see to sketch and paint. It's like recovering a part of youth.'

He had a weary way of saying exciting things, like an actor who throws away his best lines. He was, perhaps, in his early seventies, spare and wan, with the pallor of the tropics, very immaculate in palm beach trousers and a blue shirt. No jacket.

He took us for a drive through orange and banana groves and coconut, clove, cinnamon and ylang-ylang plantations.

'Who owns all these?' I asked, indicating the coconut palms.

'Arabs. By the skin of their teeth.'

He went on to explain that during the past years the Arabs had mortgaged everything to the Indians, who are the acquisitive and powerful financiers of the entire East African coast. But, before the Indians could foreclose, the Government realized what was happening and took out a bond on the threatened plantations, renting them out to the original owners for a very low sum in lieu of interest. Finally it assisted the Arabs to regain possession of their plantations on the strict understanding that never again must they mortgage them to wily Indians.

The Arabs and Swahilis often intermarry, and the children playing outside the mud palm-thatched huts under paw-paw and banana trees, were Arabian copper or African ebony. Humped cattle drew little carts lazily along the country roads, but fine cars glittered in the town. In the Public Gardens we were amused to observe a new sort of *apartheid*. There were 'women's hours' when ladies in *purdah* could disport themselves under the glorious trees undisturbed by the intrusive presence of the male.

Britain acquired Zanzibar in exchange for Heligoland under an Anglo-German Convention in 1890, but now this British Protectorate under the Sultanate, is, like every other part of Africa, preparing for the pipe-dream men call freedom.

The Sultan, who dwelt in a large white Moorish palace in the port and a small informal one on the seashore, was a monogamist in the British tradition. His son and heir was a clever boy trained by an English tutor who had hoped that his charge would one day go to an English public school and university. But one morning, shortly after his twelfth birthday, the young heir to the throne failed to appear in the classroom at the appointed time. When the tutor asked why his pupil was playing truant, he discovered that the lad had been married the night before.

'I am now a married man,' said the precocious boy imperiously. 'So no more lessons for me!'

Perhaps the young prince was only reversing the usual order of instruction. By the time he was fourteen his mind was probably once more free for further study of an academic nature.

Zanzibar was Britain's East African base against the slave trade, and the English Cathedral covers the grave of the old slave market. One wonders what dark ghosts lift shackled hands to the Cross in that House of God! But sad reflections are sent packing by the enchantment of the port. Massive teak doors, carved and studded with brass spikes to discourage enemies or elephants, open on to narrow sickle-curved streets; traffic is directed with great dash by coal-black Swahili policemen in red tarbooshes and gloves, spotless white shirts and khaki shorts and spats. In the harbour the Muscat dhows lie at anchor as they have done for over a thousand years, trading Persian carpets and Indian tiles for the spices and aphrodisiacs of Africa, and ivory, white and black. They will tell you on that coast that the slave trade still prospers, and that the European nations no longer care. The balance of interference in other people's affairs has shifted. It is Africa who tells Europe where her conduct is at fault and Europe meekly bows her head.

Mr. Dyer-Melville took us to the Zanzibar Club for a magnificent curry lunch with flaky rice and all the trimmings – chopped paw-paw, pineapple, peppers, paprika, bananas and Bombay duck, cucumber and coconut. Afterwards, we had coffee on the balcony overlooking the bay. We were joined for this feast by Mrs. Dyer-Melville, our host's Polish wife, who whisked us round-the-world-in-eighty-minutes with her supreme gift of mimicry.

'In Omsk my nose was frozen. My friends cried out, "It is white! It will break off like a piece of china if you touch it!" They took me into a farmhouse and put snow on it and massaged it very gently, then some black stuff. It hurt and swelled. For a year it was a deformity. Black, like a dog's snout!' Her hands spoke. They grabbed her hair and stood it up on end. We crossed Siberia with her in a train packed with Russian refugees in 1919; we tossed from Vladivostok to Shanghai in a typhoon with a crowd of seasick passengers who had been determined 'to eat their money's worth regardless of the elements'; we consorted with a Maharajah in Paris whose wives wore 'diamonds in ears and noses'; and had a contretemps with a London bobby, at which stage Mrs. Dyer-Melville's small plump hands turned into a policeman's feet pacing an imaginary pavement with awful deliberation. Finally, she returned us, entranced and bewildered, to the Zanzibar Club.

We sailed at dusk. A fleet of dhows passed us, their great lateen sails billowing in the evening breeze – dark ships with few guiding lights, ghostly against the stars. A moon like white fire rose among the curdled clouds; the aromatic scents of Zanzibar faded and our day among the cloves and coconut palms was as unreal as a fragment of a traveller's dream.

Our vessel spent three days at Mombasa, and we left her to stay ashore at the Nyali Beach Hotel, where we had arranged to meet friends from Kenya. Elspeth Rhodes had left her ranch at Njoro and come to the coast with her married step-daughter, Pam, especially to join us during our brief visit. Elspeth, dark and ethereal, was untroubled by the damp heat that wilted Pam and me.

Mombasa is an attractive island, though not unique like Zanzibar, and the hotel was cool and pleasant. Swallows had built their nests under the eaves of our balcony and at sunset they swooped in with a great twittering, and we'd see the forked tails quivering before they turned round and settled for the night. There was a huge flamboyant tree outside our window, its elaborate scarlet flowers ravished by honey-bees and hornets. Down on the beach you could hire little canvas shelters by the day, but we preferred to put deckchairs under the trees and sip cool drinks and talk.

Elspeth, who is a woman of mists and shadows, suspicious of the sun, made herself more than usually mysterious by wearing a straw flower-pot hat that covered her entire face, only allowing her dark eyes to look through a pair of tinted windows set at a fetching angle. When she went down to the tepid sea she stepped so lightly that she hardly left her *spoor* in the sand, and swam quietly as if not wishing to disturb the water. It was her habit to dress in protective colouring, no frills, so that she melted into the landscape. And when she scented danger she had the doe's way of 'freezing', head up, nostrils distended.

Anybody who has lived through the Mau Mau troubles in Kenya has learnt caution. Our friends had been comparatively new settlers there, but they had lived with revolvers always to hand, never sitting down to a meal with their backs to a door or a window, locking themselves into their room at night and wondering how trustworthy their farmhands or house staff might be. Would they wake to hear that their precious dairy cows had been horribly mutilated, or would they themselves be found slashed to death by pangas? When at last it seemed that Mau Mau was quelled the settlers rejoiced. Once again the future looked bright. Farms were paying their way and there was a resurgence of optimism. Few could envisage the speed with which they were to be abandoned by their mother country. Like the border settlers of the old Cape Colony, British colonists of Kenya had yet to learn that, as far as London was concerned, they were only part of a policy. In the days of the Cape Colony the policy had been expansion and the 'wall of flesh and blood' had been needed to help it on its way. Now the policy was contraction and the productive White Highlands of a young promising colony threatened to become a dying legend of endeavour, achievement – and retreat. Many disillusioned East African settlers have since come south to the Republic of South Africa where the White end of the see-saw is still high. They are our gain. One day it will all level out in Africa, but precious policies and ideals of both Blacks and Whites will have to be drastically modified before the sun shines on a reasonably fair deal for all.

One of our nicest memories of Mombasa was a trip round the harbour with Commander and Mrs. Gibbs in a naval launch. Commander Gibbs was in charge of the Naval Base and lived in a pleasant house on the waterside where we had drinks afterwards. We sailed all round the island in the cool of the evening, and, under the grim windowless walls of Fort Jesus, once a slave fortress and still a prison, we saw the dhows at anchor. Little model aeroplanes flew at their prows – strangely modern touch – and the ancient woodwork and flimsy gangways were all picked out in blue to give the illusion of tiles. When we circled round them they smelt of all the spices of Arabia and a few less salubrious aromas as well. Sombre seamen with the faces of Barbary pirates looked down upon us, unsmiling.

We bade Elspeth and Pam good-bye, and returned to our vessel refreshed by the change. Our fierce Alsatian police-dogs had been disembarked at Mombasa but our gentle pilgrims still sat in their corner aft, serenely detached from shipboard activities.

Soon everybody became excited about Aden, our next port of call, which was almost duty-free and therefore the place for bargains. But there was a strike on and no cargo could be unloaded, so we oiled out in the harbour from a floating pipe-line that made our vessel look as if she were receiving a blood-transfusion. The usual bumboats came alongside with their noisy salesmen – more Arabs than Indians now – and in the crew's quarters cigarettes were briskly bartered for tea-sets, kimonos, silk scarves for half a crown that would cost two guineas in a London store, and Japanese binoculars and cameras.

We left at dawn. The sky was streaked with pink, and the new moon was suspended above the naked hills. The pilgrims stood on deck, their faces raised to the young moon of Ramadan, their hearts lifting to the first cold dry breath of the desert breeze.

It was night and the wharf at Port Sudan was floodlit a ghostly green. White-gowned figures lay outside the row of sheds like dead men. But we had no sooner made fast alongside than a foreman uttered a loud compelling cry and the sleepers came to life and sprang on board to unload our cargo of Kenya coffee.

Fuzzie-Wuzzies came too, clad in filthy rags, their wild gollywog mops bleached by cow's urine, their mouths agape, showing both rows of savage teeth very white in their black faces. They perched among the winches and began working them like clever apes in mechanical trees. In their mops they wore what I took to be daggers, but they were really only handsomely carved primitive tail-combs good for a dig and a scratch every now and again. A young Scotsman bossed them with much gesticulation and shouting, and often he seized one by that insanitary hair and shoved him this way or that. In the remotest part of the world there is always a Scotsman giving somebody orders.

A camel caravan was encamped beyond the warehouses, a goat and a kid wandered along the wharf eating bits of paper and cigarette ends.

'The only known method of turning old scraps of paper into milk,' said Bertie. 'We must wish our pilgrims luck. They leave us here.'

'We wait here for another ship, then twenty-four hours' voyage by that; then twenty-four hours' journey by bus. Then three months in the desert,' their leader told us. His eyes behind the gold-rimmed spectacles, shone with joy.

No one met them. They walked down the gangway and past the lights of the sheds into the vast nothingness of the desert night. They were a very small group going to meet the great spiritual experience of their lives.

We could still see the Southern Cross low in the sky.

We sailed after breakfast. The arid mountains were pale amethyst, the mud town was backed by the neat pyramids of the salt-pans. The sea was transparent jade with shoals of iridescent fish; flocks of sea-birds wheeled against the cloudless sky, and the air was fresh. But, in summer, they say, Port Sudan is the 'hottest and most desolate hole on earth'.

Two days later we took our place in the Canal convoy at Suez and waved farewell to the Red Sea.

For the next twelve hours everybody was on deck with their cameras. Our passage was as quiet as that of a Venetian gondola. No waves or currents to buffet our vessel. The Egyptian bank was green and fertile with palms and towns and bathing beaches, and the camel and the ass were teamed together to plough the cultivated strips between the mud villages. On the other side was the sandy waste of the Sinai Desert.

Where the Canal widened for the Bitter Lakes and the Sweet Lakes we passed the southbound convoy, led by an aggressive British destroyer, her lean flanks stained by a blood-red sunset.

The lights of Port Said and Simon Arzt beckoned the tourists; the bumboats, filled with leatherwork, swarmed round us, and the galli-galli man came on board and took chickens out of children's ears. We bought our first English airmail papers and the wind blew colder now. At noon next day we saw Port Said recede into the distance without regret.

The Mediterranean was in an angry mood. Genoa, on its hilltop, was icy cold. Marseilles was colder still with torrential rains. Gibraltar was a noble rock seen at night against the swinging stars as we tossed in a rough sea.

Our vessel groaned and heaved through the Bay of Biscay, as did many of the passengers, and then, at last, in the early afternoon of 27th March, we entered the English Channel.

The sea was calm and the silvery sun of an English spring welcomed us back. But we were not on deck with most of our fellow passengers.

My husband was on his bunk overcome by the blinding pain of the worst headache he had yet suffered. I knelt at the porthole and looked at Dover Castle brooding over the little harbour. The sky was pale and fragile as the shell of a duck's egg, a subdued sparkle brightened the water, the sheer white cliffs were thatched by English grass. So richly green! The war years came to my mind with all their peril and endurance. Dover's ordeal – met with such stubborn courage – had been second to none. This was the England of an island people – of ships and sailors. This was Bertie's England. And he lay with his face to the wall.

We had ordered a station-wagon and driver to meet us at Tilbury next morning to take us and our baggage across London to the little service flat we had hired near Kensington High Street.

Bertie was able to raise his head from the pillow and dress himself. We were the last to disembark, and I could see that the pain was mounting again. But London was in her most alluring mood as if to banish all sensation save delight in her remembered beauty.

The Tower was mellow in the soft spring radiance, and Tower Bridge flung its graceful span of mediaeval history across the burnished Thames. Almond blossom flaunted its delicate youth among old grey roofs. The spires of Westminster rose in the heart of a once mighty empire now dedicated to the democratic vision of a brotherhood of nations within the Commonwealth.

'Darling,' I said. 'This is London at her loveliest.'

But he only answered, 'Your voice comes from far away.'

I grew terribly afraid. He is very ill indeed, I thought. What can I do now? What doctor can I get? Is there time to take our luggage into our new flat and ring up friends to ask for the name of a doctor? He's not in the Navy any more. There isn't anyone I can think of at the Admiralty. We're just ordinary people in trouble. What can I do? And then, as we drove up Buckingham Palace Road into the whirlpool of Hyde Park Corner, I leaned forward and said to our driver, 'Please stop at St. George's Hospital. Right here.'

So I went into the old blitz-battered hospital that had covered up her wounds so well, and I wondered if the matron of St. George's would be the one I had interviewed when we still had our Chelsea flat – and whether she would remember me. By some miracle she was in the hall, and I saw her come towards me.

'Joy Packer!'

The slight figure blurred, and, through my own tears, I saw her dark eyes fill with concern.

'You said if ever I was in trouble . . . I'm in bad trouble . . . My husband . . .'

'Where is he?'

'Outside in the station-wagon. We've just landed from South Africa.'

She went to him at once. He recognized her and tried to smile. After that she took charge.

When next I saw him he was in a long ward that shook as the big red buses rumbled past the Memorial and turned down Knightsbridge. It was bright and there were daffodils on the nurses' table in the centre between the cots. He was wearing white flannel pyjamas too small for him, and he had been given something to ease the pain. He managed to tell me that it had been 'an inspiration' to bring him here, and then he fell asleep.

The threads of fate are many and far-reaching and are placed in our hands for a purpose. We may tangle or break them, or weave them clumsily or well, but the design is not without meaning. It had been a long and tortuous journey from the morning when I had come here on a journalist's assignment to this moment in time – this sad homecoming on a spring day when the rampaging month of March was on her way out, gentle as a lamb. I knew, as I sat beside his bed in the long ward, that this hour had been predestined. Three years ago, when first I had crossed the threshold of St. George's, it had been written into the pattern of our lives.

CHAPTER EIGHT

SHADOWS

THE next few days were a lifetime of suspense.

For many months we had looked forward to an Easter family reunion at the Worcestershire cottage of my husband's sister, Marion, who was as near his twin in age and affection as any separate brother and sister could be. When he retired from the Royal Navy she had retired from her job in charge of the personnel of Glaxo's Laboratories, and, while we were building our home in South Africa, she was renovating a derelict Elizabethan cottage in the heart of the English countryside. His eldest sister, Dorothy, and her husband, Norman Capon, Professor Emeritus of Child Health at Liverpool University, had booked accommodation for us and themselves near the cottage, while the middle sister, Winifred, the headmistress of Craigholme, a well-known girls' school in Glasgow, would, as usual, spend her Easter vacation with Marion. We had timed our arrival in England for the Tuesday of Holy Week to give us time to take over our service flat before hiring a car and setting off for our country holiday.

And now my husband lay dangerously ill at St. George's.

But providence had been kind in our misfortune. Not only had we a personal friend in the Matron, but also in Bobby Burns, then Honorary Orthopaedic Surgeon to St. George's, who, by some fortunate chance, happened to be there in our moment of need. While Bertie was going through the formalities of admission Bobby tried to reassure me.

'You've brought him to the right place. St. George's has all the resources to look after him. This will pass, you'll have him back in a week or so and be spending a week-end with us before you know it. And now I'm going to see him and tell him what I've just told you.'

Bobby and his wife, Dorothy, the daughter of the late Lord Duveen, had a beautiful home in Windsor Forest and we had spent many delightful week-ends there. But those glamorous house-parties seemed far removed from this anxious March morning.

I went to the flat, unpacked a few things and telephoned Bertie's brother-in-law, Norman Capon, and promised to keep in touch with him. Everything and everybody else must wait.

When I returned to the hospital, the Registrar to the Senior Physician advised me to remain within call during the next twenty-four hours and Matron suggested that I could sleep in the pretty Regency Visitor's Room on the same floor as the Medical Ward.

The Registrar was youngish with sandy hair and the pallor of overwork and a London winter. He drifted in and out of the wards in his white coat and often conferred with the young House Physician. The nurses were sprightly and attractive, but firm with their patients, and the Ward Sister's word was law. I fancied that there was an armed truce between her and the young House Physician and that she accepted his seniority with private reservations, so that now and again he asserted himself to keep things on an even keel.

'You can see your husband when you like, within reason,' he told me. 'If sister makes a fuss say *I* said so!' He had mischievous dark eyes.

I was grateful for the privilege – though it warned me that my husband was very ill – and tried not to abuse it.

The official visiting hour was seven to eight in the evening. Suppers were served first. Then, when they had been cleared away, a nurse would ring the bell on the ward door, 'tring-tring', as crisp as herself, and fling it open, and in would troop a long line of friends and relatives, working-shoes or high heels clopping and clipping on the polished floorboards.

There was always some bed with no visitors, while others had the permissible two, or maybe three. Under each cot was a wooden stool on which two could sit side by side. I can still hear the scrape of the stools being pulled out and see the little girl with the fair hair and big blue bow who used to sit outside the open ward door doing a jigsaw puzzle and glancing in from time to time with quick intelligent eyes. When the visiting hour drew to its close she'd scamper down the ward, kiss her Daddy goodnight and flit out again. She was very much at home. Her father had been ill a long while. Her mother was very tall and fair with a quiet resigned face.

Bertie's right-hand neighbour was a little Cockney with a huge cage over his legs who laughed like a hyena in the middle of the night. No one ever came to see him. On his left was an Asiatic hunchback who existed by inhaling oxygen from a rubber flask which inflated and deflated with every breath. He was gay, with more than his quota of callers. Opposite was a Royal Marine veteran of both World Wars, and next to him a bus-conductor with dermatitis and bandaged hands, who served everybody teas at five-thirty in the morning. He'd wander round the ward in his white flannel pyjamas and green and red striped hospital dressing-gown, bringing people papers and magazines, buying their cigarettes and generally making himself useful. He was always full of quips and fun. In the morning, when the ward was cleaned, the cots were all pushed from the walls to the centre and people would find themselves vis-à-vis at close quarters. Bertie said afterwards that, except for the foreigners, everybody seemed to have the same obstinate Cockney faces with stubborn jaws and shrewd wise eyes, 'like a Chatham ship's company. You can't beat them.'

The number of Coloured people amazed us. Coloured ward-maids, singing West Indian calypsos softly to themselves as they worked, Coloured porters, a Coloured doctor. But for the lack of *apartheid* one might have been in South Africa.

Two days after Bertie had been admitted the Registrar told me that he was to be taken to the Atkinson Morley Hospital at Wimbledon for a certain investigation.

'We want to eliminate the possibility of any lesion that might cause this condition. There is only one place in England – possibly Europe – where this particular head X-ray can be done. It is the system of the greatest brain surgeon in this country.'

St. George's had all the resources, as Bobby Burns had said, and this was one of them. Under National Health everything was free, not only to people like my husband who had devoted their lives to the service of their country, but to any foreigner taken ill in England.

'If the investigation is negative he will come straight back here and we will follow our own line,' added the Registrar.

'And if it's positive?'

'You must be prepared for surgery. In that case it would almost certainly be there.'

I shall always be grateful for the resources of the Atkinson Morley Hospital, but certain aspects of that gaunt mansion were pure snake pit.

I went with Bertie in the ambulance. On arrival he was taken into a huge ward at the end of a stone-flagged corridor, while I was interviewed by the House Physician to give what I could of the case history. He was short and thickset, foreign, with a flat putty-coloured Slav face, probably Yugoslavian, I thought. He had a Serbian name.

It was a searching interrogation, conducted with precise efficiency and not without sympathy. When he had finished he gave me a paper to sign. As next of kin my permission was required in case immediate surgery should be indicated by the X-ray. *Next of kin.* It was like going back to the war when fear for my husband's safety had been my familiar. Fear invaded me now, as I signed my name. It was in every particle of me so that it was hard to breathe. I kept inhaling long deep draughts of air as if fear had used up all the oxygen in my lungs.

'Your husband will go for the X-ray at two o'clock. You may see him first for a few minutes,' said the physician, very impersonal.

The Atkinson Morley was originally intended as a Convalescent Home, and as such it would have been ideal. It is an old-fashioned country mansion high on a hill overlooking the green countryside. There is a secluded garden, and huts occupy part of the grounds where patients are taught remedial crafts, like basket-making, weaving and carpentry. But, although it was still used for convalescent cases from St. George's, the greater part of the establishment had been turned over to neuro-surgery and special investigations. Although the Atkinson Morley is not to be confused with a mental hospital, many of the cases affected by physical injury or brain tumours displayed distressing mental symptoms. At that time pressure of accommodation made it necessary to put investigations like my husband's into the same ward with these unfortunate people, and its macabre atmosphere is something I am not likely to forget.

It was immensely high with long narrow windows of unbreakable glass. No blinds or curtains. No frames for curtains round the beds either, only a set of mobile screens that could be wheeled from cot to cot. In the centre of that vast naked barn were four pillars at the corners of an ornate stove, near which the sisters had their table and wrote up their records. No flowers, for few of those patients would have been any the wiser if there had been flowers to tell them that spring had come.

Bertie's bed was near the door, one of about thirty others. Most of the patients had shaved or bandaged heads and some were bare-chested in the cold.

'They have high temperatures,' explained the nurse. 'So they throw off their blankets.'

Many moaned or mumbled in delirium, and in the far corner a man cackled with maniacal laughter from time to time, and then everybody capable of rational speech said 'Sshh!' Certain cots had padded arms to prevent their occupants from harming themselves. Some patients were being artificially fed. At regular intervals the nurses 'assessed' each patient, shining a torch into vacant eyes, calling loudly, 'Wake up, Mr. Jones! Squeeze my hands!' Young clear voices calling the lost back to the land of the living.

Land of the living – an old cliché. But at the Atkinson Morley it acquired a new meaning for me. It meant the sharp contrast between life and the semblance of death. It meant the world outside; the pewter sky of the late March day, grass bright with daffodils, forsythia and blossom in parks and gardens, and sticky buds of chestnuts opening green hands with the fingers right back like the temple dangers of Bali or Angkor. It meant the surge of traffic up Putney Hill, women doing their household shopping, children frisking home for the Easter holidays, the frivolity of Easter bonnets and gay displays in West End stores, and the panting of a little train that I could hear somewhere down among the misty trees. But the land of the living was here in the ward too, personified in these vital young nurses going so blithely about their tasks.

The mobile screens were round my husband's bed when I went to him. He looked at me with tired pain-filled eyes.

'You're not going away. You'll stay here?'

'Of course. Is the head better?'

'Not yet.'

A grey-haired sister came and took his pulse.

'We can't do much for the pain yet. They need his co-operation for the X-ray. He'll be going for it soon.'

She turned to me kindly. 'Have you had anything to eat?'

'I don't want anything, thank you.'

She called a nurse, who gave me a yellow card and took me to the Visitor's Room where a small fair woman sat in an easy-chair, looking shockingly weary and drawn, as if she herself had died and been left there.

'Mrs. Davis, have you had any lunch?' asked the nurse brightly.

'I don't want any.' Her voice was sepulchral, out of an Ibsen play.

'You'd better, you know. Take this lady and show her the way. She needs a snack, too. You have your yellow card?'

Mrs. Davis nodded. She rose slowly.

'We go to the ward-maids' dining-room. We can get some soup and coffee. We needn't take anything else if we don't want to.'

She seemed relieved to have someone to look after, and, when we had warmed ourselves with soup and coffee, we felt better.

'Let's go into the garden,' she said.

She was slight with chiselled features and a sad frozen face. Her fifteen-year-old daughter had undergone an operation for cerebral tumour and Mrs. Davis had not left the hospital for thirty-six hours.

When we returned to the Visitor's Room other people were there. A middle-aged man, a pudding-faced woman and a stodgy sly-looking boy of about twelve.

From the next room we heard a loud steady groaning, rising to a climax, breaking off for a second, only to be instantly resumed. I covered my ears with my hands.

'What a ghastly noise!'

'He's been doing it all night,' said Mrs. Davis. 'Never stopped. They put the noisy cases – the serious ones – into a little ward next to this room.'

'It's very upsetting,' I said. 'A very upsetting noise.'

The middle-aged man cast me a look of reproach.

'It's particularly upsetting when it's your own relation who is making it.'

'I'm so sorry.'

'It's my old Dad,' said the man. 'He's eighty-one, and he was knocked over by a bus. Stepped off the pavement right under it.'

'Don't worry,' said Mrs. Davis. 'He doesn't know he's making all that noise. He's unconscious. Not in pain.'

The schoolboy's eyes were popping out of his head. I felt that probably, for the first time in his life, he was finding his grandfather interesting. His mother gazed at him fondly.

'And poor Albert here, just home for the Easter holidays!'

I didn't feel sorry for Albert. I could imagine him imitating those groans for the benefit of horrified contemporaries at some later date.

A nurse came in and told the family that there was no change in the patient's condition. If they wished to go home any further news could be telephoned to them via the nearest police station.

Albert pounced up with alacrity and his parents rose to go, the man pausing to give Mrs. Davis a light. 'Keep the matchbox,' he said. 'You need it.' She had smoked without ceasing and had run out of matches. A nurse fetched me.

Bertie had been given a pain-killing injection at last. I stayed with him till he slept.

When I went back to the Visitor's Room Mrs. Davis was in the corner armchair again with her back to the tall window. It was dusk and her silhouette was utterly relaxed, yet it was not a relaxation one wished to see. It was as if her bones had all been broken without scarring the flesh, as Malays break the bones of their dead so that they may be supple in Paradise. Her eyes were closed and her skin had fallen in upon the sharp framework of her face. She opened her eyes.

'You were asleep,' I said. 'I'm sorry if I woke you.'

'Not asleep. I've just said good-bye to my child. There's nothing more anyone can do – except wait for the end.'

So they would stop calling her daughter back with their compelling urgency. There would be no more 'Wake up, Vera! Squeeze my fingers!' No more torches shining into sightless eyes. They would let her drift away on the ebb, through the mists, into whatever lay beyond.

I put my hand on the mother's shoulder. She scarcely moved. Ater a while she said, 'One questions God ... a young lovely girl ... Nothing can hurt me any more.'

'Don't!' I begged. 'You have another child.'

A nurse brought her hot strong tea. There was still the waiting.

'Your husband,' Mrs. Davis asked. 'How is he?'

'He's sleeping now. I'm to stay here tonight.'

She put down her cup and held out her chilly lifeless hands to take mine.

'I hope he will get better.'

Night had fallen. Mrs. Davis had been fetched home and I was alone.

There was an electric fire, yet I was cold through and through. I had been told the X-ray was negative but that my husband was 'not out of the wood'. A nurse looked in. A new face, one of the night staff.

'Lady Packer? Your husband wants you. When you've seen him we'll fix you up with a bed in the Convalescent Ward. Lucky there's a free one! The Visitor's Room is badly placed. It's noisy enough by day, but late at night it always sounds much worse.'

Poor Grandfather was still making his harrowing inhuman noises with never a pause. Nurses called out to him, and discussed him. 'Have you ever seen such a tongue? Lucky he doesn't know he's got a tongue like this, poor old boy! Wake up, Mr. Jackson!' There was no reply save the indestructible bellows producing the loud outbreathing groan, the indrawn moan.

The ward in which my husband lay was even more stark by night. Over the beds naked lights blazed on to shrunken faces, the stillness of coma or the restlessness of fever. Outside the long uncurtained windows was the cold inky dark.

The night staff was busy taking over. Nurses hurried to

and fro, twittering among themselves, always very quick or very quiet, like birds. Business-like, pleasant, getting on with the job. I wondered how deep their feeling towards this sort of work really went. Perhaps they liked the variety and drama. But a special quality was necessary for nursing such cases – a tough objectiveness that not every woman could achieve. Many girls couldn't 'take it', others found it 'so rewarding' to help rehabilitate a mind broken by injury or disease, to re-equip it to face the world once more, usefully and vigorously. All these things I had been told in this very hospital three years ago when I had gathered the material for my article on the Matron of St. George's.

I drew out the usual little wooden stool and Bertie turned his head drowsily towards me.

A pretty young nurse with gentle brown eyes fetched me for my night's rest in the Convalescent Ward. It was past eleven o'clock and here there was grateful darkness broken only by moonlight shining through the glass panes of a closed-in verandah that was also lined with beds, for this ward was on garden level, and the cases were mostly surgical and had been brought from St. Georges's to recuperate before going home.

The young nurse showed me to a bed near the verandah.

'Would you like some Ovaltine?' she asked kindly. 'Or Horlicks?'

'Ovaltine, please.'

She was on her own, for these cases needed little attention. Every now and again a sister, wearing her little cape against the cold, came in to see that all was well, and sometimes a nurse from another ward popped in for a whispered chat and the shaded light over the table caught their starched caps close together.

The heavy macintosh cloth was under the sheet and there was a curious vibration in the region of the pillow.

'It comes from the central heating plant,' explained the young nurse softly as she gave me my Ovaltine. She was very comforting.

The hot water in the pipes pulsed all night as if the life-blood of the hospital throbbed aloud in the comparative silence. The whole ward seemed to snore peacefully, except for the girl in the bed next to mine who tossed and sobbed as if her dreams were full of misery.

'She's quite all right,' murmured the nurse. 'She's really a very jolly person!'

My body was exhausted but my mind was over-active, and I felt as I had so often done during the war. Flayed of a skin. The fingers of the whole world's sorrow, anxiety and despair seemed to touch raw nerves and I was once again part of a human storm in which personal troubles are diffused and absorbed into one single calamity. Only this time the calamity was not hatred and war but the universal suffering of sickness.

How early day breaks in England! By five o'clock it was light. I had my bath and crept snugly back into bed in my underwear. The cots on the wide verandah came into focus. The garden beyond, with its lawns and trees, was spangled in the smoky bloom of early morning. People began to stir and make the deep sighing sounds of waking up. The young nurse was even prettier than I had thought in the gloom of the night.

Someone else had risen at dawn – a plain elderly woman with one of those Cockney faces one sees a thousand times a day in London, scrubbing doorsteps on a cold autumn morning, whacking out coffee in canteens, cleaning offices, serving in shops, standing in fish queues, calling strangers 'dear' or 'luv', swearing a bit at times, 'pushing out the boat' at the local, and always ready to crack a joke or lend a hand, or sit over a 'cuppa' for a nice chat about 'my operation', the neighbours, or the Royal Family. At some time Mrs. Higgins' hair must have been fashionably tinted to a dark copper, but now it was grey half-way to the roots, a sad little sign of a longish illness. She had dressed and taken great trouble with her appearance, and she was busy serving teas to the rest of the ward. There is always someone well enough to do that. Help yourselves and help each other is one of the signs of recovery.

The restless girl next to me, who had cried in her sleep, was brusque and cheerful in the daylight. Foreign – somebody's Austrian housemaid, I guessed. On my other side was a skinny little Londoner, one of the sort I had learned to love and respect in the bad days and nights of the blitz when we had shared London's long agony. She was doing remedial exercises with a good deal of clowning for the benefit of a Teddy-girl with a full sulky mouth. A retired actress, who shared her sugar ration with me, told me about her.

'She's the gay one. I've only once seen her down and out. A nurse helped her take her first bath and she was so ashamed of her poor little body! She'd undergone amputations and skin grafts, and then, in the post, she got a note to say her job had been given to somebody else.'

Financial worry, added to illness and mutilation, yet here she was making the sulky Teddy-girl laugh with her Cockney cracks about her physical contortions that didn't quite come off.

The early riser pouring tea was going home that morning. Everybody was glad for her.

'In a few months I have to go back to St. George's for another op,' she told me brightly, as if to say, 'Only one more river to cross!'

The actress informed me that she too would be leaving tomorrow to spend Easter at the Convalescent Home for Distressed Theatrical People. 'A lovely place,' she added. Time had lost its significance for me, but her words reminded me that today was Good Friday.

Those able to get up and walk about had breakfast at the long central table. Others were brought it in bed. A few had their own eggs and generously offered to share their rations with me. They wanted to know about me. Everybody was interested in everybody else. It was the war again – the sisterhood of disaster that put private worry into perspective.

For Bertie the night had been 'snake pit'. Groans, shrieks, demented laughter, wakings and 'assessings' destroying rest like a Chinese torture. But the pain was on the wane and we returned to St. George's that morning.

How cosy the long ward over Knightsbridge seemed after the bare Atkinson Morley! Open fires crackled in the hearth at either end – oddly old-fashioned and very homely – and there were flowers on the nurses' table.

The Asiatic hunchback had gone and his place had been taken by a shrivelled soot-black Tamil with pneumonia, who lay all day with his great eyes sunk in bruised cavities and looked about him with an expression of gentle endurance. He smoked a great deal, cupping his cigarette in the palm of his thin hand with the bluish nails. No one ever visited him till one evening two very dark, smartly-dressed secretaries from the Ceylonese Embassy came and stood by his bed. They stared at him for a full five minutes in total silence and went away again. He was the Embassy cook and they were evidently 'assessing' him.

My husband's ward-mates welcomed him back warmly, and the Royal Marine informed me that, in his view, the Admiral looked much better.

That night, for the first time I stayed in the tiny flat we had taken and woke refreshed at sunrise to hear the gargling notes of the pigeons flirting and bowing on my window-sill. Norman Capon was coming from Liverpool for the day and we had arranged to meet at St. George's where he was to see Bertie and the Senior Physician.

How different from the Easter family reunion we had planned so many months ago! We walked across to the park from the Hospital. The afternoon was mild and we sat on two little stiff-backed chairs. Norman was stiff-backed too because a disc gave him considerable trouble and at that time he had to wear a steel corset which he managed to treat as a joke.

'Tell me the prognosis – in simple language,' I said. 'Everything!'

He did his best, translating medical jargon into terms of everyday life and what my husband would be able to do and what he would be wise not to do. Finally he rose – awkwardly because of his tiresome back – and his humorous smile lit his face as he said:

'We all have to learn to live with our disabilities, my dear.'

'And the disabilities of our nearest and dearest,' I added.

He laughed. 'We make our adjustments.'

For the first time in what seemed an eternity, and had actually been the inside of a week, my heart felt almost light. We parted for him to catch his train and for me to go back to the Hospital. I bought a huge bunch of tulips for the ward.

The next day was Easter Sunday.

Bertie noticed that I wore a new blouse and a gay Italian scarf round my neck.

'You look very spry,' he said. 'You got that scarf in Genoa.'

I put it over my hair.

'I'm going to church to say thank you because you are better.'

'Where are you going to church?'

'Along the corridor. The most beautiful little chapel in London. There's an Easter service at ten-thirty.'

The bus-conductor with dermatitis and several other patients in their red and green towel gowns came with me. Some of the nurses were there too, and patients from other wards. There were glorious spring flowers on the altar and the silver altar pieces gleamed in the candlelight. The padré preached a brief simple sermon about the Resurrection – the wonderful consoling mystical sequel to the unbearable story of Crucifixion for the sins of mankind. It was a very short service, because those who were not patients had little time to spare from their duties.

I stole a glance at the padré's congregation – women in dressing-gowns, their hair lank, their faces pale; men stooped and bent with sickness; a few fresh-complexioned nurses; an outsize African doctor, a couple of young internes wearing their white coats; the Matron, austere head bowed, and a sprinkling of visitors like myself – and it came to me that during these last days of Holy Week we had all of us here, each in our different and infinitesimal way, shared the Agony of two thousand years ago, and paid, perhaps, a tiny fragment of our debt in the only coin there is, suffering or the alleviation of suffering.

When I returned to the ward three lady hymn singers, evidently performing with the permission of the B.B.C., were singing an Easter hymn with fine free careless rapture.

My husband gave me a most expressive look and drew the blankets up over his ears.

I wanted to laugh – and cry. Best of all, I was sure that, from now on, I would have no further excuse for not observing regular visiting hours.

CHAPTER NINE

MAGIC – ENGLISH AND AFRICAN

So we were able to enjoy our holiday after all.

We hired a car and went to see our friends and relations. We wondered anew at the glorious green of the fields and the majesty of the trees, the tenderness of the light, and the lovely lingering days of this warm early summer.

It was well into May when our family reunion at last took place.

Norman and Dorothy Capon converged upon Marion's Worcestershire cottage from Liverpool, and Headmistress Winifred gave herself a long week-end from her Scottish Girls' school in order to join us and complete the party. She stayed at Marion's cottage, which was our focal point, Dorothy and Norman went to a country hotel not far away and Bertie and I put up at the Royal Oak in Tenbury Wells, a tiny ancient inn with leaning black and white walls, and the history of Elizabethan England in every skull-cracking rafter.

The English countryside is always a delight and a puzzle to me. Such a little island with such great variety! Every county has its own personality, scenery and dialect, and its typical villages, each a tiny museum piece, highly individual in character and architecture, though faithfully following the old established pattern of the Squire's 'big house', the church and village green, the post office tucked away in a sweet-shop stationer's, and quaint cottages set in pocket-handkerchief gardens of picture postcard charm. Meadows, forests, lakes, mountains, moors and downs stretch, unspoilt, between the crowded cities and seething industrial areas. Cathedral and university towns rise out of the green landscape, aloof and provincial, and ancient market-towns still serve the surrounding farmlands.

Marion's cottage is on the border of three of England's most attractive counties – Worcestershire, Herefordshire and Shropshire – and to me it represents the very heart of rural England. She had bought it just before our departure for

South Africa and when last we had seen that tiny Elizabethan workman's cottage it had been a lonely little black and white ark in a sea of snow-covered weeds, girdled by a frozen boundary brook, unloved and abandoned. My sister-in-law put in plumbing, electricity and a telephone, and very soon it became the natural rendezvous of the family. It lies in a hollow across a bridge, and you don't see it at once because a pergola of roses hides it from the country lane. Then suddenly, there it is, beached in the lee of a high green bank, with fields, woods and orchards spreading round it.

The cottage had never looked more enchanting than it did on that summer day when we parked our car in a grassy bay outside the gate. Norman and Dorothy arrived almost simultaneously, and Winifred, who was mowing the lawn in slacks and a lumber-jacket, with a cigarette hanging from her lip, left her mower and hastened towards us. Winifred, sedately tailor-made in her role of headmistress, goes berserk on holiday and does exactly as she pleases. And there, hurrying through the rose-covered arch, came Marion, smaller and skinnier than ever. Her dog, Rags, an outsize Yorkshire Terrier, gave a flattering and overwhelming exhibition of remembering us, but was, in fact, only reflecting the mood of his mistress.

When our greetings allowed us to come up for air it was the very essence of English country air, smelling of roses, mown grass – thanks to Winifred – newly shampooed dog – Marion and Rags' combined contribution – and the may that foamed over the hedgerow. Norman went to his car to release David, an aged Corgi who circled Rags in the stylized canine behaviour pattern of age-old suspicion.

As we passed under the pergola of roses and clematis I stopped with a gasp of rapture. Waves of cottage-flowers lapped a crazy-paving shore, roses bloomed in islands on the lawn, willows overhung the brook, and birds and butterflies hovered and flitted over shrubs, reeds and herbaceous borders.

'It's magic!' I said. 'I can't believe it! You've created all this out of a wilderness.'

Marion made one of her expansive gestures, as she glanced around her with wise merry eyes.

'I painted a picture. I saw it and it came.'

She had begun to paint her picture when her tiny ark still lay marooned in its snowy field, and now the vision of summer had bloomed for our delight.

'Mind your heads,' she warned, as she led us indoors.

A little silver crucifix hung on the lintel inside the door, and, when I looked at it, I knew that no evil would ever enter here.

Marion does not need to mind her head. She is the right size for her cottage. So is Winifred. The rest of us hit our heads on splendid beams, near fossilized and hard as iron. Her coppers, pinky-gold, gleamed above the open fireplace, and sunlight filtered in through mullioned casements. Every simple piece of antique furniture or vase of cottage flowers seemed inevitable in its surroundings.

'Any ghosts?' asked Bertie.

'One or two little nuns glide about, and there's a hatchet-faced woodcutter who steals about this boarded floor suspiciously.'

'He knows it should be cow-dung,' put in Winifred.

'Is it as old as all that?'

'It's the prefab of the fifteenth century. You find them in these parts.' Marion turned to her brother. 'It has a tang of the sea. D'you get a whiff of it, you old salt?'

'Heart of oak, Mary Ann.'

His eyes went appreciatively to the massive supports nakedly revealed where she had swept a wall away to enlarge her living-room.

'That's right. The wood was probably brought from the Bristol Channel, where the wreckage of ancient vessels was salved for beams.'

She was entranced that the spirit of the sea should flourish here in this inland corner of her beloved isle.

We drank our dry South African sherry under a willow by the brook.

'There's no knowing when we'll get lunch,' Dorothy murmured, as we disposed ourselves in or out of the sun according to our tastes. 'So I've brought a tin of biscuits. Marion gets more and more casual and only eats when she thinks about it, and Winifred isn't much better.'

I was not alarmed. I had been into the kitchen and seen the cold chicken and ham and salad, to say nothing of fruit-pie and cheese.

'It'll be a feast,' said Norman who had also investigated the matter.

I asked Marion what birds and beasts shared her garden and brook with her.

'There's a family of stoats,' she said. 'I'm very fond of them. And some water-voles. Rabbits, of course, and squirrels, poor dears. The squirrels are worth a shilling a tail. The postman does quite nicely out of them. He is our vermin expert.'

'That's how Mary Ann comes to know him.' Norman's blue eyes twinkled under his straw hat-brim tilted forward to protect them from the sun. 'Her contacts with him are verminous – or social.'

'I get letters – and answer them,' she protested stoutly.

'You answer them in your head,' I said, 'at dead of night in your attic bedroom – long lovely letters that are neither written nor sent.'

'She can't help it,' put in Bertie. 'She's the uneducated one.'

'She got along in the business world,' said Dorothy, 'by dictating to a scribe. She only had to make her mark in lieu of a signature.'

After lunch, somnolent with food and cider, we each rested according to our fancy.

Dorothy, who is the graceful one, dozed in a *chaise-longue*. Winifred and Bertie impersonated people reading the Sunday papers; Marion and I talked or didn't; and after a while Norman left us.

'He's taken David into the next county,' said Marion.

He was tramping across a field on the far side of the brook, his dog at his heels.

'That's Herefordshire,' she added. 'Shall we take Rags for a stroll in Shropshire?'

We wandered through the summer green of a wood, and came to the top of a rise where we stopped to look at a scene far different from the dramatic outlook of 'Cressage' at the Cape. I lifted my arms without knowing it in a gesture that might have been one of Marion's.

'This green countryside, created for peace under a pearly sky!'

She smiled. 'You're brushing the clouds away – touching the sky.'

93

'London belongs to the world,' I said. 'This is the core of England. But secret. You can see it, as a surgeon can see a human heart, but its soul remains absolutely its own. Intangible. You have to belong to it by birth, breeding and instinct to understand it.'

'You have to love it,' she said. 'That's all.'

Our few days fled before we could count them.

It was Sunday mild and warm, with Marion's friends from round about drifting in and out of her garden, staying for a chat and departing. When the last looker-in had gone we still lingered out of doors in the long twilight, reluctant to be on our way back to London. When at last we left I turned to my husband who was driving.

'Today was lovely. I enjoyed every moment of it.'

He smiled and nodded, filled with his own memories.

Maybe Marion, alone again and listening to the plopping of her water-voles or the call of an owl, was thinking of us as we were thinking of her and the cottage. Perhaps she was smiling in her own secret way, knowing that it would be quite a while before we realized that there had been sadness underlying this lovely day. Our family reunion, in the end, had been more in the nature of a farewell. Yet not one of us had said the word Good-bye. That was her magic.

Soon, on another sunny day, we were on our way to Tilbury to embark for Cape Town. But this time none of the shabby charm of London escaped my husband.

The voyage was calm and uneventful. Bertie spent most of his time relaxing on deck between sea and sky. I had begun to work seriously once more and by the time we reached Cape Town my wild life novel *Nor the Moon By Night*, was well on its way.

Throughout the African continent White men have established great game sanctuaries to conserve the wild life that would otherwise have been killed off years ago. These conservators have done more. They have, in the past half century, altered a world way of thought. The camera has replaced the gun, and, instead of dead trophies, the modern hunter brings the living creatures of the wilds into his home and presents them to his friends on a private screen. The White conservators have trained their African assistants — not always easy, because the African is a meat-hungry man who sees wild beasts as food – and together they fight the common enemy, the poacher. Poaching, like all other forms of robbery and violence, has many aspects and degrees, from the primitive trapper with wire snares to the gangster who runs an organized racket with machine-guns, pick-up vans, accomplices in the sanctuary and markets for illicit meat in the cities. In South Africa there are the 'biltong bandits' who prefer to salt and sun-dry stolen meat before transporting it, as it is lighter to carry and will not spoil and there is always a ready market for biltong in town or country.

'There's so much I don't know,' I grumbled to my husband. 'When we've been to the Kruger Park and Hluhluwe and Wankie I've always looked at them with the eyes of a tourist. Now I want to turn the picture inside out – rangers' angle, animals' angle—'

'You'll have to go and smell it again. It needn't take you long. Fly up to Johannesburg, three or four days sniffing around, and home again. Do it like a high-powered journalist.'

'From Johannesburg it's a day's journey to the Kruger Park.'

'It'll be worth it.'

Thus it was that in the middle of August, more than two months after our return, I found myself far from the stormy Cape winter in the dry air of the lowveld where the sun burns hot by day and the nights are cold and frosty.

The rest-camp in which I had a thatched *rondavel* is called Skukusa, which is named for the first and greatest game warden of the many who have given their hearts to the Kruger Park Sanctuary, and it means 'He who turns things upside down'. There is now a statue there to the late Lieut.-Colonel Stevenson-Hamilton, who was known to the Bantu as Skukusa, and who turned a vast area and a great number of ideas upside down when, in 1903, he was entrusted with the task of developing the original Sabi Reserve of Oom Paul Kruger, the Boer President who had had the wisdom to realize that his hunter compatriots would make short work of Transvaal wild life unless he stepped in to protect it.

Stevenson-Hamilton, a professional soldier and hunter, brought a dedicated and pugnacious spirit to his task. For over forty years he fought tooth and nail against vested interests, agriculturalists, industrialists, and mineral seekers in order to expand his sanctuary until a territory of fertile well-watered lowveld bigger than Wales was set aside exclusively for the conservation of wild life. In doing so he helped to give South Africa one of her greatest tourist assets and set an example followed in many other parts of Africa where sanctuaries have since been developed to attract tourists and to perpetuate the life of birds and beasts that would otherwise have become extinct.

Skukusa is the largest camp in the Kruger Park, and, during the open season – May to October – thousands of tourists pass through it. Its thatched *rondavels*, cottages and tents are dotted about under spreading trees alive with birds. A thorn fence surrounds the area and from the high points you can look down into the jade-green gorge of the Sabi River where hippos grunt and bellow and crocodiles bask on flat rocks and sandbanks. Bantu attendants look after the camp-fires and keep the place clean, while, outside this delightful human cage, is the living tapestry of the thornveld and its natural inhabitants. Buck of every description graze in sylvan glades; herds of wildebeeste and zebras roam in company; tall giraffes nibble the topmost leaves of the acacias, or fight or caress each other with their long necks; warthog families trot in single file, tails erect; leopards and lions take their food where they find it, and further north the elephants wander through the mopani forests and leave a trail of uprooted trees and broken boughs in their wake.

By mid-August, after the school holidays, the big rush is over, and when I was there it was already late in the season and Park officials and rangers were able to breathe more freely and even to make plans for their own holidays when the heat and the rains would close most of the Sanctuary to visitors.

Bertie did not come with me when I flew to Johannesburg, the springboard for the Sanctuary.

'When you're on the job you work faster and better alone,' he said. 'And the faster the better. Don't be gone long.'

I was away a week. It was a week in another world.

I had a list of the practical information I required and am deeply indebted to a great number of people who went to considerable trouble to help me get it, but there was also an intangible *x* I was seeking, an unknown quantity, or rather quality, upon which I hoped to build not an algebraical formula but a fictional character.

My sponsor in the Sanctuary was Cyrus Smith of South African Information Services, and it was he who introduced me to one of the Park's scientists on the afternoon of our arrival.

'What he doesn't know about wild life, Natives and the Sanctuary isn't worth knowing,' said Cyrus, as he and his pretty wife, Lucia, led me across to the ecologist's office where we hoped to find this knowledgeable man.

He was there, with a cup of tea at his elbow and a huge pile of notes on the desk in front of him. The walls were covered with maps showing density, migrations and variety of game, incidence of disease, drought areas, fire-breaks, feeding grounds, water holes, and innumerable other factors relevant to the study and protection of the population.

I am going to call Cyrus's friend Jan, although that is not his name, and, as far as I am aware, he no longer works in the Kruger Park. His friendly co-operation was invaluable. He and his Bantu ranger, Nimrod, opened the door into my 'other world' and gave me vivid glimpses of the strange mystic existence of those who live close to nature and combine intellect and instinct to do their job. He was, perhaps, in his middle thirties, dark and sturdy with the piercing blue eyes of so many Afrikaners and a sudden flashing smile.

Half a century ago game wardens were usually hunters turned conservators – robbers into policemen – but now, in an age of science, many of them are university men, like Jan. Though Jan was not a ranger his work involved the same risks and journeys. When he had given us tea he explained the maps on the wall.

'People think it smart of rangers to know, to within a matter of yards, where they are likely to find certain animals – sable antelope, giraffe, lion, or whatever else it may be. In fact, it's obvious. Wild creatures don't roam about at random. They go to certain places to eat or drink or sleep, like you and me. They are consistent, repetitive and punctual unless something puts them off their stroke. They have their own territories, where they establish rights and resent interference, just as you'd resent strangers strolling into your garden uninvited. There are dangerous people, of course, who respect few laws – the carnivorae – and taking a sundowner is always a perilous performance. Some sinister customers are regulars at the water-hole. The leopard – now there's a gangster! Or elephant, who'll trample anybody. Or, behind the bar, so to speak, a hungry croc may be waiting for a juicy meal. Nobody relaxes over the sundowner. Nor like our pal, Cyrus, here – '

'Which reminds me,' put in Cyrus. 'We're going out this evening to see how the other half drinks – the four-legged people – but when we come back you might meet us for a lemonade.'

Jan's blue eyes twinkled. 'Why not?' he said in Afrikaans. 'I have a passion for that lemonade of yours! Then we'll make a plan for tomorrow. Good?'

It is a rule that cars shall be back in camp before dark, which means just after sunset, for there is no lingering twilight in this part of Africa. We returned from the river where we had watched the nervous buck tread delicately to the water's edge, a troupe of agile monkeys, zebra suddenly stampeding the other animals with a warning 'qhaha!' and the fantastic contortions of a giraffe getting its gentle antelope's head down to the cool green water, and, as we entered the camp gates, we saw the raspberry disc of the sun sink below the fragile frieze of the thorn trees. Within an hour an equally ruby-red moon came up over the eastern rim of the world. The temperature fell instantly and the quiet frosty bushveld night was upon us, sweet and sharp with its fragrance of dry grass and camp-fires and its indescribable purity.

Jan came for us in his car soon after sunrise. His Bantu ranger, Nimrod, was with him and sat in the back with Cyrus and Lucia. I was in front. We had breakfasted, and already the dew was melting on the grass and the day was warming up.

'I can't show you elephant,' he said. 'You must go to Letaba for that.'

'I don't want to see elephant. They terrify me. Some years ago I saw about three hundred in Wankie, and the Warden told me about a rogue who trampled one of a road gang. He had to go after the animal and shoot him. Anyway, I hate the mess they make of trees.'

'So do I. There – over there – are sable antelope!'

He slowed down constantly to let us see game. Once a dozen or more impala seemed to fly over our car, and went leaping away into the grass on the other side of the road.

'We scared them,' said Lucia.

He stopped the car.

'No. They accept cars as new animals with habits and routes, a certain speed, a distinctive purr and smell, ugly, no doubt, but seldom dangerous. More likely there are lion around. See those vultures on that leadwood tree? They are another sign. If they were perched like that at daybreak it wouldn't mean a thing except that they were still roosting, because they are day-birds. But now it means there's a kill. They are waiting for the lion to eat his fill. Then it'll be their turn.'

He said something in the Native language to Nimrod, who sprang out and perched on the bonnet. Jan turned the car off the road and put it very slowly into the long red grass. Almost at once Nimrod was off the bonnet and back into the car, with an exclamation and a broad grin.

'He says there are lion all right. Watch the grass!'

Sure enough, we saw the movement of a twitching ear and a ripple as a dark tufted tail lashed to and fro. Jan waited for the tawny crouching form to move away and then he drove slowly in the direction of a tree round which the grass had been grazed bare and stamped down. In its shade lay three magnificent lionesses. The vultures on the branches nearby remained undisturbed and watchful. Two of the lionesses rose and made off into the bush, while the third stared at us with hostile, intent, golden eyes. We were stationary and silent. Our windows were open. I found my mouth was dry and I was frightened. After a few moments she too went into the bush, lazy, sated and powerful.

'She's a beauty!' whispered Jan. 'As fine as any I've ever seen.'

Down in a donga, not far from the tree, lay the kill, already partially devoured.

'A blue wildebeest,' he said. 'Poor old bull! His home empty, except for the intruders and the scavengers waiting on the doorstep – the vultures, the jackals and hyenas.'

'How can you tell it was a bull? There's not much left to show what it was!'

'His signs are all round this tree. When he is old he becomes unsociable and often prefers to leave the herd and live alone. He was easy meat.'

99

He spoke as if of a human being, of some old man who was his friend and who had died alone under violent circumstances.

By mid-morning the sun was high and Jan turned the car from the game circuit on to a rough track that led us to a grove of beautiful flowering trees.

'You wanted to see the house of a ranger out in the bundu,' he said. 'Well, this is it.'

The rambling bungalow had a homely look, but it was deserted. A Bantu told Jan that the ranger was away on an inspection tour and was not expected back for a few days.

'Never mind,' said Jan. 'I have the freedom of his home and his fridge, so we'll stop off for a wash and a cool drink.'

In that lonely quiet place every scent and sound was separate and significant. The fresh tang of a citrus grove in full fruit mingled with the faint perfume of mango flowers. Paw-paws hung in heavy clusters under the sparse leaves of the palm-shaped trees. The vermilion flowers of a kaffirboom blazed against a cloudless sky. Scarlet and purple curtains of bougainvillea hung across the stoep. Magnolias, frangipani and beauhinias shaded the house. Against the inevitable thorn-fence strips of lion-meat hung to dry. 'It's for the dogs,' explained Jan, as half a dozen puppies ran to meet us, barking, fawning and frolicking round us. They were snuff-coloured like their mother, who seemed to be a cross between a ridge-back and some sort of hound.

'Does your friend kill lions?' Lucia asked in astonishment.

Jan frowned.

'From time to time rangers are ordered to thin out lion because they are taking too many buck. It is an order I hate. Lion only kill when they are hungry – out of necessity.' He added abruptly: 'Come along in!'

Once this had been a family house. Now it was no more than a young man's camp in the bush. His living-room appeared to be the enclosed stoep, and its main feature was a large table piled with geographical, scientific and natural history magazines, a few old copies of *Motor* and *Aviation*, a stack of classical records and a portable gramophone. The door into his bedroom was open and, on the wall, we could see framed photographs of football teams. A university blazer hung over the back of a stiff-backed chair, a pair of veld-boots stood under it, and on the seat was a jumble of socks obviously in need of darning.

'Shame!' cried Lucia. 'He needs a wife to take care of him.'

'Or a mother,' laughed Jan. 'He's pretty young. But you'll see he can look after himself. What's the betting we find some beer in his fridge? What we borrow I'll put back in a day or two when I pass this way again. I'm coming back for one of the puppies. The father is the best lion-dog in the Sanctuary.'

'Do the Natives eat the lion biltong?' I asked as we went on our way, refreshed with the young ranger's cool drinks.

'Some will, some won't. There are two distinct schools of thought. Some believe that if you eat lion meat you become imbued with the strength of the lion. Others think it is sacrilege and that a lion will kill you in revenge for an act of disrespect. A good many Natives won't even skin a lion, much less eat him.'

'What about Nimrod?'

Jan smiled. 'Nimrod has eaten lion meat – and he has made me do so too. You don't live in the wilds without being touched by Bantu superstition.'

It was past noon when we came to a dark jade pool where blue water lilies grew. It was fringed with reeds, parted here and there by game trails, and set about with sulphur-coloured fever-trees, festooned with the nests of weaver-birds. The wild figs, with their profusion of fruit under spreading boughs, gave lavish shade, and tall tambooties reached for the cobalt sky.

'We'll picnic here,' he said. 'Come!'

'What! Get out of the car?'

He glanced at me with a challenge in his eyes.

'Don't you trust me?'

'Of course.'

But we knew the inflexible rule. Never get out of a car. In a car a person is part of the mechanical animal. Out of it he is the old hereditary foe – man, with the smell and the shape of a human being.

'This isn't the time our friends come to drink,' he said.

I knew very well that he was familiar with every inch of this territory, but all the same, as I got out, I felt defenceless and afraid. I enjoyed the sensation of fear and deliberately savoured it. This was how my heroine would feel – my Alice Lang, who had never been out of England till she came to meet her unknown lover in a savage unknown land!

Nimrod took the lead. He was a man of the Shangaan country, like our own gardener, Sombani. He had a round bullet head, small ears, and very pink gums. In repose his face was sad or expressionless, but when he smiled it was immensely gay and alive. Whenever he moved from the car the first gesture of his long narrow hand was to the knife at his belt. The sheath was fashioned out of the hind foot of an impala and the knife slipped down the hollow skin of that slender ankle once so fleet. Cyrus followed him, then Lucia, then me. Jan brought up the rear. He carried no gun. But his eyes, like those of Nimrod, were always on the watch. Leopard, python, lion. At this time of the day they'd be lying up in the shade. Lazy. But you could never be quite sure.

'Remember, though, it's their instinct to go away, not to attack unless they are hungry.'

'They might be hungry.' Cyrus voiced my thought with a grin.

Jan chose a glade surrounded by leadwood trees, and Nimrod gathered dry sticks to make a fire, but not from the tambootie which is a 'medicine tree'. Then he sharpened a Y-shaped twig with his precious knife, and used it to impale *boerwors* for our lunch. He squatted, holding the string of sausages over the flames. He had contrived the fire in such a way that he could cook our *braaivleis* and yet remain almost entirely masked by the tree. All we saw of him was the dexterous hand and the gleam of the copper bangles on the left wrist as he turned his home-made spit over the embers. Sometimes, when he leaned forward, there was the glint of the one 'pirate' ear-ring in the lobe of his left ear.

When his cooking was done he offered us the meat off the spit and we either used our fingers or the little 'forks' he had sharpened for us. Afterwards Jan gave him what was over for himself and he ate it in the seclusion of his hiding place behind the tree.

'When we are on our inspection tours we eat together,' said Jan. 'We are often alone in the bush for perhaps a week, a fortnight, or longer, sometimes on horseback, sometimes on foot or in the jeep. We share our camp-fire and our food, our dangers and discoveries. He only talks when I invite him to, and then we share our thoughts as well. I know every aspect of him, his superstitions and tabus, and he knows mine. We are both men of the wilderness. We love and understand it, and it gives us the best that nature has to offer.'

When he spoke like this, with sincerity and sensitivity, he opened that all-important door for me. I saw the naturalist and his dark shadow allied against the poacher, and I was aware of the mysterious affinity between men and beast in nature's realm. A roller-bird of glorious plumage was performing aerobatics over the pool, with flashes of violet and blue. The weavers were busy among the fever-trees, but the siesta stillness of midday held us in its drowsy grasp. Lucia said, rather enviously,

'I suppose Nimrod works in your house too.'

'Never!' laughed Jan. 'He is my companion of the veld. Here he cooks my food and doesn't let me lift a finger. But, when there is danger, we share it. I never expect him to do anything I would not be prepared to do myself. He knows that.'

'What about your wife and family?' asked Cyrus. 'Does he like them?'

'He respects them. In his eyes a man without a woman and children of his own – especially daughters – would not be a proper man. His daughters are his bank. A father can get twenty to thirty head of cattle for a good and beautiful girl. Cyrus, you'd have had to pay thirty beasts for your little blonde nooi!'

We returned to our rondavels for the rest of the hot afternoon, and, towards evening, we went out again. Once more we broke a rule for we were out after dark, but in official company the rules laid down for tourists do not apply.

That night of the full moon I fell under the spell of the lion.

At midnight I was scribbling in my writer's note-book.

Night. August, 1956. Skukusa.

We saw her in the dusk. That is the time when animals like to take it easy and walk along the empty man-made roads. The soft dust is patterned with their spoor – pan-like hoof-marks, great pugs of lions and the lesser tracks of hyenas, jackals or wild dogs.

We rounded a bend and there she was! Minnie-the-Moocher, mooching along with that unhurried incomparable grace which is the personification of latent strength, great muscles relaxed, tufted tail dangling almost to the ground, stride long and purposeful, on the way to the hunt.

It will not be so easy tonight, for the moon is at the full. She was alone, yet there were others of her kind not far away, for the baboons were swearing and scolding in the trees on the river-side. Bark, hoot, chatter – a noise full of threat and fear.

Jan slowed right down, only his side lights on. She seemed oblivious of the 'new animal' so close on her heels. She did not so much as turn her head. We followed her at her own pace – perhaps five miles an hour. Presently he put on his head-lights, but dimmed. Even then she did not turn. At a fork in the road she hesitated, considered the idea of going to the right, changed her mind and settled for the left branch away from the river. In that moment some animal on the river bank was reprieved from death and a victim on the higher parkland was doomed.

'That's our road, too,' said Jan. 'We'll have to pass her.'

She was on the left. So was I. Jan kept the car beside her, pacing her. The window was open, she was within patting distance, my heart was thumping and I felt as if my nerve was being tested. For about fifty yards we walked hand in hand with Minnie-the-Moocher and then the bonnet drew ahead very slowly still. She looked up, without stopping, straight into my eyes. The noble face with its pride and indifference humbled me. There was none of the expression of the tame animal here. None of the aggressiveness or subservience of the dog, not even the selfish egotism of the cat, only the sublime arrogance and infinite menace of the potential killer who knows her strength and the mistrust of a wild beast confronted with an unusual situation. The 'new animal' seldom moves at night with glaring eyes. She was suspicious but still mainly intent on her own business.

When we had left her behind I felt weak. Jan said something to Nimrod, who answered without hesitation. Jan translated.

'Nimrod says she was not dangerous to us. He looked into her eyes.'

'So did I,' I said. 'To me she looked very regal and very dangerous!'

'To someone else. Not to us.' He has this way of speaking of animals as people – *someone* else, not *something* else.

'A Native knows,' he added. 'He speaks the language of the eyes. He looks into the eyes of a wild animal or a man and he knows the mood. He sits in silence with his woman, but they speak with the eyes. At a certain moment her eyes say "I am ready", and then he says "Come!" and they will make love.'

It was my last day in the lowveld.

I had visited the attractive little police post where the Sergeant in charge had shown me the cruel traps and snares that maim a beast without killing it. Helpful officials had given me some idea about the immense organization required to make the Sanctuary the great tourist attraction that it is, and on that final morning Jan took us to see a lonely Native picket-post in the bush where a young woman and her baby waited for her husband to return. She had been there without human company, except for her child, for a week. She amused herself playing with the baby or decorating her hut with primitive clay pictures of wild beasts or making bead necklaces. Only the high thorn-fence protected her from marauding animals. As we left her we met her husband and his fellow ranger returning on their bicycles hung with cooking-pots, water-bottles, food and a sleeping-sail. Jan stopped to talk to them in their own language. All, it seemed, was well. He made them laugh and their strong teeth gleamed in their dark faces. Seeing them like that – the White scientist and the Bantu rangers so friendly – I was sad that the world should always think of my country as being disrupted by hate between men of different races.

'What do you suppose they talk about on their tours?' I asked Jan.

He laughed. 'Women, cattle and shop.'

We met women walking along the roadside, calabashes balanced on their heads, and piccaninnies slung across their backs in blankets, their pace measured and stately like that of the lioness.

'They are taking maroela beer to their menfolk in the

squatters' camps or picket-posts,' said Jan. 'The women brew the beer.'

'Aren't they afraid to walk in lion-country?'

He shrugged his shoulders. 'It is their country. They know it well.'

We bade him good-bye at Numbi Gate. Yet we were not losing our contact with the Sanctuary just yet, for we were on our way to lunch with Lieut.-Colonel and Mrs. Stevenson-Hamilton at their home, 'Gibraltar', near White River. I had, of course, read his classic books about the birth and growth of the Sanctuary and before I left 'Gibraltar' these beautiful volumes were autographed with his neat signature.

The first and greatest warden of them all was old and frail when we met him that day – a little man, crippled with arthritis, who walked with the aid of two sticks. One of his bright lively blue eyes was blind, but he was still the fighter I had expected him to be, brisk, independent, alert and candid. His wife, tall and tawny, with a charming speaking-voice and great humour, is an artist and illustrator of distinction. Her enchanting animal designs on many of the fabrics to be seen in the Sanctuary are full of life and character.

'Gibraltar' overlooks a sheet of shining water and the hills and vales of the Colonel's 'Eden' were spread before him. But he had no wish to return to the Sanctuary.

'I like to remember it as it was in the beginning,' he said.

I told him that it had amazed me to see the women walking with their children in lion country, evidently unafraid.

'Everybody is afraid of different things,' he said. 'A man from elephant country fears lion and a man from lion country fears elephant. I knew a snake-catcher who went after mambas to milk them for their venom and who insisted on having a ranger with a rifle go with him – not because he feared the deadliest snake in the world, but because it was lion country and he was terrified of lion.'

We ate a most delicious lunch prepared by Mapuli, the cook, whose wife was a witch.

'Mapuli was sick not long ago,' said Mrs. Stevenson-Hamilton. 'He was convinced somebody had put a spell on him, so his wife said she'd make a better magic. She boiled a cauldron full of steaming muti and made him lean over it while she massaged his neck and shoulders. Some of the ingredients in the cauldron were tops of coca-cola bottles plopping about, a couple of old electric light bulbs and a dead mouse – I wouldn't know what else! At all events the answer was a cure!'

'Mapuli's wife had other tricks,' added the Colonel. 'She could make lions. A man would go to her to buy a magic lion to kill an enemy. She charged the princely sum of five pounds for the lion, which was a piece of paper with a very impressionist lion drawn on it. The man was then instructed to go to some place his enemy must often pass – a place in lion country, of course – and blow on the paper and throw it into the air. When his enemy appeared the paper would change into a man-eating lion. You may be sure she took good care to see that the enemy in question was informed of the spell put upon him because the African sorcerer is nothing if not a psychologist. A man believing himself doomed to be a lion's prey loses his head and invites disaster.'

'How does he do that?' asked Cyrus, fascinated.

'Simple. He is returning from work in the Sanctuary. He sees the movement in the grass, the twitch of an ear or a tail. Instead of continuing on his way quite quietly, he is panic-stricken. He cries out and begins to run. Fatal.'

Mrs. Stevenson-Hamilton had once tamed a lion cub whose mother had been killed. She had kept it with various domestic animals.

'He was a darling,' she said. 'But he soon began to stalk other creatures. Once he went too near a donkey with a foal and the donkey bared her teeth. The lion fled. He did the same when an impala stamped at him. But, by the time he was twenty months old, we knew that there would be a disaster if we kept him.'

We didn't ask what happened to her pet. I had a feeling that he would never have been placed in the captivity of a zoo.

We were sorry to leave the pleasant house above the water. The plantations on the distant slopes were cool and dark; beyond them, on the far side of the ridge, was nature's kingdom for which our host had fought with a warrior's courage and tenacity. It was mature and established now, no longer the threatened paradise of those early years of endeavour. But we knew that to him it would always be the 'Eden' of which he had written with such deep knowledge and love. He would remember it untouched by the eyes of the world, before the camps and the cars and the cameras. He would remember it as it was when it was ruled by the lion – and by him.

CHAPTER TEN

MOONSHINE

AFTER my return home the book went fast.

The title for *Nor the Moon By Night* derives from the reaction of my English heroine, Alice Lang, to Velaba, the fictional wild life sanctuary which South African brothers – idealistic Andrew and earthy Rusty – are establishing in a remote and unspecified part of Southern Africa. Alice falls under its spell on her first night alone in camp with Rusty. She looks across the thornveld, silvered by a burning moon, to a range of sombre mountains, and the words of the familiar psalm come into her mind.

'*I will lift up mine eyes unto the hills from whence cometh my help ... The sun shall not smite thee by day, nor the moon by night ...*' She is aware that the sun and the moon of Africa are not like the sun and the moon of England. They are potent and dangerous.

Up to the last chapter I did not know the ending. I could hardly wait to find out!

Early in 1957 I sent the typescript to my publishers, and, a few weeks later a jubilant cable arrived from my agent. By some prodigious stroke of luck I had brought off the 'double'. *Nor the Moon By Night*, like *Valley of the Vines*, had been made a Literary Guild of America selection. In England it was chosen by Foyle's Book Club, and in time the foreign editions came along too. My penetrating Finnish publishers re-named it *Leijonan Aäni*, which I always assumed means 'Lion Magic', and produced it with a gorgeous glazed white jacket decorated with an emblematic navy-blue lion on a crag overlooking three little scarlet rondavels obviously symbolizing the eternal triangle of love. The film rights were bought by the Rank Organization and I signed a contract which reduced me to nothing and made me feel like the man who sold his shadow to the devil.

Towards the end of the year John Stafford, the producer who was to make the picture, flew to South Africa and came to see us.

John Stafford is large with shrewd eyes, an attractive speaking voice, an engaging smile and a confidence inspiring manner. Beverley Baxter once wrote of my husband that 'in an emergency he flies into a great calm'. In command at sea during the war this quality was invaluable. John Stafford possessed it too, and, during the making of *Moon* – as we now abbreviated the full title – he certainly needed it.

There were various ways in which I could help him with the contacts he required to produce the film on location in South Africa and exploit the wild life resources of the country. His approach in this respect was endearing and entirely sincere.

'This film must not sacrifice or seriously inconvenience even one wild creature.'

He honoured the spirit of this resolution faithfully, though it must be admitted that a porcupine was reluctantly dragooned into service and a cobra was mildly inconvenienced. Even the rogue elephant, Dumela, who died in the eye of the camera, was not killed for the film but destroyed in a foreign African territory where a herd was being thinned by the local authorities as a matter of periodical necessity. The camera merely witnessed an inevitable event.

Over a cup of tea John showed me the script.

I found it amazingly fresh and new. The basic situation and a few names and places were vaguely familiar. I recognized none of the dialogue and only part of the action, but the story sounded exciting. Here and there I protested.

'This couldn't possibly happen! No ranger in his senses would allow this girl to ride through lion country by herself—'

'I'll make a note of it.'

He made many notes before he departed, and a fortnight later Ken Annakin, the director, appeared, script in hand.

Ken, tall, striking and masterful, was probably in his early forties. His hair was steely grey, so were his deep-set eyes. He wore spectacles and spoke with the accent of his native Yorkshire. He had found his way into films by chance, through a life of adventure, roughing it all over the world. His enthusiasm for his job, his patience and determination were boundless. Apart from the preliminaries, his job was to extract the best possible performance from the cast and anybody else to do with the production. Where John soothed Ken attacked.

He stood looking through our landscape window. It was evening and the amber light slanted on to the granite buttresses of the mountain, leaving the kloofs dark and mysterious. The Flats to the north lay bathed in the last of the sun and beyond them the Drakenstein range reflected the rosy western glow.

'The colour and the light of this country,' he said. 'It's God's gift to the screen.'

He began to talk about *Moon*.

'It's to be our great outdoor picture of the year – a picture of youth. All the cast are young and adventurous – a do it yourself cast. Here, for instance, in this swimming scene, Belinda Lee can swim—'

'Belinda Lee! Oh, *not* Belinda Lee! She's all curves and flowing fair hair. My girl is dark, intense, skin and bone—'

'It has to be Belinda. She's available. She's under contract to Rank's. But she'll play Alice convincingly. She's very intense – is Belinda!'

'But look, there isn't any swimming scene. How could there be? Rusty would never let Alice swim in a crocodile infested river – to say nothing of bilharzia.'

'He does in this picture. He sits on a rock with his gun loaded and watches her. He wants to see her in a swim-suit. So does the audience.'

I groaned. 'Why not the altogether and be done with it?'

Ken's eyes gleamed. But he shook his head. 'The censor, my dear.'

I took up another vain stand.

'Must you have this veld fire? It's so *ham*! I've never yet seen an animal picture that didn't have flames and the thunder of stampeding hooves—'

'And why? The audience will go home cheated if we don't give them fire and fleeing beasts.'

'But our big problem is poaching. Every sanctuary in the African continent, from the Sudan to the Cape, is at war with the poachers, black, white, individual or organized. Even up there, on the mountain, the poachers go after the little buck and the birds—'

'Relax! We'll have poachers – all sorts. We'll have everything in this picture – plus the fire and the swim-suit *and* the kitchen stove.'

'What do you really want from *me* then?'

'We want to be sure that nothing in this script could offend South African susceptibilities. The colour angle. After all, it's a mixed cast.'

Ken left me fascinated and pulverized. Africa had gone to his head and Alice was to be spared no conceivable or inconceivable adventure.

'Well?' asked Bertie later.

'It's going to be Tarzan of the Baboons!' The idea was rather alluring.

Meanwhile Ken was ranging through Africa in search of the ideal terrain for the enterprise. Lonely places were out. 'How d'you s'pose we'd hold down a unit with scores of technicians in the back of beyond where they can't get any amusement off the set? They only put up with being on location because they get three times the money they'd get at home.' There was even a fantastic moment when it seemed that a considerable part of the picture might be made in Spain because the Organization happened to have some Spanish currency over from the last Graham Greene film John and Ken had completed there a few months ago. However, finally Ken discovered the glories of Zululand within easy reach of Durban, that city of civilized charms, and by January 1958 shooting was well under way in the beautiful Valley of a Thousand Hills.

My husband and I were invited to be the guests of the Rank Organization to see the unit on location.

In the middle of January we touched down at Durban airport at six-thirty on a hot humid evening. Natal in midsummer is as enervating as it is crisply bright in winter.

We were met by a short sturdy man wearing slacks, a

startling check sports vest and a yellow shawl about his shoulders. Jack Martin had evidently fallen for the blanket costume of the inhabitants of Zululand. He was the production manager, responsible for finding whatever might be needed, from the Pietermaritzburg fire brigade to a nice-natured lioness. He had a round humorous face and a quick manner as if life might slip past him if he didn't catch it by the coat-tails. In fact, very little slipped past Jack Martin. He had worked with John Stafford on and off for over thirty years, in Hollywood and England and wherever else John might happen to be filming.

'John's in Johannesburg with the second unit,' he said, 'the one that's doing the wild life stuff. He'll be back in Durban by the night train and he'll pick you up tomorrow morning to bring you to the camp.'

He led us to a Hillman Minx.

'Sorry it's not our big car. Moses smashed it up last night. It's a write-off. He's very upset. Porter, put the bags in the boot! Shall I drive, Moses?'

Moses, a small Zulu, blessed with bountiful curly whiskers, said that he would prefer to drive. Jack nodded approval.

'Best way to get his nerve back. He's quite a character. He's known as the Zulu with the *mustash*.'

Moses retrieved his nerve by driving as if Beelzebub were after him. We were to stay in Durban for three nights, but our two days would be spent with the unit in action among the Thousand Hills.

'Is there a lioness – the Sheba of my book?' I asked eagerly.

'Sure, sure. You'll meet her tomorrow. Her name's Suzie and she's magnificent but temperamental. She belongs to a local farmer, van Rooyen, and naturally he's with her. She has quite an entourage – three Bantu handlers – who wouldn't dare handle her – and a dog. She didn't settle at first, but yesterday we reckoned she was all right. She wrestled with her dog and slept well, and today she performed. When she's performing the set is picketed. No one not actually in the scene is allowed near.'

'What are the human stars like?'

'Ken finds the boys good – Michael Craig and Patrick McGoohan. Pat's grappling with lions somewhere near Johannesburg, so you won't meet him. Annie Gaylor's sweet with the animals, but we aren't so sure of Belinda.'

'Nor am I! She's not my Alice.'

He grinned. 'Nothing will be yours by the time we're through, my dear. In any case, the animals are going to steal this show. Two lovely cheetahs and a crane left the camp yesterday. We have to send the wild stuff back as soon as we've used it. Can't keep it around. The porcupine was a wow, but had no clues about acting – had to be driven into Belinda's tent. And did she come out fast! That was something! The baboon was a honey and Annie's crazy about her vervet monkey, but she's still a bit nervous with Suzie. The first time we had Suzie on the set she clawed up all the furniture – Suzie, I mean – though van Rooyen says she's perfectly house-trained in *his* home!'

The lights of Durban flashed along the Esplanade and twinkled up on the Berea. Moses drew up at the hotel with a flourish, his nerve evidently restored, and a few minutes later we were in the exotic air-conditioned 'Chinese suite' which Rank's had appropriated during the period of filming. Jack looked round.

'I think you'll find everything here. There's booze in that lacquer cabinet. You can get dinner up to nine-thirty. Be seeing you tomorrow.'

Then he was gone, on his way back to Cato Ridge where the unit was dispersed between four hotels on the long spine that commands a breathtaking view of the tumbled Valley of a Thousand Hills.

We dined sumptuously and slept soundly.

The next day dawned bright and beautiful. John Stafford fetched us and drove us up the dramatic winding road to Cato Ridge. There he introduced us to his wife and daughter who were both in love with Africa.

'Are you coming with us to the camp?' I asked them.

Dorothy Stafford glanced at her daughter and laughed. 'That would be against all the rules. We might interfere with routine! You'll find that even you won't be allowed to do that. On the job, Ken is inhuman.'

Jack Martin appeared in an emerald-green and ruby-red shirt flowing free over khaki shorts, and soon we were on our way to the camp.

The Valley of a Thousand Hills, where the unit was on

location, is a Bantu Reserve, and, as such, it is necessary to have a permit to enter it. This had many advantages from a filming point of view as it eliminated the sightseers who would surely have interfered with work anywhere else.

The soft green country with its hills and vales is unbelievably lovely, broken by blue rock-crowned koppies, and watered by two rivers with foaming rapids and deep quiet pools. The rushing water filled the warm steamy air with its murmur, but, apart from that and the twittering of countless birds, it was silent and still. Zulu kraals were scattered over hillsides where cattle grazed with herds of goats. Stately women, clad in blankets or dried goatskin skirts, with babies slung on their backs and burdens upon their heads, trod the winding tracks, their feet bare save for bead anklets. Their firm naked breasts were dark and glossy as indigo satin. Their bead headdresses and necklaces were significant adornments with messages for the initiated. Their menfolk wore many different garbs, from bizarre shirts or drab khaki to the traditional blanket. Many carried guitars or more informal instruments such as old cans flattened and fitted with strands of wire.

'Just right for a skiffle band,' said Bertie.

John Stafford smiled. 'They're very musical – these people of the Valley of Vital Statistics.'

At the foot of the tender hills, on the banks of the Umgeni, we came upon a native store near a rambling wooden bungalow with a large notice outside it. TEA ROOM CLOSED FOR ALTERATIONS. Which was, undoubtedly, the understatement of the year.

'There!' said John, stopping the car and looking pleased with himself. 'What do you think of Boryslawski's ranch?'

'Just right – from outside.'

Inside was pandemonium. The large main room was packed with a conglomeration of cameras of all shapes and sizes, arc-lamps, electric cables, cans and containers filled with electrical equipment, a couch with lion-clawed covers and broken springs, a couple of easy chairs, a table covered with recording apparatus, a number of upturned boxes, and a great many hot human beings. Technicians – and there were many of these – sat or lounged about, smoking, reading or killing their abysmal boredom by flirting with the dressers. They wore khaki shorts, no shirts, and some had chains round their necks with medallions or religious symbols. The old-timers, who had been on location in the Far East, were heavily tattooed. Among these electricians, camera crews, carpenters and decorators, roamed the art director, the props man, the publicity man, the make-up man, the hairdresser, the wardrobe mistress, the stand-ins, and, most essential of all, the continuity girl. A few of the cast not in action, relaxed on the wide stoep.

The moment I was flung into this hurly-burly I had the most extraordinary sensation of having been here before. Which was certainly not the case. It was a memory generated perhaps by the mess of paraphernalia, shabbiness, improvisation, foreigners billeted here and there and the locals out to profit from the invasion. Suddenly, the penny dropped and I was back in Italy in 1943 in the Psychological Warfare Branch of Allied Headquarters, a propaganda unit even crazier and more mixed than this one. So strong was the impression that I pursued it in my writer's note-book that night.

The real reason, I think, why I felt so at home this afternoon on the set – so back in the curious unreal but compelling atmosphere of P.W.B. – was the fact that here too is a human menagerie with everybody drawn from a different walk of life, sharing nothing in common except the job and a certain degree of lunacy. When I say they have the job in common I don't mean they care tuppence about it. They are interested only in what it offers each of them personally. It was so in P.W.B. even though then there was a war to be won and a world at stake. And here too, each individual is only a small piece in the jigsaw, oblivious of the whole. Only the director has a vision of what he hopes to achieve – a God's eye view.

It amused Bertie and me to find that nobody, except the producer, the director and the South African hospital nurse in charge of the unit's health, had even dipped into the novel, Nor the Moon By Night. Till I appeared on the scene they had never heard of the author, but, when we were introduced, they were friendly and seemed to bear me no grudge. The cast worked entirely from the script, and I doubt if any of them had glanced at all of that.

Not long ago I read a New Yorker 'Profile' of John Giel-
gud, in which he said: 'Many actors never know what's
going on in the rest of the play; they only know what is
happening to *them*. I once discovered that a certain star
didn't know who her children were in her play.'

Most of the cast were chiefly interested in their publicity
and Belinda, of course, was consumed with a personal grand
passion about to reach its first tragic climax.

None of the cast bore the faintest resemblance to my
characters.

My dark repressed Alice was transformed into tawny-
maned Belinda, her curves bursting out of swim-suit or
pyjamas; Rusty, a leonine fellow with reddish hair, was
played by dark, handsome Michael Craig; Andrew, the the-
orist, had become a great doer of deeds; my villain, as slim,
flexible and dangerous as his sjambok, was fat and heavy;
my teenager, Thea, the daughter of a missionary and naïvely
in love with Andrew, was a knowing French girl now the
daughter of the villain! Only the lioness was herself, beautiful and gloriously dumb.

Outside, in the hot sun, we stood for a few moments and
watched the cameras pursue Anna Gaylor perched like a
blonde mosquito on a huge white horse galloping across the
veld, while others followed Michael Craig and his Bantu
game-guard down to the bank of the fast-flowing river.

'Belinda Lee – Joy Packer and Admiral Packer,' said John
Stafford.

She came to join us in the shade of the big mango tree.
She was wearing a simple blue cotton dress and no make-up.
Her hips were a little too big and her legs not quite long
enough for true grace, but what one noticed was the beauty
of her green cat-tilted eyes, her mane of red-gold hair and
the young firm contours of her throat and bosom.

She was quiet and composed, easy to talk to, with a sleepy
well-educated voice. I asked her if she found Africa exciting.
She smiled.

'I've discovered a dressmaker up on the Ridge who copies
my expensive models for eight guineas a time. That's exciting.'

She had a way of tossing her hair constantly as if she could
not forget it. He's told her that it's wonderful, I thought –
and so it is!

She was unaware of Africa, unaware of her surroundings or her job except when she was actually performing. People said that she was unapproachable. Perhaps she was, because she was wrapped in the shining cocoon of an illicit love affair. Her heart and soul were in Rome with her forbidden lover.

The publicity man came over to us.

'Lady Packer, will you and Belinda come across to the lioness and be photographed with her?'

'In the den?' asked Belinda.

'Yes . . . just you two, and Suzie.'

'I'm not keen,' she said.

'Van Rooyen says it's safe. He should know.'

'I don't believe in courting that sort of danger. But, if you insist, then . . . yes.'

'I think it's all right,' I said, as we strolled through the long grass towards the fenced outhouses where the animals had their temporary abode. 'Mr. van Rooyen took me into the shed to talk to Suzie about half an hour ago. She wasn't hostile.'

'Did you pat her?'

'No, it's a question of looking. No touching.'

'Good,' said Belinda.

Mr. van Rooyen, Suzie's owner, was a big man who carried a stick which he used to guide the lioness, not to chastise her. He was attuned to every mood of his dangerous pet. His contract allowed Suzie one donkey a week and, for the rest, horse-meat. Even so, she had not been happy at first.

'The valley is too hot for her,' said Mr. van Rooyen, 'but she has acclimatized, and, once she began to play with Zimba again, we knew all was well.'

Belinda and I looked through the wire netting of the large cement-floored shed where Suzie lay with her friend, Zimba, the dog. It was a case of Beauty and the Beast. Zimba, the gentle and agreeable Beast, had to be seen to be believed. He was a cross between a ridgeback and a bull-mastiff, and somewhere along the line some dauntless and enterprising dachshund had clearly left his mark upon Zimba's ancestral tree. Those front legs could have no other explanation. Suzie's three Bantu handlers, dressed as game-guards with wide-brimmed felt hats turned up at the side, stood nearby. They carried long whips which they cracked in order to

117

drive her in the required direction. Not so much as a flick of those whips ever touched her, but she responded well to the crack.

Belinda and I followed Mr. van Rooyen into the shed while the photographers remained close to the entrance.

'Will she mind the flashlight?' asked one of them, tensely.

Everyone seemed to feel that the human voice in her vicinity was a mistake, and only Mr. van Rooyen spoke normally.

'It'll be all right, but don't take too long about it.'

'Shall I pat her?' I whispered.

'No,' said Mr. van Rooyen.

We gazed at Suzie and Suzie gazed back. She stared straight into Belinda's glorious feline eyes so like her own, opened her mouth to its full extent, showing a terrifying denture and a long pink rasping tongue, and yawned her head off. The cameras clicked, the arc-light flashed, the photographers bustled out as fast as they could and Belinda and I followed suit with sighs of relief.

Later that afternoon, between her siesta and her 'hunting time', Suzie performed. Suzie alone selected her time for being on the set. 'Not before four o'clock,' said Mr. van Rooyen, 'and not after five. It's too hot early and after five she wants to go hunting.'

When the set was cleared for Suzie it was the rule that everybody not absolutely necessary to the shooting of the scene should go over to the adjacent native store.

We sat on a low stone wall, in company with some enormous ants, and talked to all sorts of people. The fire brigade from Pietermaritzburg was there, so was Ben, the young Afrikaans police sergeant who was playing the part of the police sergeant in the film. Ben had a curious and difficult task requiring considerable tact, and he accomplished it with good humour and judgment.

He was tall, broad and excessively handsome, with an ingenuous smile showing a fine set of teeth. His normal job was to keep the peace in this Zulu territory of some forty thousand black people, and it had now become his business to see that the film unit in the valley did not upset them. When some incident looked like causing trouble Ben would go to Jack Martin and talk to him firmly, politely and chummily –

a man-to-man approach – and the trouble would be ironed out.

Ben told us that he had had real difficulty learning English well enough to get into the Police Force. 'Man, that's a hard language to master!' So he was quite glad of the opportunity to practise it continually in the unit.

'Even in Natal most of the Police come from Afrikaner homes,' he said. 'The English-speaking boys just aren't interested. I don't know why. It's a good life – but not good enough for *them*!'

There it was – the touch of irritation, the suggestion that the British South African was arrogant. Yet the young man's smile cancelled out all malice.

'In some ways I'd rather work for the English-speaking,' he laughed. 'If an Afrikaner loses a tickey you've got to find it for him, if it kills you. He won't let go. He's *hard*! The English just shrug their shoulders after a bit.'

A fireman standing near us said to Ben, 'Hey, man, when are we going to do our rain-making stuff?'

'After the lioness is through.'

'Why must the fire-brigade make rain?' I asked. 'Heaven has made too much already – according to the papers.'

'One drop of rain on a camera light and it explodes – pft! And forty quid down the drain. They have to control their rain.'

Not far from us sat Doreen, the Zulu girl chosen to play Oasis, the wife of the mutilated game-guard. The baby cast for 'the little warrior' was on her lap. She played with him most of the day so that he should be happy and at home with her. He was as delightful as his name, which was Innocent. Half a dozen genuine mammies squatted around the store, suckling their babies or feeding piccaninnies mealiepap from bowls. They were nothing to do with the film. They had come to make their periodical purchases and now they waited to see the added attraction of the lioness.

'Oasis is very pretty,' I said to Jack Martin, who had appeared in his sudden way.

'Doreen? She's Oasis the second. Oasis the first photographed like the Black Hole of Calcutta. This girl is good. She was a student nurse, but already she's showing star temperament. They pick that up fast!'

She was small and slight with dainty features, not too dark. She wore the stiff little pigtails and bead headdress, which, like her black goatskin skirt, denoted the status of a married woman. In real life Doreen was not married. She and the rain-makers were next on call.

'Look!' Ben pointed down the grassy slope from the river to the tea-room converted into a temporary ranch. 'There they come! Man, that's a nice lion!'

A little procession, headed by Mr. van Rooyen, approached. Anna Gaylor was at his side. Like the Zulu girl with her film baby, the little French actress was required to be constantly with the lioness to accustom them to one another. Suzie and the dog, Zimba, followed at their leisure, tumbling each other in the long grass and stopping from time to time to lie peacefully on their backs with their paws in the air.

'*Kom, Suzie, kom!*' urged Mr. van Rooyen, when this happened. And the Bantu game-guards on either flank and in the rear, cracked their long whips and called to the lioness to be on her way. Suzie understood Afrikaans and Zulu and was learning French endearments from Anna, but she was not to be hustled.

'No collar, no lead?' I was surprised.

'Og, she's tame, that mooi animal,' said Ben, who loved and admired her.

'All the same,' growled the fireman, 'a lioness that age isn't a safe pet.'

'She's eighteen months old and weighs three hundred pounds,' said Jack Martin, who knew everybody's vital statistics. 'And I was responsible for finding her and meeting her food bills. Next time you write a lovely book, Joy Packer, leave out the lions!'

'And the rain,' added a senior electrician. 'My cables fuse.'

The fireman looked hurt.

Suzie went up the steps of the ranch on her own. Zimba lay humbly outside. Anna was close on Suzie's tail, and Mr. van Rooyen kept them both in sight but was careful to remain out of range of the cameras.

Inside, on the set, Suzie's entrance was awaited tensely. A camera man, prone on the floor to get upward shots, moaned as her hot breath seared his neck while she sniffed at him. 'Did I sweat!' he said afterwards.

Colonel Pierson, the owner of the converted tea-room and the native store, lurked in a specially constructed gallery with a loaded gun.

'I'd never dare use it,' he confided to me later. 'A lion's too quick, but it gives the folk on the set confidence. Anyway, if I shot Suzie, I'd have to shoot van Rooyen too in self defence!'

Ken Annakin was dripping when the scene was over. He lived in dread of some catastrophe. 'These lion sequences take years off my life! And Suzie's impervious to direction.'

Ah, the lovely animals! That was *their* magic. They were impervious to conventional direction and no one could put foolish or banal lines into their savage mouths.

Suzie 'worked well' that day, but she was playful on her way home. She loped towards the store with its crowd of sightseers. Those tasty children and plump mammies would make a more interesting meal than the old blind donkey now being skinned in preparation for her supper.

When at last she had been safely returned to her shed with Zimba we went to watch the rain sequence. This was Doreen's great moment. With Innocent in her arms she crept out of the fire brigade rain on to the stoep bent on nefarious business. The rain was stupendous and the brief scene endlessly repeated. 'Rain! ... Action! ... Cut!' Soon both mother and child were half drowned.

'Innocent must have a dry shawl' commanded Gladys, the continuity girl, firmly. While she fetched one, Nick, the props man, dried the drenched baby with the assured dexterity of experience.

'How many has he got at home?' I asked Jack Martin.

'Four.'

'Why doesn't Oasis carry her baby on her back? She should do.'

Jack grinned. 'She prefers not to. She feels that she is no longer a tribal woman. She is educated. Her calling as a nurse and her dignity as an actress would suffer.'

'But she's not herself when she's performing. She's Oasis – a very tribal woman indeed.'

'Tell her that when she's a great actress – and then she'll

believe you.' His eyes twinkled. 'By the way, do you mind if she goes down to Durban in your car with you when Moses takes you?'

'Of course not.'

'One never knows here,' he said. 'It's as well to ask.'

Ken Annakin and John Stafford and his wife and daughter were to join us for a late dinner. We had had a full day and were ready to go back and relax for half an hour.

But only a lion can hurry a Zulu. Doreen kept us waiting. She sat beside Moses in front, very trim in her blouse and tailored skirt. No beads and goatskin now. The 'Zulu with the mustash', his nerve no longer impaired, drove like Jehu and never stopped talking to his companion, using his hands like a Greek as he did so. I guessed that they were putting on a sophisticated little act for our benefit since they did not speak their own language. Moses was to call for us next morning, Doreen with him.

'I must be at the hotel at eight-thirty tomorrow,' he said to her. 'So I fetch you at eight-fifteen.' He had an exact somewhat explosive way of bringing out his words.

'Yerz,' she drawled. 'That will do nicely.'

'On second thoughts, make it eight o'clock.'

'I doant get up so early. Why eight o'clock?'

'It will give us a quarter of an hour to go backwards and forwards.'

'Backwards and forwards?'

'Back for what you will tell me you have forgotten – "Moses, my coat! Moses, my handbag!" – and forwards aftah!'

'Uhuhuhu!' The little laugh and shrug surely belonged to the new world of the screen. 'You are a seelly man.'

Moses fetched us at eight-thirty without Doreen.

'I went for her but she had some shopping to do. We will meet her in the main street.'

We waited for some time. She appeared with a well-dressed ebony boy friend carrying her parcels. She dismissed him, gave us an amiable 'good morning', and took her place beside Moses.

'You are late,' he remarked.

She half turned her head, presenting us with a flat attractive profile.

'Sorry to have kept you waiting.'

Within twenty miles the car coughed and stopped. We had run out of petrol. Moses was humiliated.

'The other car – the big one I smashed – *had* petrol when it registered empty. This is a rotten car – no reserve tank – nothing!'

We got a lift to Cato Ridge and left Moses and Doreen to their own devices. John Stafford was cooling his heels at the hotel with some impatience.

Jack Martin sorted out the car situation and we drove to Pietermaritzburg to see rushes of *Nor The Moon By Night* recently developed in London and flown back to South Africa.

It was then that I realized how beautiful the colours were and how fascinating the scenery and the wild life pictures. If all else failed this film should be able to ride home on the photography.

The blind Old Chief was played by Moses' uncle, a librarian over eighty years of age, and the witch-doctor was a man of horrific appearance.

'A wonderful make-up,' I congratulated John.

He laughed. 'He was his own make-up man, I can assure you. He is the local medicine man. We fitted the Old Chief with contact lenses – milky, to look like cataract – and, when he took them out after the sequence, I wish you could have seen the witch-doctor's face! A man who could take out his eyes – what a magic!'

On the screen and with her hair drawn back, I was astonished at the impressive beauty of Belinda's face.

'Her face is strong on the screen – older looking,' I said to Dorothy Stafford, who knew her well. 'You might almost call it austere.'

'The camera reveals its own truths. Belinda is very determined and wilful – very warm and feminine too. At this moment she has set her heart on flying to Rome for a few days with or without leave.' She sighed and laughed. 'That's John's headache! Austere? Perhaps her honesty reflects that way. She's one of the most honest people I've ever met.'

Presently, while the Staffords waited to see more rushes, Moses drove us to the camp in the Valley.

'Are there crocodiles in this river?' I asked him.

'Only holes,' he said. 'A man was drowned close by the place where Belinda was in swimming.'

Belinda. Not *Miss* Belinda? Or Miss Lee? Ben, the Afrikaans policeman, would feel that boots were pinching a bit. 'They get too big for their boots,' he'd said with his pleasant grin. This free and easy unit was leaving its mark here and there.

'What about snakes?'

Moses waved an airy hand. 'A few mambas flying about! But Belinda doesn't mind about mambas. She screams if she sees a grasshopper.'

'I suggest you chat later,' Bertie told me firmly. 'We want to get there.'

Moses not only answered questions with his hands, but turned round to be sure of the effect of his replies.

A reporter was interviewing Belinda when we arrived. When she consented to speak to reporters she did so with candour.

'What sort of parts do you *like* to play?' he asked.

She considered the matter.

'Passionate exotic parts. I don't want to be the girl next door, or somebody's sister.' She turned to me with a smile. 'I don't really like being a simple decent outdoor girl either – good at heart, even when she's swept off her feet!'

Yet, in her cotton dress, with her tanned unpainted face and attractive English voice, that was the impression she left. Only the expressive green eyes gave that healthy outdoor look the lie. The hidden voluptuary slumbered there. She tossed back her loose tawny hair in the gesture I had already come to know, and I guessed that she was no longer with us in this sunny valley of the Umgeni but on the banks of the Tiber, where the known and familiar trend of her life had irrevocably changed its course.

A week later, when we were back in our own home, with the Thousand Hills and the world of film fantasy far away and forgotten, I picked up a newspaper and saw those disturbing tilted eyes looking at me from the front page.

Belinda Lee, star of *Nor the Moon By Night* at present filming in Natal, is seriously ill in a Rome nursing home.

She is believed to be suffering from an overdose of sleeping tablets. Prince Filippo Orsini, a member of the highest Italian nobility and till recently her close friend, has been taken to a private clinic with slashed wrists.

But death was not ready for Belinda. She still had three years to wait before the Ides of March, 1961, when a car smash on Highway 91 between Las Vegas and Hollywood did what those sleeping tablets had failed to do in 1958. With her then was Gualtiero Jacopetti, the Italian journalist and film director she was to have married. He survived the crash that killed Belinda.

In the three years between seeking and finding death she made a fortune in foreign films, playing the 'passionate parts' she had craved, culminating in Messalina, the beautiful wicked wife of the Roman Emperor Claudius. The background of violence, intrigue and debauchery was Rome, the city in which this young British star had discovered her own fiery potentialities as a woman and an actress.

But, at the height of her wealth and notoriety, Belinda Lee – always so honest – spoke like the 'simple decent girl' she had never wished to appear.

'This fortune – more money than I can use – what does it mean? What have I really got? Anybody with babies is better off than I am.'

CHAPTER ELEVEN

'INTERESTING TIMES'

How John Stafford extracted Belinda Lee from her Roman nursing home under the twitching noses of a pack of scandal-hungry news-hounds is his story, not mine. Whatever the means, that imperturbable man succeeded in bringing the heart-broken star back to South Africa disguised as Mrs. Jones. But, although Belinda completed the picture, the 'suicide scandal' cost her her career in British films – which she did not appear to regret – and Prince Filippo Orsini was obliged to resign from a privileged position in the

Vatican which had been held by members of his family for many generations.

When the picture of *Nor the Moon by Night* finally made its bow it was taken apart by the London critics, though most of them allowed that Eastman colour, the scenery and the wild life were fool-proof. One gloomy fellow, however, refused to concede even that. He complained that the performers were wooden, the rogue elephant was plastic and the lioness was a man in a fur rug! What Mr. van Rooyen would have said to that I hate to think. I have often wondered what happened to Suzie, that gentle lioness, and her dog, Zimba. It pleases me to think that she was taken to the Kruger Park, where she learned to fend for herself and mated with a magnificent wild lion. Possibly Mr. van Rooyen goes there from time to time and calls her with the crack of a friendly whip. Maybe Suzie answers the signal by strolling out of the long red grass, followed by her cubs. Maybe not. I can't dream up a satisfactory solution for Zimba, but then neither in life nor in story-telling can one hope for a happy ending for everybody.

Zimba was a dog whose fate was linked with that of a lioness. He owed his modest measure of publicity to Suzie. But that same year of 1957 – the International Geophysical year – other more distinguished dogs were in the limelight. Far away in Russia 'Little Lemon' was rocketed into outer space and simultaneously into the imagination of animal lovers the whole world over.

On a summer night in November my husband and I stood on our lawn and watched the satellite, Muttnik, approach above the dark mountain.

'There she comes – that small white light over Constantia Nek moving towards Table Bay.'

He had his powerful German night binoculars trained on the Russian moon, but she was easily visible to the naked eye, rather like a bicycle lamp and appearing to move at much the same pace. I had expected the silver streak of a shooting star or the drama of a comet trailing a tail of fire, but Muttnik, in no great hurry, kept steadily on her course and presently disappeared over the flank of the mountain to the far horizon where sea and sky meet.

The brief but impressive manifestation of man's scientific genius reminded me of the film life of Our Lord in which the

Star of the East 'went before' the Three Wise Men, across a luminous cinema colour sky, leading them to the stable in Bethlehem where they 'fell down and worshipped'. Where would this Russian robot star lead the people of the earth? To the conquest of new worlds or to total annihilation? Some children, allowed to stay up that night to see Muttnik, had no profound thoughts or fears. Miracles of science they already took for granted, but they voiced a universal reaction when they said, wide-eyed and pitying, 'There goes the poor little doggie!'

The 'little doggie', imprisoned in her capsule, blazing the trail for Major Gagarin, the earth's first human astronaut, stole the picture from science.

I wrote in my note-book.

Nov. 1957. 'Cressage'.

I find the new developments and possibilities frightening and enormously exciting. But the dog-in-the-moon is so sad. What makes it worse is the knowledge that Limonchick (Little Lemon), the clever little dog in Russia's artificial moon, must have accepted her fate confident that her master would soon let her out of her capsule. They say a dog has no sense of time – that waiting in a car, for instance, means the same to the animal if it is reckoned in minutes or hours. So no doubt Limonchick waits for her human to come and release her from captivity. She will wait with patience and confidence. But only death will release her faithful spirit.

I think it is the loneliness of her fate that makes it so distressing. When I harped on it, Bertie said at last,

'Listen, of course it is unpleasant, but she isn't the first dog that has been used as a guinea-pig for science, nor I fear will she be the last. Does that cheer you up?' He looked like a sad old dog himself as he said it, caustic to cover up his hatred of the whole business.

I was very emotional though.

'If any animal is used in scientific experiments – at least he is petted by human hands and has human friends near him all the time.'

He shrugged his shoulders with his giving-in movement.

'Little Lemon has nobody,' I went on, 'but nobody!

Even those poor apes the Americans sent up in their first rocket to carry a live creature into space had each other. There were three of them. And somehow, it doesn't seem so bad to do dreadful things to a creature that is not a *natural* friend of man – that doesn't trust man and that knows him for an enemy.'

'I expect the apes were fond of their trainer,' he said.

In the night I woke and thought, There'll be a parachute. They'll bring her down in a parachute. I felt better then and went to sleep.

Later:

The whole world has felt as I did about Limonchick, Little Lemon. At first there was lots of parachute talk. Then that died out. Now, Nov. 13th, the paper says: 'A lecturer of the Moscow Planetarium yesterday told questioners that the space dog, Laika – known also as Little Lemon who went up in Russia's second satellite nine days ago – was evidently dead. For days people have crowded the planetarium – a vast model of the universe – to ask the lecturer about Laika.'

So the Russians have hearts as well as satellites. How long will it take for science to evolve a uniformly cold heart for every human being?

It was good those summer nights to sit out on our terrace under the fragrant little lemon tree which – except in name – had no sad associations with the animal in her flying coffin. Our own simple safe domestic dog and cat sat nearby, Snowy on the low stone wall with his tail uncoiled and limp as a fishing line and his gaze fixed on the valley where the dogs bayed to the moon and the coons played their guitars. The white cat brooded at the top of the terrace steps, crouching like a miniature sphynx on the tread-plate of my husband's most famous and well loved 'grey mistress', H.M.S. *Warspite*. When they broke up that grand 'Old Lady' of the sea the name-plate from the quarterdeck at the head of the ladder was sent to him as a souvenir, for he had shared her fortunes in two wars. It was now no longer burnished brass but weathered to a sombre gunmetal, darkly at home in the slate crazy paving, and at the end of the day it continued to radiate the sun's warmth, which was no doubt why the cat favoured it.

I wondered sometimes what vibrations of peace and war that tread-plate held. The thin echo of a Sailor King or an Admiral of the Fleet being piped aboard? The thunder of battle at Jutland? Was my husband re-living bygone battles as he sat reflective in the summer dusk? Was he once more a very young officer in charge of the only turret still in action as the great ship circled helpless in the grey North Sea, her helm jammed, a target for the German High Seas Fleet? Or did he recall the bright Mediterranean where once again this ship had buried her dead and limped back to port through 'the dangers of the sea and the violence of the enemy'? No, more likely he was wondering whether to give the lemon tree trace elements to combat those signs of yellow and curly leaf, for my man of the sea had returned 'in safety to enjoy the blessings of the land', among which he rated the peace and quiet of his garden very high.

Every morning it was his habit to carry out an inspection of the grounds with Sombani, pointing out this and that with the smooth wattle pole he carried like an Alpine stock. That pole lived in a corner of the sun porch with his straw sun-hat and my flower basket and secateurs, for in the cool of the evening we liked to stroll down to the rose-beds and cut off the dead heads, while we planned a new colour scheme in a border here or a flower-bed there. Our white animals accompanied us, playful and gay in the failing light. Sometimes it seemed to us that our home was contained in a charmed circle of peace, a place apart from the rumblings of a restive world.

There is a Chinese saying: 'May you live in interesting times.' It is a subtle curse. Our times were certainly interesting. Christmas changed its face and character in that year of the Russian moons. Father Christmas came to Cape Town toy-shops in a space-ship and sledges and reindeers were forgotten. But in the new year sledges were back in the news and dogs once again proved themselves pioneers. These were the husky teams of the successful Commonwealth Trans-Antarctic Expedition led by Sir Vivian Fuchs of England and Sir Edmund Hillary of New Zealand. With the aid of their old fashioned sledge and huskies and their new fangled snow-cats and scientific equipment, the two leaders crossed the frozen continent from coast to coast and clasped hands at the South Pole.

To us at the Cape the Antarctic triumph was of special interest, for Cape Town is one of the world's most important springboards for the white south.

Every year in late November the whaling fleets of Europe assemble in Table Bay to take in stores before sailing for the summer season in the ice. The annual departure and return of the whaling expeditions and their tales of adventure, hardship and hazard are part of the life of our port. Small wonder, then, that the dashing whalermen found their way into my third novel.

What was surprising was the manner in which one of them taught me the importance of a minor character. As far as I was concerned, Bok Makiérie, the young Coloured whalerman, sailed off with my third novel, *The High Roof*. He not only absorbed me as a personality but he came to symbolize the frustrations of his people. He was the lad with the love of high places – the mountain top or the masthead – but his life was conditioned by the limitations of *apartheid*. He meant no harm to anyone, yet he struck his head against one of those unyielding ceilings and was warped into a criminal.

I learned a great deal from Bok.

I saw him first on a bright windy afternoon when the Netherlands whaling fleet was in harbour before going south.

The catchers – fourteen converted Canadian corvettes – had spent the winter refitting in our docks, or engaged in coastal whaling, and the factory ship, the refinery, *Willem Barendsz*, had arrived from Holland and was taking in supplies and signing on crew. The Netherlands company was one of the few to take on South Africans in Cape Town and most of them were tough Coloured fishermen. There was no *apartheid* in the *Willem Barendsz* or her catchers. It was equal pay for equal work and the same living conditions for everybody.

Our kind friend, the Dutch Consul-General had arranged for me to go over the factory ship, and my mother, when she heard of this, said:

'I'd like to have a look at that ship myself, and I'm sure

Gudrun Digre would. Arend can take us down to the docks, and then, while you're on board, Gudrun and I will go for a drive and come back and fetch you later.'

Mother and her Norwegian neighbour, Madam Digre, were always thrilled by the whalers. Mother loved any activity in the docks and to Madam Digre the arrival of the whalers always brought a keen longed-for breath of her native fjords and mountains, for, no matter what nationality the fleet might be, the gunner-captains of the catchers were invariably Norwegian. Although she had lived over thirty years in the cottage next door to 'Tees Lodge' and had brought up three sons and a daughter to be good South Africans, her own heart still ached for the land of her birth. When the soft autumn days came to Cape Town she would tell us of the coming of spring in her far away country and of the many delightful customs that celebrate the end of the long northern winter.

We arrived opposite the high ungainly *Willem Barendsz* in advance of my appointment. She was loading stores into the newly-painted catcher alongside her, and on the quay was a queue of Coloured seamen awaiting their turn to go on board, pass their medical examination and sign on for the expedition. Arend got out of the car and went over to them, for several were personally known to him.

A few squatted in the lee of a pile of timber out of the blast of the south-easter that whipped the white horses of the bay and rolled the Niagara of cloud over the granite face of the mountain. They played cards or gambling games while others danced to keep warm. Encouraging the dancers and strumming his guitar as he sang the words of old Cape *liedjies* was a gay wild-looking lad with a sailor's copper tan on his high sallow cheekbones. He danced in the supple double-jointed fashion of a coon, every inch of him acting, from his bold black eyes to his nimbling scuffling feet. He was a born entertainer, magnetic, carrying his audience with him. He paused for a few moments to laugh and chaff with my mother's old chauffeur who was himself a personality well-known among his people. In company Arend was a wag and a mimic with a keen eye for a pretty girl, but he was also a patriarch and a martinet in his own home which swarmed with his innumerable descendants, for, like Father Abraham, he had been blessed in that his seed was multiplied 'as the stars of the heaven and as the sand which is upon the sea-shore'.

Whatever witticisms might be passing between old Arend and the young seaman were evidently highly amusing, and I watched fascinated as the light and shade of laughter and mock solemnity crossed the lad's face. Already Bok – he could have no other name – was establishing himself firmly in my mind. I could feel the tentacles of my imagination reach out to grasp his entire background, his triumphs and tribulations, and a faint glimmering of his ultimate fate.

'A friend of yours?' I asked Arend, when he returned to the car. Bok was moving on with the queue. He had reached the foot of the gangway.

'Las' year he was courting a fren' of my granddaughter.'

'Did he marry her?' inquired my mother, who liked romance to lead to the altar.

Arend's eyes twinkled in their ancient folds of plum-dark flesh.

'He was too long away, Madam. Four, five mont's down in the ice . . .' He raised expressive shoulders as if to imply that we must all appreciate the frailties of human nature and the temptations of sailors' sweethearts – as, indeed, one of us did. But my mother, who had led a sheltered life and seldom been absent from my father, did not pursue the conversation. It was Madam Digre who caught my eye and laughed as she said to Arend,

'And when he is coming back with money burning holes in his pockets, what then?'

He grinned. 'De whalermen comes back an' de women is waiting for them. But not my granddaughter's fren'. She is married an' it's too late to change her mind.'

At the head of the gangway the Dutch Consul-General was about to take leave of the Captain.

'I must go,' I said. 'Will you come back for me at five o'clock?'

'We'll go to the Doll's House,' said Mother. 'That'll fill in the time nicely.'

The Doll's House was a drive-in snack and coffee bar on the shore by Mouille Point Lighthouse. Customers were served in their cars, sea-birds wheeled overhead and the air smelt of coffee, fresh toast and ozone.

Arend turned the elegant vintage car, her home-made flag

shuddering and stiffening in the wind. Through the back window I saw my mother's gleaming silver head, immaculate and hatless, as always, and Madam Digre's aristocratic profile under her dashing wine-coloured hat. They were very old friends, deeply content to be in each others' company. 'Sometimes we talking, sometimes we just keeping quiet together,' Gudrun would say. When my mother didn't want to be bothered chatting she simply touched her hearing-aid, shook her head as if she were dumb as well as deaf, raised her lovely grey eyes heavenwards and smiled apologetically, then Gudrun would nod, smile back, pat the old lady's hand, and they would both relax into companionable silence.

Climbing the steep gangway of the *Willem Barendsz* was like going up Lion's Head. The Consul-General waited to introduce me to the Captain, a gnarled man of the sea with a slow kindly smile.

'There's a catcher on the other side,' said the Consul-General. 'She's loading stores and harpoons. How would you like to go over her? You'd have to be lowered in a basket.'

'I'd love it.'

'It shall be arranged,' promised the Captain.

The bridge and officers' quarters towered over us for'ard as we stood on the long deck littered with supplies, the winches and hoists working as crates and harpoons were swung over into the little catcher bobbing on the wind-churned water far below. Soon this deck would be a gigantic slaughterhouse, slippery with blood and ice as the monster mammals of the deep were prepared for the refinery and the huge pressure-cookers that reduce the blubber to whale oil, the base of the world's supply of margarine, or, as in the case of the rare sperm whale, of cosmetics. No part of the whale is wasted except his stomach contents which are fed to the fishes.

'They stink,' said the Captain, 'but the Japanese use them for something – I cannot guess what!'

I went all over that astonishing ship from heel to head and got some idea of the great floating industrial enterprise where the whale is processed while you wait, twenty-four hours a day non-stop.

The young Hollander in charge of the refinery spoke excellent English as did the Captain. From him I learned that the whale-killing season begins roughly in early December and continues for about ten or twelve weeks until the international signal goes out that no more whales are to be killed because the quota has reached its limit. Every factory-ship has two international referees on board to see fair play.

Whales generally breed in the tropics and travel to their feeding-grounds in the Antarctic during the summer. Browsing and sluicing as they go, they feed mainly on krill, a sort of shrimp which moves about in shoals. Krill is greasy and creates the valuable blubber which yields fish oil.

A factory-ship carries the most varied complement of experts you could wish to find at sea, from the scientists in the laboratory to the flenzers who slice off the blubber. It also has a first class hospital and a well qualified surgeon because whaling is a hazardous occupation and the casualties during a season may be many and severe. Steel hawsers drag the monsters inboard. Huge saws are used to cut through bone that will one day be used as agricultural fertilizer, and the long sharp knives of the flenzers are designed for massive surgery. In fact, everything intended to take a whale to pieces could make short work of a careless man, and I daresay the ship's boy could easily slide down a chute into the pressure-cooker to be 'tried out' with the blubber.

The wife of the surgeon on board the *Willem Barendsz* was a trained hospital nurse and accompanied her husband on the expeditions. She was a great asset, not only for her professional qualifications, but because she was blessed with a motherly personality. The men told her their troubles and prayed with her on Sundays and Christmas Day when she took short simple church services on board.

The crew loading the catcher clopped about on their wooden sabots, and their apple-cheeked faces split into broad grins as they helped me into the big basket, which already contained harpoons and biscuit boxes, and prepared to lower it over the side. Like the Captain, they came from Terschelling Island in North Holland where they worked in agriculture during the European summer. I firmly believe that most sailors are farmers or nursery-gardeners at heart. The Captain told us with pride that he had a small farm which his wife managed during the unproductive winter months.

As the basket descended I felt rather like Alice in Wonderland when she fell down the White Rabbit's hole into a strange new world.

One of the catcher's crew was greasing the blunt menacing gun in the bows, and, as the basket settled shakily on the deck, the Norwegian gunner-captain clicked his heels, bowed over my hand and led me along the high narrow catwalk to the gun-platform. He was short and broad with pale hair and eyes, very light against the tan of his skin.

It was while he was explaining how the harpoon-gun worked that I suddenly began to hate the whole business.

I remember Wendy-the-Whale and her baby who had charmed us all when they played for hours in the waters of False Bay the first year we were at Admiralty House, Simon's Town, and the other mother who, with her calf, had amused and entertained the inhabitants of Hermanus this very summer. Whales are the most affectionate, devoted and playful of mothers and their calves are always near them. The harpoon was no longer abstract to me. It was dreadfully real and immediate, a heavy steel weapon containing an explosive charge to open out the wicked grapple instantly upon entering the body of its victim. How different from the days of Moby Dick when men and whales fought it out with a fifty-fifty chance of death or survival! Now men hunted their prey in warships, shot them with invincible guns, inflated and flagged them, reported their position by wireless so that the buoy-boats would be able to pick them up and tow them to the factory-ship to be hauled up the slipway on to the long bloody block for dismemberment. The world must have fish-oil, I told myself, and vitamins – liver extract – and bone meal and animal food and whale meat, but already the squeamishness that was to jeopardize the family whaling interests of the hero of *The High Roof* was at work inside me, preparing for its timely transference to the principal character of a novel as yet unconceived.

The gunner, unaware of my reactions, pointed to the crow's nest swaying and dipping some fifty feet above us. In his mouth the soft W became a V.

'Up there is the spotter. He sees far over the vater. Our best spotters are the Cape Coloured fishermen. They can always distingvish the vhale from the spume. They give the vord and the chase is on. You follow the herd and pick your vhale. A good gunner kills vit' the first shot or the vhale may drag the ship which is very dangerous.'

My mood switched as my eyes followed his to the crow's nest. Perhaps young Bok would be up there, a key man scanning the surface of the sea for the give-away spout. He'd call in Norwegian, the language of whalermen, 'Hval blast', and give the direction to the helmsman. How did he feel up there? Godlike? He was a leading player in this drama of death in the deep, at no disadvantage with his fellows! No niggling regulations here would remind him day and night that he was a second class person – a man who must live in areas assigned to his people by the authorities, sit on benches labelled *'nie blankes'* or 'non-Europeans', occupy certain seats in buses and trains, or enter public places by doors which would not permit him to rub shoulders with the white-skinned master race. In this man's world he was a man like any other, sharing the work and adventures of his comrades to the full. Would it occur to him that his White shipmates – the Hollanders and Norwegians who treated him with little consideration and less patronage – were, in fact, true Europeans as opposed to South African Europeans who claimed that desirable definition only by virtue of their origin and who had, down the years, evolved an ingrained confidence in their superiority over the indigenous 'darkies' upon whom their ancestors had bestowed the blessings of western civilization? I doubt it. People like Bok take a good deal for granted until something particular gets under their skin. The nature of that special corrosive I had still to discover. Already Bok was beginning to tell me about himself, but there was still so much to learn.

By the time my mother's car was reported alongside my mind was a vivid jumble of mixed impressions.

The squeamishness was buried by layers of excitement and visions of undreamed of beauty. Haze over the sea when the herd is spotted; the thrill of the hunt; a blue whale marked down and making for the ice-pack at twenty to twenty-five knots; a tough little catcher in pursuit; the clean clear world of seals and sea-birds; fantastic formations and colours of cliffs and coast, for the contour of the white continent is fashioned by the changing pattern of ice and painted by prismatic reflections more glorious and profound than any rainbow. No whalerman would concede that the black sky and unwinking stars of space and the glowing colours of earth seen from infinity could be more impressive than the indigo seas with their frozen shores and the fragile castles and cream cakes and Christmas crackers of floating ice-bergs.

And the gunners – those daring specialists who have inherited their knowledge of whales from their fathers and grandfathers right back to the days of the Vikings – they too lay hold on the imagination. When I asked one of the scientists about the gunners, he grinned.

'What are they like? Headstrong, arrogant, egotistical and tough as hell. All they think about is whales, women and cash, and they get a surfeit of all three in a seasonal sort of way. There's tremendous competition for top score in dead whales. The winning whale-killer goes home bursting with prize money and prestige. In his home port he has the status of a successful bullfighter in Spain, and when he has gained the highest whaling score he is a hero – a matador strutting round the ring holding the bull's ear on high!'

Of course, many of them forfeit this acclaim to stay at the Cape and do a winter season of coastal whaling, and quite a number retire in South Africa and swell the Norwegian community. They take on other shipping jobs, but when they talk of 'going to the ice' their eyes glitter and they are once more in their man's world apart where few can follow them.

Before I got into the car I looked back for a moment at the *Willem Barendsz.*

A girl in a yellow sweater and full skirt waited at the foot of the crew's gangway, her face uplifted, her frizzy reddish hair tossed across her cheek by the south-easter. The lad with the guitar bounded down the ladder, slipped his arm through hers, and half danced her away. They were laughing and elated, vital and young. So Bok had been taken on. Tomorrow he'd be on his way. Tonight belonged to love. Her resilient breasts bounced under the tight sweater and the high heels of her shabby shoes tapped to the dancing rhythm of her step. She was a tiger-lily girl, amber skinned, provocative.

'That girl in the yellow jersey,' murmured my mother in an undertone not intended for Arend's ears. 'White or Coloured?'

'Borderline,' answered Madam Digre without hesitation.

Ah, borderline! Suddenly I felt the chill of the wind. Today they were lovers. Tomorrow what? The aura of menace and persecution shimmered round the carefree intimacy of the Coloured boy and his borderline girl.

CHAPTER TWELVE

END OF AN ERA

ALL summer I worked on the new novel, *The High Roof*, but certain key pieces in the jigsaw of my story still eluded me. Then one day I went with my mother and Madam Digre for one of those 'airings' they both enjoyed. Arend drove us to the top of Signal Hill with its superb panorama of Cape Town, Table Bay, and the distant ranges that form the first jagged step to the plateau of the north. My mother never tired of this fine view, nor, indeed, of any of the beauties of her beloved Cape Peninsula. Now, in her late eighties, she had grown frail and the strong afternoon light showed up the pale transparency of her skin.

'Where could you beat all this?' Her grey eyes sought the far blue peaks. 'When I count my many blessings I never forget our glorious scenery.'

She counted her blessings every day, as if they were the beads of a rosary, each imbued with a different quality of contentment. Arend, Madam Digre and I had our place among them. Fidelity, friendship and filial affection were precious to her for she was a woman who basked in love. The only blessing she ever treated with impatient hostility was her hearing-aid, the 'darned contrivance'.

I left the two old ladies in the car and went to stand alone by the guard rail on the wooded crown of the Hill.

By a coincidence the Dutch whaling fleet happened to be steaming into harbour, the bold excitable catchers, scarred by the vicissitudes of the summer in the ice, escorting their clumsy mother ship, the refinery, *Willem Barendsz*.

I thought about the crews, so long out of touch with civilization, and wondered if they had had a good season. Would the girl in the yellow sweater – Lily Laguna – be waiting on the wharf to greet her Coloured lover? Suddenly, I knew that she would not.

I felt the curious breathless thrill that every author knows when a knotty situation begins to unravel itself. Hang on to the thread, don't lose it! Here was the key to the central theme of my novel. When Lily Laguna failed to meet Bok on his return from the ice she settled the fate of a great number of more important characters. And the reason why she would not meet him was contained in the one word, 'borderline'.

During Bok's absence down in the ice I was convinced that Lily, his borderline light of love, had succeeded in passing herself off as White. She had officially crossed the Colour line and her newly acquired identity card was stamped with the coveted W. Unlike Bok, she could now move freely in the world of 'Europeans only'. She had become a first class citizen with the right to live on the sunny side of the fence, but there was a price for this glory and the price was Bok.

The embittered love of Bok and Lily – two minor characters in *The High Roof* – was pure fiction, but it might just as well have been poignant fact.

The Population Registration Act had recently come into force for the purpose of advancing 'positive *apartheid*' yet another step. Everybody in the country was registered and placed, once and for all time, in the appropriate racial category. Many people of mixed blood, who had been tacitly accepted as European all their lives, now suddenly found their social and economic future in jeopardy. A word in the ear of the authorities and entire families had to go before a Board established to investigate 'borderline cases'. The inquisitors conducted their hateful and well nigh impossible task with compassion and *in camera*, but, even so, many of the victims – while not disclosing their names – aired their grievances.

'What's the good of secrecy?' they said. 'All our neighbours know and talk about it. Our eldest boy is classified as Coloured and his brothers and sisters as White! How can a family live like that? One child forced to go to a Coloured school, while the others are Europeans.'

Marriages were broken on the wheel of the Act. If a husband were classified as European and his wife as non-European both parties would be breaking the Immorality Act, which is a criminal offence with no option of a fine. Even couples married before the Act was made law would suffer because one or the other would be contravening the Group Areas Act which forbids a non-European to live in an area zoned for Whites or vice versa. Thus the White partner must be degraded to Coloured status if the marriage was to survive.

In many respects our country sets a civilized example to the rest of the African Continent, and it is no exaggeration to say that never before in the history of African benefit has so much been done for so many by so few. But the remarkable advances in non-European welfare and education are masked by daily individual humiliations, great and small. A man wounded in his pride is mortally wounded, and these wounds are inflicted continually and relentlessly by the policy of legalized discrimination.

How my characters, Bok and Lily, tried to solve their problem and the far-reaching effect of their solution upon the major characters of *The High Roof* convinced me anew that integration of our lives – no matter what our race – is inescapable.

'Darling,' said my mother, when I returned to the car, 'what were you so thoughtful about – all by yourself over there? Your new book, I suppose.'

'Yes, in a way.'

'When will it be finished?'

'Not for months. You know how slow I am – always tearing up and beginning again.'

'Don't be too slow. I want to see it in print.'

She was smiling, but her eyes were apprehensive and the hand she laid on mine was light and cold. She no longer wore her rings because she complained that they were too heavy and slipped round with the jewels facing inwards to her palm. Only the smooth gold band on her wedding finger never came off. I pressed her hand lightly.

'I'll do my best.'

*   *   *

My mother never saw *The High Roof* in print.

She died peacefully in her sleep on the eve of its publication.

As a young woman her interests had been many. Her political affinities, greatly influenced by her youngest and favourite brother, Wilfred Marais, had always been nationalist and, like Wilfred, she longed to see South Africa a Republic. This was not surprising, since she had been born in Pretoria in the time of the first Boer Republic. Her wish, granted to her brother, was denied to her, but at least she was spared the turmoil and tempests that marked the last lap of the road to an independence so absolute that it is near isolation. In any case, as her long life drew to its close, the world outside the Victorian iron railings of 'Tees Lodge' had become remote. She had returned, childlike, to the safety and intimacy of the home, the family circle and those who looked after her with such unfailing devotion.

It was Teena, who had been with her for more than thirty years, who summed up her quality.

'Madam never raised her voice to us. When Madam was angry or upset it was in her eyes.'

'With all of us it was the same,' I said.

Often, towards the end of her years, when she lay dozing with the evening sun slanting through the big bow windows of her bedroom, her shining head on a shell-pink pillow, her pearls gleaming round her throat, and the little hearing aid on the bedside table, Teena would come to the door, which was always ajar, and stand watching her.

'Is there anything you want, Teena?' I'd ask.

'No, Miss Yoy. I jus' like to look at Madam so long.'

Serene in the silence of her deafness and the drowsy peace of her declining years, my mother was unaware of us. Teena's dark gentle gaze would drink its fill, she'd smile at me, and go quietly back to her kitchen. There now, I'd think, she's put the good eye on Mummie. And the old house would draw me into itself once more, back into my childhood when Teena's sister, Cookie, had reigned in the kitchen and German Nannie had controlled my nursery existence as she had done from my birth and as she later controlled my infant son's.

Nan, grown old and lame, with her lion's heart and fighting spirit still unimpaired, was as much a part of our lives as ever, though she no longer lived at 'Tees Lodge'. But Cookie, who had come to this house as a girl in her teens, married in middle age, and borne one daughter, delivered by my father, had died here after forty years of faithful service. My mother had attended the funeral and bowed her silver head with the dark mourners at the graveside. Until her marriage Cookie's daughter had worked at 'Tees Lodge', and, on the young girl's wedding day, the old lady and her little grandson, Peter, had been at the church service. She had written to me afterwards in far away China to tell me that 'the bridesmaids looked like a bunch of flowers in their gauzy hydrangea-coloured dresses'.

Marriage, birth, death. These fundamental events had been shared in the families of the *nooi* and her domestics.

These reflections would pass through my mind on those afternoons when I sat in her room watching over her as the sands of her long life trickled gently and peacefully through time's hour glass.

At six o'clock Angeline, the sturdy housemaid from the country, always brought in the *nooi*'s supper tray with a nip of sparkling wine. We'd plump up the old lady's pillows and she'd reach for her 'darned contrivance' and fit the plastic bead into her ear. She'd smile serenely.

'I've been lying dreaming. Have you been here long, Joy?'

'Not very. I've been dreaming too.'

The dreams and ghosts of other days were always with me in my old home. Nowhere else would ever contain so many unforgettable years. A whole era was embalmed in this house where time stood still while the world moved on at its ever increasing pace.

Three months after my mother's death 'Tees Lodge' was sold with its contents by public auction. The domestics, now pensioned, lived there to the day of the sale. The buyers wanted the site for a block of modern flats. When their bid was accepted 'Tees Lodge' was doomed to destruction.

The last carpet was rolled up, the last massive piece of furniture was loaded into a van and the last tin of carnations taken from the derelict garden. The big teak doors were locked and the shutters closed. Angeline had gone to her home in Darling, and Arend had taken his grey sorrowful face into the outside room labelled 'Arend Esq'. It was his refuge from his large family, his place of peace and quiet where his grandchildren had always brought him his midday sandwiches. He had liked to eat his meal and drink his coffee in the dappled light of the vine over the open door, his spectacles on his broad nose, his newspaper spread on his lap. To pack up the belongings he had collected in 'Arend Esq' was to say a last farewell to forty years of his life.

Teena stood on the stoep in her neat grey flannel suit and black hat and gloves, her few remaining possessions in a large carrier bag over her arm. She was waiting for me to drive her to the home of the niece whose wedding my mother had attended so many years ago.

'Are you ready, Teena?'

'Yes, Miss Yoy.'

'Come then.'

Neither of us looked back at the shaggy lawns and creeper-covered gables. We would never return to this house. For both of us a way of life had ended.

The wind blew across the Flats and raised clouds of golden dust round the cottage in Kensington. Teena's niece came out to meet us. I leaned across and opened the door of the car.

'Will Miss Joy come in for a cup of tea? Miss Joy must be tired.'

'It's very kind of you, and I am tired. So is Teena. But I must get home.'

Home. Now that had only one meaning. 'Cressage'.

Teena wanted to say good-bye, but the word stuck in her throat, and I couldn't help her. She paused uncertainly, her carrier bag over her arm, her gloved hand holding on to her hat as she swayed in the tireless wind.

I watched them walk up the sandy path to the door and noticed how lame Teena had grown over the years. Her niece had taken the carrier bag and her auntie's arm. We would meet again, of course. But I knew that, in truth, old Teena was walking out of my life.

CHAPTER THIRTEEN

A LONDON REFLECTION

My husband and I were on a visit to England in the year my mother died, and that summer in London I began to be aware of the full force of disapproval and disgust engendered abroad by South Africa's official racial policy of enforced segregation.

For the first time in their lives individual travellers found themselves being held responsible for the 'un-Christian attitude' of their Government, and so contrary is human nature that again and again I found myself attempting to justify certain aspects of our traditional way of life that at home I would have decried.

When toothache drove me to the dentist I listened to his views on South Africa while he drilled a molar. He had the best of that argument. Even at the photographer's I was involved in a defence of my country.

To me a session in the studio is even more terrifying than one in the dentist's chair but my publishers were adamant and insisted upon making an appointment.

'All you have to do is turn up at this address at 11 a.m. on Thursday,' said the editor-in-chief. I took the slip of paper from her with dejection.

'I freeze at the sight of a camera.'

'Never mind,' she said easily. 'Perhaps you won't freeze on Thursday.'

The name on the card was John Vickers and the address appeared to be somewhere in Belgravia, but the taxi-driver couldn't find it.

'This is the street,' he said, 'but there's no 29B. We've 'unted 'igh and low.'

We had indeed. We stood on the pavement in the pale May sunshine, looking up at the pillared Georgian portico of Number 30. The numbers were all haywire. Somebody had shuffled them like they'd shuffled the houses. The odds and evens, the high and humble were all mixed up, with embassies and junk-shops hobnobbing the way they do in London, and luxury flats a stone's throw from tenements.

The little black taxi panted by the kerb, ticking up three-pences. The driver removed his peaked cap and scratched the back of his head with a rasping noise.

'No sign of any 29B is there, mate?' He appealed to a painter who was having elevenses down in the area of an empty mansion.

The painter shrugged. He was, he explained, 'a stranger in these parts'. But he came up out of the area and conferred with another painter drinking a mug of tea outside another mansion that was also receiving its spring coat of cream.

'29B?' The second painter was puzzled. 'No b's around here. Who did you want?'

'John Vickers,' I said. 'Would there be a telephone directory in your house?'

He obligingly went in search of one.

'Oh dear,' I said, as he returned in triumph. 'That's A to K. It's Vickers.'

'Vickers John,' he sounded aggrieved. 'You said John Vickers.' But he went indoors again and came back presently with S to Z. The driver and the painter watched me look it up. I read out the address.

'—*road*,' they echoed in disdainful chorus.

'That's *over* the river!'

The taxi-driver's face, old and lined in the sun, cleared. At least he had not failed in his knowledge of London. The painters returned to their tea-drinking and we rattled away from the weary elegance of Belgravia towards Pimlico.

Even here we had our difficulties. Then suddenly I spotted a tiny sign pointing down some area steps into a basement. 'John Vickers. 29B.' This house, too, must once have been a Georgian mansion, though its grandeur was remote and would never come again, for it had gathered dull companions round it. No eccentricity here, no brightly lacquered front doors, no odd little dwellings to catch the eye and lay siege to the imagination.

'He hides,' said the taxi-driver. 'But we found him – this Vickers, John.'

'We ran him to earth,' I agreed as I paid him.

'I better wait a minute till you're in.' He had lost faith in the existence of Vickers, John. At the bottom of the area-steps I collided with a Frenchman who said 'Pardon' and 'Bon jour' and turned back to open the door for me before going on his way. I glanced up, waved good-bye to the taxi-driver and stepped out of the deep well of silvery London light into the fox-hole of John Vickers' studio.

I looked round for the usual display of studio portraits. There was none – except for one framed photograph of an Italian-looking girl in a sweater. It seemed to have been taken 'on the wing'. It was tremendously alive. The sharp breasts breathed, the dark eyes *looked*. There was one other photograph, the subject of which I don't remember, and a copy of *The New Statesman* lay open at the photographer's advertisement: 'Reduced prices for women with beautiful souls.' What would be the qualifying test? I wondered.

I had a brief impression of red walls, black lamps, cameras and cobwebs, a vision of corpses under the cellar-floor, bats and black magic and the blind-worm darkness of a burrow in the ground. Then a very young man plunged into this gloom from a cupboard which might more likely have contained a skeleton.

'Lady Packer! Would you wait *here*, please. Mr. Vickers won't be a minute.' His voice was young too, and his smile flashed as he opened a door into the recess under the stairs – always 'the safest place' during the blitz. The ghosts of war-time fears, forgotten these many years, pressed in upon me as the door closed and I was alone.

'No!' I said, and opened it quickly. But the young man had vanished and there was nothing but 'the place under the stairs' masquerading as a dressing-room, and the dim cluttered blood-red studio beyond.

I sank down on to a divan under the slanting ledge and thought, Yes, it's here they would have cowered all those years ago. 'They' – the dwellers under the sky of death. This part of London had taken heavy punishment. Opposite the divan was a narrow dressing-table with two electric candle-lights on either side of it. I combed my hair and wondered what next?

I looked up and saw John Vickers leaning against the flimsy door between 'the place under the stairs' and the studio. I received an impression of an aura of frizzy grey-blond hair, searching blindish eyes behind strong spectacles, a nose too big for the face, a head too big for the body, a hesitant voice and a mouth that twisted when its owner talked. He wore an old alpaca jacket over grey flannels, and a floppy bow tie.

'There's some coffee coming. Will you smoke?'

He offered me a cigarette from a torn packet. Real smokers don't transfer cigarettes into cases. It takes too long – they'd be filling cases all day. I shook my head.

'I smoke very little. Look, Mr. Vickers, I'm awfully bad about this photograph business. Will this do – this plain black velvet?'

I was wearing a severe black velvet suit.

'It doesn't matter,' he said. 'This picture is for your publisher. Not family. Family like more of the person – to the waist. So!'

He folded his arms and made his face look like every studio portrait since the camera was invented. Smug, suet pudding, self-conscious, a 'half length' to stand on the piano.

I laughed because the little act was funny and released a tension that had been building up inside me – the prelude to the freeze.

'I don't give my family photographs of me, nor my friends. I don't give anybody photographs.'

If that sounded rude in the fox-hole of a photographer he didn't seem to mind. The hands of the apprentice who had received me appeared out of the gloom beyond the door and set a narrow tray with two little cups of black coffee on the dressing-table. Somewhere above the electric candle his smile flashed and was gone.

John Vickers said, as he helped himself and me to sugar, 'I haven't read any of your books. Tell me about the one with the attractive title – *Valley of the Vines*.'

He had drawn a stool into the doorway. He perched there with the light on his glasses and his hair.

'It's about South Africa. Have you been there?'

'If you gave me a ticket and offered me a free tour I wouldn't go. I should get angry and I don't like being angry. It's so destructive – unless, of course, it leads somewhere.'

Oh dear, I thought. Here it is again – this reproach, this wrath against the South African – any South African.

'I am South African,' I said, 'and *Valley of the Vines* is a happy book. A love story.'

147

He brooded on his perch, like a sleepy, big beaked, crested bird with untidy feathers. His eyes had become narrow and impersonal, the lids drawn down. His neck sank into his shoulders. He was squat like a bird preparing for the night. I had pulled the black curtain over his cage with the words 'happy' and 'love'. I had lulled him into boredom and somnolence. There is no happiness for the true creative artist. There is torment in plenty and high leaping moments of elation, passion with an aftermath of sickness. As for love, that is the will-o'-the-wisp luring genius into the quagmire of domesticity. Suddenly I caught it off him – the suspicion and mistrust of happiness. Was it, perhaps, more destructive to the artist than anger? Was it the feather-pillow gently pressed over the warm breathing mouth of inspiration? But I defended it – my faith in happiness – even the happiness of dark people in my own country.

'There are happy people in South Africa! Not only those you would call – privileged, but many others too. I wish you could see our Coloured Coons at the Cape dancing and singing in their brilliant costumes – happy in a simple way, in the sun and with music and rhythm in their blood – or the children of the Transkei Native territories in their little ochre blankets waving as your car sweeps through their cattle-lands . . .'

His eyes flicked open, condemning the glitter of the White man's car trailing its wake of red dust in those sun-drenched uplands grazed bare as worn plush.

'What are they like – these territories? Forests? Jungles?'

'Grass-lands,' I said. 'The Native is a cattle-man, a nomad. Hunger and soil erosion are the problems we have to fight on his account, and it's so hard to teach him to help himself. He doesn't want to contour plough, or restrict the number of his cattle, or settle round the nucleus of a civilized community – a church, a school, a store, and some sort of medical centre. He would rather wander with his herds, grazing them where and how he pleases, or go to the mines as a sort of initiation, and leave his women to cultivate the soil in the easiest way, regardless of the future. You don't learn collective responsibility overnight. If his territories were not reserved for him exclusively they would very quickly fall into the hands of unscrupulous White men or Indians. Why, a Swazi chief sold his country to the British for greyhounds and champagne. Giving it back to the Swazi – even in part – has been quite a major operation.'

John Vickers said thoughtfully: 'Social responsibility takes a couple of generations to learn – like receiving full value for education. There was an African on television the other night. Interesting. He explained how his people could be educated – there are grants and scholarships that allow a great many to come to Universities in this country – and then there comes a point when they have this priceless gift of education and they don't know how to use it or what to do with it.'

He made a gesture with his hands – and it seemed for an instant as if they were black hands holding between them the tarnished Aladdin's lamp of learning. He looked down into those hands holding the invisible gift, and he was no longer John Vickers, theatrical photographer, but a puzzled young African intellectual wondering how to summon the slave of this magic lamp, education.

'I've had them here, working for me,' he went on. 'They learn it all – the technical stuff, the craftsmanship – and then they don't seem able to apply it. They can't get full value out of it.'

'In South Africa it's very hard for them,' I said. 'A lot of education is a dangerous thing for the African there. He gets it – the key to the door – *but the door remains barred*, and that burns him up. Naturally!'

'You should talk on television,' he said, suddenly. 'Your face comes alive, and the lighting is from below. Well now, I console myself by thinking that maybe this thing that goes on in your country is a stage of evolution the African has to go through before he can find himself – and equality – so let him get it over as quickly as possible.'

'The sad thing is that most White South Africans can't really visualize equality as a reasonable condition between Black and White. It's our blind spot. We're blind about it in a hysterical way. We won't see the possibility. We could if we made up our minds to, but we are afraid of what such a picture would present. You see, there are so many of them and so few of us – eight million against two million. Yet in South Africa the White man has never behaved as emotionally as he has in America. There has never been a lynching in our country – never any Klu Klux Klan or Flaming Cross. Look – about this photograph, I hate the left side of my face.'

'Now, why?' he asked.

'It's taken all the bumps of my life. It's the hard side. All the things I'd rather forget are written in the left profile. We're all Jekyll and Hyde, aren't we? I'd rather you photographed Mrs. Jekyll than Mrs. Hyde.'

He laughed – a husky bitter little sound. 'You don't really believe you are only two people, do you?'

'Fundamentally, yes. Many more on the surface.'

'Fundamentally, *one*. And that one is all the rest as well. I am forty years old. At forty one begins to know human beings. And oneself.'

'Oneself. Does one ever?'

'At forty – yes.'

'I doubt it. You'll go on surprising yourself all your life. That's half the fun – the excitement of living. Not knowing what one will do next.'

'I want to write,' he said. 'Novels, plays. Chiefly plays. Just write. Give up photography. How do *you* write? Where?'

'In a room with a view – a glorious view. Across a wooded valley to a mountain with deep kloofs and ravines. In bed – in long hand – till quite late in the morning. Then outside on a sun-porch. Always with a view. I type the second draft. My desk is by a landscape window.'

He said: 'I couldn't write that way. I should have to write by electric light – bury myself and write.'

He blinked owlishly and I saw that he was a creature of the dark and of lamps – lights slanted on to faces from queer angles, torches trained suddenly on to various aspects of human nature, flashing this way and that.

'Like Simenon,' he said. 'Simenon is sociable, meets his friends, likes to talk, to sit on the boulevard and drink a glass of wine and study the world he writes about. Then suddenly he disappears into the dark shuttered room with the electric light; trays of food are put outside his door at certain hours and he takes them in or doesn't, and he works and works, and one day he comes into the daylight again – with a novel. That's the way I should want to write.'

We were two different animals, John Vickers and I. He

was a burrowing animal, and I a climbing creature.

'The photograph,' I reminded him.

'Ah, yes! Perhaps you are pressed for time?'

His tone was a reproach. Time was not important. One is too aware of time – the bully, the nagging mistress of our lives.

He slid off his stool and moved from his borderline post between the 'place under the stairs' and the studio. He made his way round the heavy unlit arc lamps towards a shadowy camera. Daylight seeped through heavy curtains. I followed him into the room with the blood red walls.

'You like music?' he asked.

'Yes.'

'I have some long-playing records. Old French folk-songs.'

'No, not old French folk-songs. I like rather emotional music. Rachmaninoff – Tchaikowsky.'

He looked disappointed. We were such very different animals, he and I.

'*Prince Igor*, then. I haven't got the others.'

Like the trip to South Africa, I felt he wouldn't have them if you gave them to him.

Music filled the studio. What language was the opera sung in? I don't remember. Russian, perhaps. The singers were Russian. He told me their names. They conveyed nothing to me.

All at once, everything came to life. Lights blazed into my face, on to my hair, behind me, in front of me, to the side, as I sat on a slender cushioned chair with arms. I saw the sultry face of Diaghilev glaring at me from a frame in a corner by a screen. Diabolic. I looked away from the portrait. Above it, slender wires were suspended from the red ceiling in an abstract design vaguely resembling the half-finished model of a little boy's aeroplane, or echoing, perhaps, the first winged whisper of inspiration trembling in the brain of Leonardo da Vinci.

The camera drew near. I took fright.

'It's nearer than they usually are!'

'It's conversationally near,' he said comfortably. 'I wouldn't talk to you further away than this.'

The dazzling glare of the lamps high-lighted the blaze of the little man's frizzy hair and the gleam on his glasses. The disembodied voices of the Russian singers vibrated in the background.

'Look!' said John Vickers. 'About here' – I could see his hand, pale in the dark behind the glare '—about *here* someone you love is coming towards you!'

The warmth of the thought filled me. I looked for the person I loved and believed him present.

There was a sinking *clonk-clonk*.

'Oh dear,' I said. 'That was the bomb dropping.'

Strange, but the feel of the 'place under the stairs' was still just a little bit with me – a memory of the fear of showing fear. And then I was nervous of the camera again – my enemy.

But he moved his lights about, unconcerned, I closed my eyes to shut them out and saw, on an orange screen, strange Japanese water-flowers bloom and fade and blossom again. The pattern changed as the lights receded or approached.

'The things behind one's lids!' I said. 'Amazing! Blue and purple blobs floating down against an indescribable background.'

'Have they got legs?' he asked, interested.

'No. But there are tiny snakes weaving about, like the things you see under a microscope. It's all in colour.'

'Like pictures of music? Music in colour and design?'

'Yes, very. Like the abstract bits of Disney's *Fantasia*. Do you think being blind, yet aware of light – of where there's a window in a room, or a chandelier – is like this, a brilliant pattern behind the skin of the eyelid, behind the shutter of blindness?'

'No. I think light is a feeling – a vibration – to the blind. Or a warmth. Much of my work – developing and so on – is done in total darkness, but there are lamps, very dim blue, not enough to make colour behind the lids, or heat. When I have recently shaved I can close my eyes and go towards them in the dark because I can feel where they are through the sensitivity of my skin.'

I was sitting with a pool of darkness over my left shoulder. Into this pool he flung a large white gauntlet glove – the sort of glove a welder wears.

'The pattern of the future!' he said.

I stared at it, seeing the gloved human hand pressing the button or pulling the lever that would release heaven alone knew what energy to set miraculous machinery in motion. I looked away and up at the flimsy wires, the effect of a primitive flying-machine heading for the age of inter-planetary communication.

He drew my attention with a wave of his hand.

'The person you love – *about here*!'

My eyes followed his hand. The person I loved – dreamlike and ghostly – smiled at me from the darkness behind him.

'And now the last one,' said John Vickers. 'Shall it be the left profile?'

'No!' I said. 'That is my own business. Never the left profile!'

'As you like.'

'I must get a taxi,' I said.

'I'll come up with you. Sometimes it's not easy to find one.'

We climbed the area steps into the sun. He blinked in the noonday light and I knew that he longed to plunge back into the burrow where he made his own sunshine in his own way.

He hailed a prowling taxi going in the direction of the river. As he opened the door for me, he said:

'Yes, you're right about black velvet. It does suit you, doesn't it?'

I laughed and looked at him, and wondered if we would recognize each other if we were to meet again.

'I like it. I feel safe in black velvet.'

'*Safe!*' His eyes widened behind his glasses and filled with horror. 'To be safe is to be dead.'

CHAPTER FOURTEEN

OF BEASTS AND MEN

PERHAPS, as John Vickers had exclaimed with such unmitigated scorn, safety is akin to death. But to me it is the lull between one storm and the next. Life batters human beings with so many storms – the hurricanes that are not of their own making and those that are personal and come from within and are no less devastating.

1959 went her way and, in South Africa, 1960 was born under a summer sky in which the new man-made moons played hide-and-seek with the timeless constellations.

For us the next few weeks in the Cape were blessed with the same tranced quality that had held England spellbound twenty years earlier during the summer before the blitz. Now, as then, nature was at her most tranquil. Never had the weather been more balmy, the sea more sparkling, the woods more cool and fragrant, or the crops so good. One glorious day followed another, offering calm and – yes – safety. It seemed to most of us that danger was everywhere else. We, in our paradise, existed blissfully in the euphoria of a ruling race as yet not seriously challenged.

In our own immediate neighbourhood the sole threat to peace was a pack of roving dogs led by a Bull-Mastiff and a Terrier belonging to people who had gone abroad, leaving their fierce dogs in the care of an irresponsible Bantu. The animals ranged as far afield as Constantia, attacking cattle, poultry and domestic pets.

Our own little dog, Snowy, had developed an affection for some Golden Spaniels further up the hill. These lovable creatures belonged to a friend of ours who was amused at Snowy's constant visits.

'He trots up after tea to play with them,' she laughed. 'Saucy as you please, a gleam in his eye, his tail coiled left-about, and he stays till I give them their food, when I shoo him off home. I don't feed him, of course.'

'He's always back before sunset,' I said. 'He's scared of the dark, as well as hungry.'

We could count on him to come jauntily home for his evening meal and that reflective hour afterwards when he sat on the low stone wall in the dusk that thrilled with bird-song and smelt of lemon flowers.

But one lovely evening, as night was falling, I whistled in vain for our little dog, up through the woods and all round the garden. Bertie was worried too.

'He always comes pounding along when you call him.'

Puzzled, I telephoned the owner of the Spaniels, but she had chased him away as usual and had watched him trotting off in the twilight, homeward bound.

Finally, we had to go to bed with Snowy still absent. We hoped it was only 'woman business' that had kept him. The moon was at the full and a good many neighbouring dogs were baying their appreciation. Pools of indigo shadow lay on our lawns and banks; the long white goblets of the moonflower tree glimmered in pale profusion; the Fernwood and Protea Buttresses of the mountain, bleached like ancient bones, towered against the heavens ablaze with stars.

I stood at the window and saw the white cat move secretly among the rose bushes. It was past midnight, but I whistled softly for our little dog. He might be down there in the shadows. Kitty paused and looked up, her eyes phosphorescent. There was no other answer.

In the morning we received a telephone call. Snowy had been found.

We went up to the garden of the Golden Spaniels. Their mistress was out, but the Coloured gardener met us as we got out of the car.

'Look at the mess those dogs have made! All my flowers knocked flat. Might be lions! Madam's gone to report it to the police. People should chain up such fierce dogs at night. It's the big one and the Terrier, they lead the pack.'

Their spoor was everywhere, the light and heavy prints of several animals bounding across the flower-beds in pursuit of something.

The gardener led us to a shrubbery of azaleas and camellias. In a small clearing the pack had caught up with its quarry.

'I found him here. I haven't touched him. You'd never believe he was a white dog, would you? I can bury him if master wants.'

The police van came then with its wired windows and the words POLICE and POLISIE in their luminous frame in front. A young policeman sprang out and stood staring down at what was left of Snowy.

'They've gone savage,' he said. 'When they hunt in packs they act like wild dogs, killing for the hell of it.'

As far as we were concerned, that was the only act of violence to mar that lovely summer destined to lead into so much tragedy.

* * *

For our gardener, Sombani, that summer was a season of mixed blessings. He had already been home to his country twice since he had worked at 'Cressage'. The first time he had introduced his nephew, Amos, into our garden to take his place during his absence, and the second time he had smuggled his wife back with him. Sombani's explanations were always involved. When he stood twisting his cap in his supple hands, smiling coyly, we knew that a long session of unravelling his problems was bound to follow.

Sombani introduced Amos with customary dignity. The young man was his kinsman and he was also known to the Big Old Man up the Hill – the imposing parson-butler of our friends. Amos had not worked at the Cape before but Sombani and the Big Old Man would vouch for his character. There is no better reference. A good employee does not risk losing face by recommending a man he cannot trust.

Amos, at that time, knew little Afrikaans, less English and no gardening. He stood seriously by, rather tense, his eyes on the ground while his uncle spoke for him.

'He is of the Bavenda. One time the Bavenda and the Shangaan people kill each other. Now they marry. The mother of Amos is the cousin of my brother's wife's mother, and I am his uncle.'

As Bantu relationships and obligations are far too complex for the uninitiated to follow, my husband merely nodded gravely. Amos had worked for a while on the Rand where the lingua-franca of the mines is a sort of Esperanto compounded of many Native dialects, but now he wanted to see more of the world. He was athletic with the neat features and tiny ears of many of the South African Natives and he had a coy trick of ducking his head with a suppressed titter when he was amused. He could be very gay or absolutely deadpan, and he was only one degree less temperamental than his uncle, who suffered all the mood-changes that make the private life of any Bantu such a turbulent affair. When he worked about the garden he sang to himself, for he came of a musical race.

The rate at which he picked up English from us, Afrikaans from Mary, the cook, and a knowledge of plants and sprays and electric mowing machines and such matters was phenomenal. So when, one day after nearly six months away, Sombani returned, my husband announced that he had decided to keep Amos on. 'I can use two of you in the garden.' This pleased everybody very much and part of the pine wood was cleared to make a fine vegetable patch.

Sombani, of course, had returned with a tale of woe. Everything always happened to him.

'My heart is sore,' he told us. 'I was asleep when the train stopped at Kimberley and the man next to me got out and took my suitcase with him.'

We shrugged our shoulders. There was nothing to be done. In Sombani's world a man who cannot watch out for his property must kiss it good-bye.

Even his ordinary daily bus-ride from Langa to Claremont was not without its hazards. Once, when he was late coming to work, I noticed that his face was swollen and his cheek lacerated as if with a saw. Sickness and accidents in our household came into my province.

'What happened?' I asked, as I disinfected the jagged wound.

He grinned sheepishly. 'A man bit me.'

'He had strong teeth, that man!'

'He had a bad smell. I did not like his smell.'

He proceeded to explain that he had been sitting in the bus with a carrier-bag containing his jacket which he was taking to the one-day cleaner. Near the Mowbray terminus he had felt the bag move beneath the seat as someone behind him edged it back with his feet. In the scrum of the terminus the thief had got out fast with the carrier in his hand. Sombani plunged after him and struck him down.

'The man fell with his head on the pavement and lay for dead, and other men caught me and held my arms. I cried out, "He has my parcel! Ask him what is in it. He will not know!" Just then the man woke and jumped up like a dog and bit me in the face.'

The audience now held the arms of Sombani's assailant as well, for they recognized the wisdom of Solomon in the argument that the man who knew the contents of the carrier owned it.

So our gardener was let loose with congratulations and his carrier, while the biter vanished into the tarmac jungle of Mowbray.

When such incidents could happen in the course of a few miles it was little wonder that the four-day journey by slow train from the north was fraught with peril.

Sombani's country, just south of the Limpopo River, is rugged and beautiful with mountains and forests where wild beasts abound – though the hunter and the poacher reduce their numbers every year – and with villages that melt into the thornveld, for the huts are made of reeds and grasses and are as perfectly constructed as the nests of certain weaverbirds. In this region the local flora and fauna plays an important part in the lives of human beings. So does witchcraft. Certain sorcerers are famed for their knowledge of herbs and for being able to transform themselves and others into animals or reptiles. Such gifted men are much esteemed and feared.

My husband gave Sombani his return ticket to his homeland biennially, but during his months away he was not paid, so it was not surprising that soon after his departure urgent letters began to arrive at 'Cressage'. Some local scribe penned them and they made their point.

> Sir, I inform you that I reach home very well. All what I come to prepare I am bussy doing. I inform you only that I found my family staving and the mealies not well in our fields. Money is shorted. Please send me only £15, otherwise I cant be alright because they say I must pay money and they worry me. There is somebody who worrees me. Please help me about that money. I will be very happy when you send that money. When you send that money use telephone so that it will be very quickly. I have nothing in my pocket. I will work and fine you when I come bag . . . I have no more words to write.
>
> By-by my master. I remain
Sombani

'He's always fining me,' said Bertie, with resignation. 'I think I'd better send ten pounds and use the telegraph instead of the telephone.'

The acknowledgment, which came after some weeks, was more relaxed. It was evidently the work of a different scribe with a flowery script and a more sophisticated approach.

> Admiral Sir Herbert Packer KCB, CBE.
> I am very pleased for the money. Dont groan because it

has taken me a long time to reply your letter. I am busy here at home to build and plough. I am really very thankful for the money as well as my householders and for the present of £5.

Here we had rain for a very long time. It was daily rain from 15th Feb till 9th March.

As for crops in our lands this year is really very bad. I hope next year may prove better. I am expriancing a very high cost of Leaving Allowance just because of our bad mealie crop.

I am anxious to be back soon and I think everybody of my household should try to work hard.

Greeting to Amos. Pass my greetings to your lady Sir.

> Happy life and success
> I am
> Sir
> Obedient Servant
> Sombani.

His return was invariably heralded by a final appeal for 'money for food on the train'. This was dispatched, and then one day he would appear in the garden once more for another term of comparatively profitable exile.

His second return to 'Cressage' produced an embarrassing surprise.

I had been doing my week-end shopping, and, when I came in, Bertie met me with an expression half amused, half irritated.

'Sombani is back. You'd better have a look in the vegetable garden.'

Sitting in the lee of the tomato-trellis was a young comely woman, clearly a 'blanket-Bantu' not yet accustomed to the European clothing she wore. Her bare legs stuck straight out in front of her and a toddler, sturdy and bright-eyed, played near her. The scent of the pines was resinous in the noonday sun.

A memory stirred. Another primitive mother and child, up in the Wild Life Sanctuary, sitting in the shelter of a tall thorn-screen in the heart of lion country, alone and unafraid, while she awaited the return of her game-guard husband from his regular patrol. Save for the lions behind bars at Groote Schuur Zoo, there were no wild beasts beyond our woods, but I could well believe that this young woman from a tribal territory was more afraid of the savagery of the city to which her husband had brought her and her son than she would have been of lions roaming free. Here, in the White man's city, everything was menacing and unfamiliar.

'His wife and son,' said Bertie. 'And he has no permit to bring them here. He's smuggled them in and taken a chance that I can pull strings to get them permission to stay.'

We would normally have been glad that our gardener should have his wife and child with him, but it isn't always as simple as that in South Africa, any more than it is in the Navy where certain jobs are stipulated as being 'unaccompanied'. At the Cape the migrant Bantu labour force was not allowed to import dependants, so, unless a permit could be obtained for Sombani's wife and child, they would certainly be sent back to their Native territory, at their own expense, which inevitably meant at my husband's.

Mary, the cook, came into the kitchen-garden with a jug of milk and some biscuits for the mother and child. The little boy, Thomas, drank it thirstily, stealing laughing glances at Mary as he did so. Sombani beamed at the child proudly, his eyes shining with pleasure.

'Let's go and talk it over.'

I linked my arm in Bertie's, and, as we left the little family in the kitchen-garden, I pleaded for them, laughing.

'I'd have done the same in their position. I've always managed to get to places where I wasn't officially allowed.'

Before a temporary permit could be obtained Sombani had to prove that his wife was his legal spouse, and here the Big Old Man up the Hill – being a parson – could help. He was able to satisfy the authorities that Sombani had been married by tribal custom. So the young woman was granted a permit to live with her husband – though it had to be renewed each month – and the couple was allowed to put up a shack in Nyanga.

'Influx control' was then less stringent than it became later when the Western Cape was zoned as the 'ethnic homeland' of the Coloured people and the Bantu began to be shifted back to their tribal territories despite the protests of Cape industry and agriculture, and regardless of the fact that those territories were not yet ready to support many thousands of unwilling repatriates.

Mrs. Sombani certainly did not realize her good fortune in being granted a permit. The precious piece of paper was merely a nuisance to her. So it was not long before her husband informed us, with a light wringing of the hands, that she had lost it.

'She put it in the pocket of her dress,' he explained. 'She washed her dress and the pass was all washed up.'

'You make us groan,' I said. 'You must teach your wife the importance of bits of paper if she is to live in the city with you.'

Permits, or if you prefer, passes – those 'bits of paper' – were becoming more and more significant. They symbolized oppressive laws and the curtailment of liberty. What person could call himself free if he could neither work nor move, not even exist, without a pass? It was just possible to explain to a man that his pass-book was a sort of protection, because, if nobody carried such identification papers, many thousands would flock in illegally from African countries beyond the borders and compete with him for his job; but it incensed him beyond measure that his womenfolk should also be compelled to carry papers. Passes for women was an old grievance revived with unfailing regularity in the Bantu townships, the breeding-grounds of dissatisfaction and political agitation.

In fact, one of the aspects of city life most repugnant to Sombani's country wife was the fear and resentment engendered by the violation of personal privacy. There was the 'knocking in the night'. And why? Because of passes. Sometimes, at two or three in the morning, the police came banging on doors, 'Open up! Open up!' demanding to see passes. Other nights men came pretending to be police. They would order Mrs. Sombani to march next day in a procession of women – 'a protest march against passes for women'. Sombani would advise her to stay at home and lock her door. But they were both afraid, for the men were men of threats and violence and were later to be known as 'the spoilers'. Few people dared to disobey their orders. It was often difficult to be law-abiding in Langa or Nyanga.

Her exile in Nyanga must have been hard on Sombani's wife. Instead of her dark bare hut in her own country she lived in a *pondokkie* in the sandy wastes, where even the scores of sturdy little houses being completed daily by the authorities were not enough to shelter the families crowded there. While they waited they made do with *pondokkies*.

The core of Sombani's home was a prefab garden shed we had given him. He had added on to this, and, somehow, with the aid of friends, had made a weatherproof temporary abode. The family acquired a dog and a few hens and planted some mealies. But his wife was miserable. She did not speak Xhosa and turned up her nose at the Xhosa women who predominated in the location. She was not easily persuaded to use the clinics and welfare organizations and preferred to take her problems to the native herbalist.

Her main problem was fundamental. She had only consented to accompany her husband south because they wanted another child, and during his leave she had failed to conceive.

The herbalist brewed strange concoctions for Sombani and his wife and threw the bones to tell them their fate. He was reassuring. They would have a daughter and they would call her 'Happiness'.

So one day Sombani came to me with a radiant smile. Thomas had a sister – a big beautiful girl – and he wished to name the child for me. Two days later I went to see my namesake at Nyanga. Many of the shanties among the shifting dunes beyond the wattle screen were gaily painted with elaborate decorations on the outside and their open doors revealed colourful advertisements papering thin walls and partitions. Piccaninnies played cheerfully in the sand, for sand is a playground as natural to children as the branches of trees are to birds and monkeys. They looked healthy and full of fun.

Sombani's *pondok* had been painted a vivid blue, picked out with scarlet. Inside, it was as dark and cool as a native hut. A few garments hung on pegs, shelves were reasonably stocked, and a curtain separated a primus stove, a table, and three wooden chairs from the sleeping quarters. A bed stood against one wall and Thomas, the little boy, laughed when I looked at it and expressed amazement at finding it empty. It was a 'prestige' bed and I doubt if it was ever used. Thomas's mother lay on the floor beside it. She was rolled up in blankets, for the spring day was chilly. I made a sign to her not to move and put some fruit beside her. Unlike her three-year-old son, she had not learnt any words of English or Afrikaans and very little Xhosa, but she smiled slowly. I made a gesture to ask where the baby was. She drew aside the blanket. The infant was lying close against her breast. Even its head was under the blanket and I wondered that it did not suffocate. My namesake was a splendid specimen with a mop of woolly black hair.

We admired her and I took my leave.

From the time of the infant's birth Sombani's wife sent him to Coventry.

'She will not speak to me,' he complained, his hands twisting his cap miserably. 'She wants to go home to her mother.'

'Women are sometimes difficult after the birth of a child,' I said. 'Be patient.'

But her silence defeated him and finally he put her in charge of a friend and sent her back to her country with her children.

What loneliness, homesickness and apprehension she endured to achieve the little girl who would one day be worth many cattle, and whose name was Joy, one can only begin to guess. She was a foreigner in a foreign land unable and unwilling to adapt herself to her situation or her company.

Not long after her departure the telephone rang and I answered it. A woman's voice asked for Sombani.

'Who are you?' I asked. 'Sombani works in the garden. He does not come into the house and talk on the telephone.'

The sing-song answer was confident.

'I am Sombani's wife.'

'Oh no, you're not! His wife has returned to his country. She is far away.'

'I am his town wife,' announced the voice.

I put down the receiver. In any walk of life this was an age-old pattern of living – but not to be encouraged.

After his wife's departure Sombani was, for a time, erratic in his behaviour. One Monday morning, when he had failed to come to work, we received a message from Phillipi Police Station requesting two pounds to pay the fine that would release him from gaol. As my husband was playing golf that morning it was I who responded to the S.O.S.

Phillipi Police Station is small and well built. The

sergeant on duty was a cheerful beefy young Afrikaner. I told him that I had come to pay our gardener's fine and asked what the charge was.

He shouted to a Bantu clerk who thumbed through an enormous ledger.

'Ja, here it is,' said the sergeant. 'One of our drunks. Drunk and disorderly, lady, very truculent with the constable who arrested him.'

'He's a good fellow, really,' I said.

The sergeant grinned. 'The best of them get into trouble once in a while, especially on Saturday nights when the knives flash.'

I handed over two pound notes and the sergeant gave an order in Afrikaans to the Bantu constable. Then he said to me, 'They don't know *how* to drink. They just can't stop once they get going.'

'A good many of us are like that.'

'Ja, but we don't drink the stuff they do! If you want to know what knocks them out, come this way.'

He led me into a small store-room full of home-made weapons and bottles of confiscated *shebeen* liquor.

'This is the poison the shebeen queens brew. Each has her own recipe and some of them add a few odds and ends for witchcraft – an ear or a toe, or worse. This bottle is wit-blitz.'

He picked up a bottle of something that might have been milk.

'Looks innocent enough – straight from the cow or the goat,' I said.

'Smell it, man!'

He uncorked the bottle and held it under my nose. It was sheer anaesthetic.

'Ugh! What a bouquet!'

He grinned and put it back on the shelf.

As we went back to the charge office I saw Sombani following the Bantu constable across the courtyard. He gave me a shamefaced smile. His inflamed eyes bulged and he stank to high heaven.

'Come,' I said. 'Your fine is paid.'

'I cannot come yet, my lady,' he answered in his slow soft voice. 'I have not got my papers or my bicycle.'

The clerk gave him his passbook. His bicycle was tethered

to a post in the yard. He gazed at it with a fiery desirous eye.

'We can't put that in the boot,' I said.

The Afrikaans sergeant pooh-poohed my objection.

'Yes you can, lady. See!'

He wheeled the bicycle to the car, opened the boot and folded it in with a deft twist of the handle-bars while Sombani watched in admiration.

'There you are!' So off we went. I opened the window wide.

'Master is playing golf. That's why I came.'

He said, 'Master will be little bittie cross. I will work on Saturdays to pay my fine.'

'What happened?' I asked.

'On Saturday night my friend – man of my nation – went back to my country. He will not come to Cape Town any more.'

'So it was a farewell party?'

'Yes, my lady.'

After a time I said, 'Soon it will be the turn of Amos to go home.'

Sombani shook his head. 'He will not go, my lady.'

'Why not? He saves money for lobola to marry the girl who waits for him.'

Sombani shook his head and winced. His thoughts, combined with the effects of the witblitz, seemed to pain him.

'Amos will not marry her. He likes too much a Coloured girl.'

This was a problem. Our government insists that people should stay in their own carefully labelled boxes.

We were in the respectable Coloured area of Lansdowne now. The people who dwelt there in the sturdy little houses were ignorant of tribal custom and disapproved of pagan polygamy. The women would never dream of carrying bundles on their heads or babies on their backs, but few would deny the existence of the *tokolosh*, a hairy dwarf who may be the dread familiar of a human being, compelling that person to murder in order to satisfy his bloodlust. And none would deny the power of the evil eye or of the African witch-doctor.

'What do her parents say?' I asked.

'Her father and mother like very much Amos.'

Times have changed in spite of the fetish of 'racial purity', and inter-marriage between Bantu and Coloured is no longer as rare as it was.

'What about the girl? Is she a good girl?'

Sombani smiled as if to say that no man could answer such a question. Instead he said, 'She is young.' His expression approved her.

'And the girl in his own country?'

Now his face became sad. This was a heavy thing.

'That girl is also good. Amos was in school with her. They learn together. For five years all the time she write to him. She waits for him.'

Amos is a handsome lad. It was the usual story. Boy goes to city, girl stays at home, boy falls for a more sophisticated type and girl waits in vain.

'And now? Does she still write?'

'Now she is littie bittie tired. She stop writing.'

'Is her father important? Has he cattle?'

'He has many cattle. He is important.'

'Is he a chief?'

'He is a doctor,' said Sombani heavily.

I shivered. In the country of the tribesman the 'doctor' may well rank higher than the chief. It seemed to me that Amos might indeed be in a mess and well advised to remain at a safe distance from this young girl's father.

'If Amos goes home and does not marry the girl what will happen?'

'Her father will kill him,' said Sombani.

The extreme penalty for breach of promise! But face was involved and stock. The girl, at twenty, was on the shelf, her value in cattle depreciated. I turned the matter over in my mind.

'That would be murder. He would hang if he did such a thing.'

'This doctor can kill without murder.'

The medical profession among primitive people is not limited in its scope by any Hippocratic oath and the witch-doctor's talents are certainly not dedicated solely to curing the sick. His wisdom is inherent and his knowledge inherited. He is a herbalist, a psychologist and a hypnotist. His spells and potions are his closely guarded secrets, and he is as often a slayer as a healer – a highly paid instrument of vengeance. His affinity with animals and reptiles is renowned.

'This girl's father is of the crocodile people,' added Sombani, as if that explained all.

In fact, 'crocodile men' in Africa are dangerous fellows. They are able to swim safely in crocodile infested rivers, such as the Limpopo, and it is believed that they can turn themselves or other people into crocodiles. It's a two-way street for the magician, he can resume his human form after living – and eating – as a crocodile, but for his victim it's a case of once a reptile always a reptile.

'There was a man in our village,' went on Sombani. 'And he made the doctor angry. Afterwards nobody sees that man. One day his wife, she is washing her blanket by the river, and her husband is lying on a big rock. Now he is a crocodile.'

'How did she know him if he was a crocodile?'

'He has the face of her husband.'

'What did she do?'

'She call everybody. The people come to the river. They recognize the woman's husband. He roars and slides into the water and we never see him again.'

No wonder our younger gardener felt it prudent to postpone his return to his homeland!

Bertie and I made a joke of it.

'One of these days we'll find a crocodile mowing the lawn!' I said.

It was about then that I began to write *The Glass Barrier*. Amos and Sombani naturally came into it, bringing their vendettas and their African sorcery with them. So did a great deal else. All the highlights of 1960 – South Africa's year of fate – forced their way into my latest novel, and I found myself, against my will, reflecting the tragedy and tumult of a time of transition.

I write in my note-book: '*A passing thought*. What is Life? A medley of world events, personal drama, comedy and trivia. It is also the raw material of my craft.'

CHAPTER FIFTEEN

THE STORM BREAKS

MARCH 1960 was a turning point in the life of our country, and, consequently, for many of us in our private lives too.

The simultaneous riots in the Bantu townships at Sharpeville, near Johannesburg, and Langa, near Cape Town, hit South Africa like an earthquake. Ground that had once seemed firm and safe was split asunder that night. Pits and crevasses opened under our feet and ideas toppled as the mighty underground rumblings of African discontent erupted in blood and flame. Mob defiance was countered by police shooting and the eyes of the world turned in horror upon the black dead.

Although the Sharpeville disaster was numerically so much greater, the shock of the Langa riots was no less disturbing. Mass violence had been, until then, unknown at the Cape.

Only a few weeks earlier I had accompanied the Mayor of Cape Town, Mrs. Joyce Newton Thompson, on a tour of Langa and the adjacent Coloured town of Athlone. The tour had been arranged for the famous author-journalist, Dame Rebecca West, representing the London *Sunday Times*.

Rebecca West, who was new to South Africa, had recently been ill with 'apricot sickness', but I had the impression that her assignment had got her down even more than her upset tummy. To go to a complex multi-racial country, about which you know nothing at first hand, assess its problems and pass enlightened judgment upon its government and its people, is not easy for a sincere and conscientious writer, and Dame Rebecca West had to live up to a reputation for presenting responsible, penetrating and well-balanced pictures of contemporary events and personalities.

The author and the Mayor had a good deal in common. They were of approximately the same vintage – grandmother status – and both were honest, outspoken human beings holding strong views on most subjects of importance.

t, as the mayoral car bore us from the City Hall along the
 front towards the Paarden Eiland entrance to Langa, it
ickly became apparent that they were interested in two
ally different aspects of the city's dark life. While Rebecca
est wanted to know about the Africans, Joyce wanted to
 her about the Cape Coloureds. Dame Rebecca brushed
de all references to our large indigenous population of
xed blood – which is so significant because it is the natural
k between White and African – and concentrated her
estions upon the urban life of the Bantu from the north
o have infiltrated the Cape during the industrial revo-
ion of the past half century.

'Why should they come all this long way?' asked our visi-
. 'Surely they can get work nearer their own
ritories?'

'They can,' agreed the Mayor, and added with pardonable
ide, 'but, like everybody else, they want to travel, and the
pe is famous for its good working conditions. The Afri-
ns get higher wages and better treatment here than any-
ere else. We have a tolerant attitude towards other races.
ou have to remember that the Cape is an older civilization
an the rest of South Africa. It was first colonized in 1652
 the Dutch East India Company while the Transvaal and
range Free State were opened up by the Voortrekkers
arly two centuries later, and Natal later still.'

It is always difficult to make strangers to South Africa
alize that our entire country was not established all in one
ce at one and the same time.

The Mayor pointed out the squalid *pondokkies* of Wind-
mere, her face expressionless.

'I knew you would want to see these squatter slums,' she
d. 'They are being cleared and rebuilt but it can't be done
ernight. Do you want to take photographs here?'

Rebecca West covered her eyes. 'Oh, no, no! That's
ways being done.'

'That's why I asked you.' But the Mayor's face cleared.

At the entrance to Langa township the driver showed our
rmission to enter.

'Can't white people go freely in and out of the African
cations?' asked Dame Rebecca.

'Not without a pass,' said the Mayor firmly.

In the older part of the township our visitor express
surprise and pleasure at the shady square and shopp
centre where people stand and gossip, or squat under the
trees, the women with baskets over their arms and bab
strapped to their backs.

'All this part looks lived in. It seems to have develope
communal life and character,' she said.

'It's the heart of the place. The rest followed. For thi
years Langa has been growing.'

We inspected schools and clinics and peeped into mod
churches and play-grounds and were invited into neat li
family houses by the housewives. Many of these houses w
well furnished with a radiogram in the living-room, a
with a car outside the mealie-patch.

'Nobody has TV?' remarked Dame Rebecca.

The Mayor said, 'There is none in South Africa – yet.
are told that bilingual TV would be an uneconomic a
unpractical proposition.'

As we came to the pretty Police Station and the bl
Bachelor Quarters near the Vanguard Drive entrance
said: 'This is where the migrant bachelors live. In fact,
course, they are neither migrant nor bachelors but part c
permanent labour force separated from their families.'

I wondered what Dame Rebecca was thinking beh
those limpid observant eyes, and I felt constrained to po
out that some 'bachelors' had more than one wife at home

'It is perfectly legal by tribal law, but if they brought th
all here the piccaninny multiplication rate might be ala
ing, to say nothing of a housing problem even more ac
than it is at present. In any case, the women and children
needed in the territories to plough the land and herd
cattle. The men don't necessarily want their country wive
the city.'

She nodded, but I knew that she had already arrived
the proper conclusion that if they *did* want them they sho
be allowed to bring them, no matter what the difficulties.

'Do you get much discontent? Strikes? Trouble?'
asked.

The Mayor proudly responded that we had never h
serious trouble at the Cape. 'But if we did, it would be
here and might easily spread into the Coloured town of A
lone. That's what worries me.'

It worried her with very good reason as we were soon to learn.

Rebecca West went her way to Johannesburg, and while she was there she attended the prolonged and much criticized treason trial in Pretoria.

Dame Rebecca was much impressed by the martyred dignity of ex-Chief Luthuli who was the winner of the Nobel Peace Prize for that year. The award was, in itself, a strong straw to show the way in which the wind of popular sympathy was blowing.

Luthuli, once a school-master in Natal, was the President General of the banned African National Congress in 1956 when he, with over 150 others, was arrested for high treason. The trial dragged on for over four years and, at the end of it, most of the defendants were acquitted of the main charge, Luthuli among them. His health impaired, he is now officially confined to a limited area in the Stanger region of Natal. He is not allowed to attend meetings or make speeches.*

It was Luthuli's avowed intention to bring about the full emancipation of his people by passive means and for the good of South Africa as a whole, but the A.N.C. had its hotheads who presently broke away to form the Pan Africanist Congress under Robert Mangaliso (Wonderful) Sobukwe, a Bantu lecturer at Witwatersrand University. Sobukwe preached 'Africa for the African by 1963' and no co-operation with other races. This movement, which was also banned, went underground when its leaders were arrested after the 1960 riots, only to emerge again in 1962 as Poqo, a terrorist organization meaning 'pure' or 'alone'. Poqo has much in common with Mau-Mau.

As a journalist Rebecca West had one very lucky break. She was still staying in Johannesburg when the Sharpeville riots made world headlines. Thus she was able to scoop the foreign correspondents who swarmed in afterwards.

It would be absurd to say that the March riots blew up out of a clear sky.

Only a few weeks earlier Mr. Macmillan had made his famous 'wind of change' speech in the Union Parliament in Cape Town. That speech drew attention to the storm of African emancipation blowing through the dark continent

*Luthuli was accidentally killed a few years later.

from end to end and it did not leave Britain's attitude in doubt. As far as the mother country was concerned, the White settlers in Southern Africa could go with the rising wind. That day the African leaders rubbed their hands in glee, Dr. Verwoerd listened to the urbane Scottish statesman with a stony countenance, and the tie with the Commonwealth was frayed to breaking point.

In South Africa the endless protests of both Europeans and non-Europeans against the injustices and irritations of *apartheid* had reached a crescendo. Demonstrations were the order of the day. There were demonstrations against job reservation, transport *apartheid*, the government closing of the open Universities to non-Europeans, and above all, against the pass laws and the tough police methods of enforcing them.

The most effective of these protests were staged by the women of the Black Sash, whose Federal Chairman at that time was Molly Petersen, the wife of my brother, Norman. This non-party-political band of women was pledged to uphold the humanities and to draw attention to repressive legislation by every passive means in its power, an obligation which it faithfully continues to honour.

Non-European frustration was at its peak, and, in the Bantu locations, the agitators of the extreme Pan-Africanist Congress were inciting the people to burn their pass-books and march on Police Stations, demanding to be arrested. That, they declared, was the first move. A general strike would follow, and later, if necessary, violence. The African, like the Afrikaner, is a natural orator and the Pan-African leaders had some rolling phrases. 'Upon what meat does this white man feed that he grows so strong!' Throughout the land the Bantu agitators were telling their people that the Pan-Africanists stood for the complete overthrow of White domination. By 1963 South Africa would be the Black man's country, and the Whites would be 'the slaves'. Africa for the African!

The first day of the strike was set for Monday, 21st March.

It was a beautiful bright autumn day. Neither Sombani nor Amos came to work.

There was something brewing. I was uneasy and disinclined to settle down to my new novel, but my husband remained philosophical.

'Sooner or later we'll know what it's all about,' he said, as he prepared the sprays for his roses.

From my writing desk with its distractingly splendid view I saw him moving in his leisurely way among the lovely blooms, his straw garden hat on his head and his big gauntlets protecting his hands from the spray and the thorns. The cat sat on my papers and made it still more difficult to concentrate. I began to pick her soft fluffy white hairs idly out of the typewriter.

The Glass Barrier was a story with the emphasis on youth. I reflected that youth didn't change. Down the centuries it ran true to form, rebellious, always eager to go against the stream, and these days there were many streams up which it might swim and leap, or perish in the attempt. No wonder young politically conscious Africans of the mid-twentieth century were intoxicated with waging war against White authority! They had something to bite on there – and limitless hordes of ignorant savages to follow them. So back I came to the problem. There was no evading it. All lines of thought seemed to lead to the Black-White conflict – the invisible war. And down in the garden my man of peace tended his roses while his gardeners were being sucked into mercy knew what vortex.

The cat began to purr very loud and rub herself against my arm.

'Oh dear, I'll have to feed you in a minute,' I said. 'Stop drooling on to my note-book, there's a good kitty!'

Although the cat's appetite and my scattered thoughts were not conducive to work, I jotted down a few notes. It was part of my working discipline. But Sombani and Amos, absent from duty, were constantly present in my mind, and it was then that they found their way irrevocably into the pages of *The Glass Barrier* where they became people of importance like Bok of *The High Roof*.

All day suspense mounted steadily. We discovered that the Bantu house-servants of our friends were nervous, uninformative, and inclined to lock themselves in their rooms, while those who had been in the locations on Sunday had not returned to work. What was simmering down there on the sandy flats? Even our Coloured cook and maid, Mary and Sybil, were worried, although what went on in the Bantu township was, strictly speaking, no concern of theirs. They did not fraternize with Natives, and even our gardeners would never have dreamed of entering the kitchen but always took the snacks and coffee Mary gave them at a table in the yard. This *apartheid* among themselves was customary and of their own choice.

That evening before dinner I had occasion to telephone Mayor Joyce Newton Thompson, at her private home, 'Newlands House', once the country seat of the early Cape Governors. I knew by her voice that something was seriously amiss.

'I think I've chosen a bad moment to ring you. It can wait.'

'Well, perhaps,' she agreed. 'I've had disturbing news about Langa. Call me tomorrow.'

I put down the receiver and went to the window where I had tried and failed to work earlier in the day. The sunset still painted the sky as the first lights of the northern satellite towns pricked the gloom. But there was something else.

'Bertie!' I called. 'Come and look!'

He came from his dressing-room and stood beside me, his hand on my shoulder.

'It's not a veld fire,' he said, puzzled. The smooth white contours of the great Athlone condenser glowed red in the dusk as angry fires leaped into life around it. 'It's Langa!'

The night of terror had begun.

That afternoon the leaders of the Pan-Africanists had called a meeting of the people in Langa square. The police had reason to fear trouble and the meeting was banned. Their patrol vans broadcast the banning order throughout the township, but nevertheless the people gathered in many thousands till the square and every roof around it was densely packed. When the crowd failed to comply with the command to disperse the Bantu police charged them with batons. Someone on a roof-top fired two shots at the police, stones hurtled through the air, and the terrifying yell went up in Xhosa. 'Kill them! Kill them!'

Mob control – the discipline of the maddened many by the armed few – requires experience and fine judgment. Both were lacking on this occasion. The young officer in charge gave the order to open fire on the angry crowd.

Scores of people, including women and children, were wounded and two men were shot dead. The pretty leafy square became a shambles.

Bricks and petrol-bombs were thrown, offices were set alight and bonfires were made of the hated passes. Churches, schools and clinics were burned down. Two reporters who had gone into Langa to get a story were lucky to escape with their lives. Their car was stoned and overturned, and the Coloured driver was dragged out, murdered and mutilated, for no better reason than that he was not a Bantu and happened to be in charge of a car which had carried White men. The fever of the pack was in the mob that night. They were ready to destroy any life or property remotely connected with a White skin. As the young policeman had said when he had looked at the filthied body of our little white dog, Snowy, 'When animals hunt in a pack they kill for the hell of it.' Men, too.

Buses entering the location were stoned and their windows broken. The infuriated mob surged out on to the speedway between Cape Town and the Airport. They stoned passing cars. Some nurses were seriously injured and taken to hospital. The night shrieked with the sirens of fire engines and ambulances and the yells of the rioters.

In Athlone the Coloured people locked themselves into their houses and trembled lest the raging black tide should engulf them.

Old Teena and her niece were among those physically and emotionally rocked by the explosion of that night.

'Oh, Miss Joy!' they said afterwards. 'You can't think what it was like! Here, on the road outside our place, we saw and heard terrible things! Beatings and fighting – stoning and yelling! We've never been so scared.'

Yet by midnight the immediate situation was under control. Langa and Nyanga were cordoned off by police reinforced with military and naval units, roads and vital points were guarded, and we heard over the radio that all was quiet.

Next morning at eight o'clock, Sybil brought my tray upstairs as usual. Coffee, toast, marmalade, and orange juice, while Bertie's breakfast waited for him in the dining-room on the hot-plate.

From my window I could see the rays of early sunlight

reach down into the milky lagoon of mist shrouding the flats. Even the big condenser was hidden, but an unfamiliar helicopter circled above the Bantu locations. The granite buttresses of the mountain sparkled in the clear light and the green tapestry of bush and forest glowed softly on the sunny slopes. Doves crooned and flirted on the stone wall, and our pair of Cape sparrows, Mr. and Mrs. Mossie, chirped to one another from the elm to the oak. Down in the pine woods the ringing call of a bokmakierie drew an elaborate stanza of answering song, a thrush said 'chip-chip' as he hopped about the dewy lawn. The robins, always the first to greet the new day, with their musical whistle 'so-sweet so-sweet', were still vocal although once the sun was up they would fall silent. But the sound I listened for and did not hear was the harsh swish of a rush broom and the calypso in a minor key that told us Amos was sweeping the terrace, his first task of the day.

Mary came up to my room for housekeeping orders, but when I asked if the garden hands had come she shook her head.

'No, my lady. Nor the paper boy, nor the milkman, nor the dustman. They didn't come yesterday either.'

'It says on the wireless they've all knocked off work. There'll be no delivery men on the job. It's a general strike. I wonder if Nellie will come?'

Nellie was the Coloured laundress who did our household washing and ironing.

'She will try to come,' said Mary.

Nellie, a widow, had four children to provide for. She needed her day's pay. When she arrived on the early bus she told me that many of her neighbours had been threatened that if they went to work they would be 'punished'.

'Are you frightened?' I asked.

She shrugged her shoulders with a resigned smile. 'What's the good of being frightened? We can't all stay at home, we must go to the shops to buy food for our families and we must earn the money to pay for it.'

'What they want – the people who started this thing – is that everybody should stay at home. A general non-European strike.' To make us realize who does the lion's share of the work in this country, I thought, and added, 'What will your friends do?'

'I expect they'll work,' she said.

In fact, the majority of the Coloured people, though frightened and intimidated by their own agitators, did defy the strike order, and all essential services were maintained. The Citizen Force was called up in strength and a State of Emergency declared.

Later that morning Bertie and I went to Claremont village to buy food, milk, a newspaper and other items that were usually delivered as a matter of course. Banner headlines hit us between the eyes.

KILLED. 54 ON RAND 2 AT LANGA
DAY OF BLOOD IN TWO AFRICAN LOCATIONS
Fifty-six Africans were killed and more than 230 injured in a day of blood yesterday in two African locations – at Langa, near Cape Town, and at Sharpeville, near Vereeniging – on the opening day of the Pan-African National Congress anti-pass campaign . . .

The Pan-African leader, Mr. 'Wonderful' Subukwe, had been arrested in Johannesburg; there had been trouble in other locations throughout the country and in the Bantu territory of Pondoland. It was clear that the P.A.C. was well organized.

At the treason trial in Pretoria ex-Chief Luthuli had been giving evidence on the methods of the banned African National Congress of which he had been President General.

'I myself would never be a party to the use of violence,' he was quoted as saying. 'To resort to violence to achieve the Africans' political aims would be national suicide.' Non violence, he declared, was the accepted policy of the A.N.C., which used demonstrations, civil disobedience and stay at home strikes as its weapons, but there had been splits. For example, the Pan-Africanists had broken away over the issue of nationalism, refusing to agree to the concept of South Africa as a multi-racial country in which the various races must co-operate.

In fact, it read as if the only powerful African voice of reason, restraint and moderation was being silenced when it was most urgently needed in this transition period between the decline of White *baaskap* and the gradual evolution of the multi-racial state which many thinkers, Black and White, consider to be the inevitable solution in South Africa.

When we got back home we found Sombani sweeping the terrace. Amos had not appeared.

Sombani's face was ashen and beaded with sweat, and he was obviously seriously shaken. He told us that at dawn police patrol vans had gone round the locations broadcasting that anybody wishing to go to the job would have protection. 'Go now,' they said, 'and we will see that you are safe.'

It had been an awkward decision. Many had felt themselves to be 'twixt devil and deep blue sea.

'If the spoilers see me go to the job they will beat me up. If I stay in Langa the police are taking too much people away and perhaps they want to take me too. They do not ask "Are you a good man?" They say "You come" and throw you in the van. Some people think one way and some another, but when the police say "Go to the job now and we look after you while you clear out", I run. Then we, who have run outside, see that the buses are all broken and have no drivers. We must walk all the way to Mowbray before we can find a bus to take us. It is a suffering way to come to the job.'

It had all been a 'suffering' experience. When he spoke of 'the hitting and stoning and the burning' his face was contorted and his long expressive hands writhed in their characteristic gesture of distress.

'What about Amos? Is he safe?' my husband asked.

'I don't know, master. I have not seen him.'

'Have you got your pass-book?'

For the first time his face brightened, pleased at his own cunning. He showed us the cap he held under his right arm. 'It is here.' His papers in the thick shiny wallet were hidden in the lining. 'If I keep it in my pocket the spoilers find it and they will kill me.'

He made a sign of hands frisking his jacket for documents or weapons.

'The spoilers say we must burn our passes, but they always have papers themselves.'

'These spoilers – who are they?'

'Tsotsis – men who hide by day and prowl by night. The

strike leaders tell them what to order the people to do, and they know how to make us obey.' He grinned then. 'Some go round in cars, looking everywhere to see who is working.'

'Intimidation gangs,' put in Bertie. We saw them later, lurking corner-boys and car-loads of thugs, driving with reckless arrogance, sure of being apprehended sooner or later, not caring. Their sign was a finger drawn significantly across the throat. 'What about your wages? Do you want me to look after your money for you?'

'No, master. On Friday, Amos and me, we keep some money for meat and the rest we give to my uncle, the Big Old Man up the Hill. He keep it safe.'

So the parson-butler was also a banker.

'Did he know there would be trouble?' I asked.

'People spoke of it. They were afraid.'

'Many strike leaders have been rounded up,' I said. 'They are in prison.'

'Others will spring up. They grow like weeds, my lady. One goes and ten more stand in his place.'

I was profoundly sorry for him. He did not want trouble. It came from outside and drew him into its toils.

'You'd better stay here for the present,' said Bertie. 'You can sleep in the garage or the tool-shed.'

'Yes, master. I am frightened to go to Langa now. I will sleep in the house in the wood.' This was the tool-shed.

'Will the intimidators find him there?' I asked Bertie.

He smiled wryly.

'It's hidden in the trees and it's an armoury – axes, spades, shears, pitchforks, even a crowbar and a saw. He could withstand a siege.'

So we gave him blankets and an old hammock-mattress and he settled in.

We had entered a lunatic interlude in our country's existence.

It saddened me to read daily of the wanton African destruction of churches, libraries, clinics, schools and community centres. At the same time, under the State of Emergency, many thousands of people – European and non-European – were taken from their homes overnight and detained without explanation or trial for an indefinite period in gaols bursting at the seams. Panic-stricken political personalities fled the country by escape-routes quickly exploited by enterprising air services, and the British Protectorates of Bechuanaland, Basutoland and Swaziland, became the acknowledged rat-runs for nervous fugitives. Ships bound for Australia and New Zealand were loaded with young South African immigrants seeking a more stable future for their families. The Canadian Consulate was besieged with inquiries about emigration.

'It's like the war,' I said to Bertie. 'Everybody looking for security for their children.'

'Things'll settle down here,' he said. 'This is a time for stock-taking, not for acting in a panic.'

I smiled. I had never known him act in a panic. But my heart was sore, as Sombani would have said, for I felt that our own contentment had suddenly become vulnerable to forces beyond our control. We were all in this mess, one way or another. A State of Emergency had not only been imposed upon our country. It was within every one of us.

CHAPTER SIXTEEN

ISLANDS OF PEACE AND FEAR

Our old Nanny celebrated her eightieth birthday that March. She had all the German veneration for anniversaries, and, as she put it to me, 'Eighty is an important birthday. I want to give a party for the people in my life.'

There were a dozen of us. The youngest 'people in her life', our grandchildren, were not present because it was an evening party and they were asleep in their beds. My husband came into my room ready for Nan's great occasion.

'Will I do?'

'You should be wearing your medals. Nan loves medals.'

He grinned as he adjusted his tie. He would be on her right, and he intended to propose her health.

'What will you say – to link us all? German, South African, English – three generations!'

'The link? Affection for Nan. She's lived for others all her life and she's done it with courage and gusto. And she's a

180

giver – the socks and pullovers she knitted for Piet and me—'

'And for the little boys, and her son-in-law and her grandson – you, all of you, are the men in her life, my dear.'

I laughed, but the backs of my eyes prickled. The picture of Nan's busy knitting hands was sharp in my mind, for they were essentially herself – strong, gnarled, capable, joints swollen and fingers twisted by arthritis, helping hands that had never shirked a task.

What preparations was she making now in her small square room in the home for the aged? It was a pretty room with the possessions of a long life-time pared down to the minimum, but every one of them reminiscent of some pleasant aspect of bygone days. Her Dresden china was in our home now.

'I can't keep such things in my room. There is too little space.'

She was gratified at my pleasure in the angels and flowers of her birthplace. She liked her gifts to be appreciated.

Even the view from her window incongruously enshrined the past. It commanded a small intimate cemetery, the last resting-place of my parents. At first I had been dismayed by this outlook, but how little we know one another! It held no grim associations for her. She loved to look down upon the coarse green grass where the wagtails hopped and the gulls planed over weathered tombstones and the old Coloured caretaker tended the graves with his dog at his heels. It was a garden of remembrance for her, an oasis in the city's busy life, inviting tranquil meditation and communion with the spirits of those departed and at peace, all earthly ills shredded away.

'I look down at your Daddy's and Mommy's grave and only wish my hubby's could be there too, so that I could give him flowers every week as well.'

This was a self-appointed tribute. Every week she arranged fresh flowers for my parents. When she became too lame to carry the heavy vase to the near-by tap she called the caretaker to do it for her. Her own husband was buried further afield at Maitland. To Nan no one dearly loved was ever lost or truly absent. That is why she was never lonely in the little room that contained the last lees of a long eventful life.

'How can I be lonely? I have travelled all over the world,

I have so much to remember, and my people are always with me.'

Her people, the quick and the dead from many lands, were made welcome, invited to enter that small room and keep her company and share once again the best of the past. They were her allies against the pains and depressions of advancing years.

The birthday party, held in a private room of a Cape Town hotel, was a great success, and several times when I looked down the long table I saw my husband and our hostess deep in conversation, and knew from her absorbed and happy expression that they were speaking of her homeland, the Germany she loved to remember, when, as a very young woman, she had first learnt the care of infants in the orderly nurseries of spacious homes. Those were the leisurely days of carriages and courtesy, when the young respected their elders and betters and all who were set in authority over them, and Nan still sighed after those pleasing conventions. She had once looked after the baby son of an officer in the Kaiser's bodyguard and she still retained an inflated regard for military discipline in all its forms. But such formal days belonged to the Europe of the turn of the century and nothing would ever be the same again. Nan's Germany lay buried beneath the débris of two world wars. Her adored birthplace, Dresden, hid its wounds behind the Iron Curtain, and none of her family have survived the holocaust, except one married niece in the smiling prosperous Rhineland. This niece wrote to her aunt faithfully, but although her letters gave the old lady great pleasure she had no wish to go back.

'To me Germany is as I remember it,' she said. 'It is best that way.'

Seeing her now, in her blue silk dress with her white hair carefully waved, with my husband and her son-in-law at the head and the foot of her birthday table, I was touched anew at her robust quality. Her world might disintegrate and her heart might break but she would battle on, fortified by her awesome determination never to give in.

That's what they have in common, I thought, she and my Admiral. Each salutes the warrior in the other. Peace is their goal, peace is what they want above all else, but not peace at any price. They're prepared to fight for it and go down fighting.

Love is the indestructible force, and, because she had loved it, the Germany of the past was still hers.

It awaited her in the little room where my son and his wife left her after the party. And all those who had shared it and added to her joy in it were there too. We, her guests that evening, were only a few of 'the people in her life'. Along the road of eighty years there had been many others, still radiantly alive in her tenacious memory. They, too, were there that night to congratulate an old friend on a 'special birthday'.

On April the 19th at 3.15 p.m., the country received its second shock. The Prime Minister, Dr. Verwoerd, was shot at point blank range in the presence of a vast crowd as he was opening the Union Exposition in Johannesburg. His assailant was on the grandstand near the Prime Minister's box and before he could be overpowered he had shot his victim twice in the face. By some miracle Dr. Verwoerd was not killed.

Only three weeks had elapsed since the riots and South Africa held her breath as she waited to hear the identity of the would-be assassin. A long sigh of relief seemed to pass through the entire country when it was learned he was not an African.

David Beresford Pratt, a fifty-four-year-old English-speaking farmer from the Transvaal, was brought to trial later that year. Wealthy and eccentric, he refused to plead insanity, and during that part of the trial which concerned itself with his state of mind, he delivered a lucid and remarkable speech from the witness-box – 'At last I have a platform!' – in which, for an hour, he associated the advancing stages of his mental derangement with his growing conviction that 'apartheid was a stinking monster, gripping the throat of South Africa and preventing her from taking her rightful place among the nations'.

It was finally proved that in shooting at the Prime Minister he had aimed to destroy Dr. Verwoerd, 'the symbol of apartheid', and not Dr. Verwoerd, the man. Pratt was an epileptic whose second wife had recently left him. He was cultured and brilliant, a musician, a philosopher, and an aspiring politician, who had lived for years on a razor's edge between eccentricity and insanity. The happenings of March

1960 had given the final jolt to his unbalanced mind. He was committed to a mental institution as a Governor-General's patient, where he later hanged himself.*

As so often happens when violence is the weapon employed to serve an end, it defeats its own purpose. Dr. Verwoerd by his dignity and courage became an object of sympathy, and his 'miraculous' recovery undoubtedly increased his followers' belief that he was a man of destiny divinely appointed and preserved to lead the country in her 'hour of liberation', for it was thus that they regarded the coming birth of the Republic. So, more than ever, they rallied round the fatherly personality of their leader.

It is possible that Dr. Verwoerd himself may have felt his remarkably fortunate escape to be a sign of infallibility and of a dedicated task still to be completed, for, no sooner was he on his feet once more, than he delivered a broadside at those who had optimistically hoped the Government might see the writing on the wall and modify its policies. *Apartheid* – separate development – was to be speeded up and intensified. It was the 'granite wall' between life and death, and there must be no breaks in that vital wall. But the policy must be applied with humanity, generosity and responsibility and in a truly Christian spirit, according to the Will of God and of the people. The will of the people – *volkswil* – of course excluded the four to one black majority of South Africa's population. The Bantu territories must be developed at no matter what cost to the White man, and the Bantu must be lured or pushed back into his own tribal homelands, there to develop according to his ethnic potentialities. The Bantustans would, in time, be independent and autonomous, ruled by the Bantu for himself. He would be our good neighbour and owe his future prosperity to his White South African sponsor. Oh yes, he could still work for the White man in those industries where his labour was absolutely essential to the country's economy, but there was to be no integration. None whatsoever.

Dr. Verwoerd, whose father came from the Orange Free State, was born in Holland and educated at the Cape and in

* Six years later, in 1966, Hendrik Verwoerd was stabbed to death in the House of Assembly during a debate. The murderer, a schizophrenic messenger named Tsafendas, claimed to be 'possessed' of a diabolical tapeworm which hypnotized him into assassinating the Prime Minister.

Rhodesia. He subsequently studied at three German Universities, Leipzig, Hamburg and Berlin. Later he was appointed Professor of Applied Psychology at Stellenbosch University and also of Sociology and Social work. With this interesting grounding he graduated into politics and was made Minister of Native Affairs in 1950 and Prime Minister of the Union of South Africa in 1958. His interests were farming and fishing. He had seven children and a number of grandchildren, and to both his family and his followers he represented a father-figure with an aura of indulgent omniscience. To his supporters Dr. Verwoerd's 'granite wall' utterance brought reassurance. *Ales sal regkom* – everything will come right. Pa says so! But to his opponents it had the ring of fanaticism.

Many people at that time were planning lines of escape – escape from the law, escape from future physical danger, escape from financial loss or even escape from a nagging conscience. My own escapism was an attempt to keep the serenity of our home unimpaired. In this way my husband supported me without even knowing it. He wanted peaceful living in his retirement – the simple joys of his garden, his recreations and friendships uncomplicated by politics. So we cherished our islands of personal peace as we had done in World War II. In those bitter days time together between one danger and the next had been a priceless gift, whether it was a week's leave or just the glory of a spring afternoon in a Hampshire wood. Once it had been a snatched wintry hour in the captain's cabin of a pugnacious battle-scarred cruiser. Outside the scuttle a frieze of birds waded in the misty Humber marshes and gulls cried on the wind. Night, grim and menacing, brought the moment of parting in which good-bye was a word unspoken, fear never voiced, and faith and love were the only amulets against the fury of the enemy.

Now, here in the lovely Cape – our haven of retirement – the devil's teeth were showing once again. Hate bayed round our lives and incipient fears blossomed into ugly moments of suspicion.

For instance, there was the time when I chanced to be in the little outside laundry in which I also kept flower vases. I had gone there to select one, and Sombani had followed me with some trivial request. He stood, blocking the doorway, his cap respectfully in his hands, no notion of harm in his head. Yet, just for an instant, I felt cornered and claustrophobic. When did one stop trusting them? When did they turn into enemies? At once I was ashamed. And there was the time I took Nellie, our laundress, back to her home on a chilly May evening.

The air was damp under the mountain and dead oak leaves danced in a wind that smelt of rain. It was the 'burning season' and smoke wreathed up from many gardens, mingling its bluer shades with the pale ground mists.

In Wynberg Main Road we met the woodman.

He was walking beside his horse and cart, a thin shabby little Coloured fellow with a battered hat, and a torn open shirt under his worn jacket. His horse looked well nourished and so did the large Coloured man who drove it. There was a heavy load of wood on the cart.

The little man had eyes everywhere. He wanted to get rid of his load and go home before nightfall. I slowed down – hesitating, wondering what the wood was worth. In an instant he had sensed a possible customer and he was beside my crawling car. He called through the window.

'Wonderful dry wood, Madam! Strong thick wood that will burn for hours. Take the lot off me and I make you a good price.'

I stopped the car and went to the cart which had come to a standstill.

'I don't know,' I said. 'Master orders things like wood in our house.'

'Where do you live?' His voice was quick as his eyes.

'Up there – up on Bishop's Court Estate.'

He glanced at his horse. 'Is it too steep for my horse?'

I explained exactly where it was.

'Is the Master in?'

'Yes.'

'When the Master sees this wonderful load he'll give me ten pounds for it.' It was half statement, half question, wholly optimistic. 'Hey, Cookie! You know the best wood when you see it. See, there's fifty logs here – all dry and ready for burning!'

Nellie shrugged her shoulders. She knew his sort. He'd make his price according to his client's pocket and gullibility. I said:

'Master certainly won't give you ten pounds. You can save your horse a trek.'

I put the car in gear and drove on, but in the driving-mirror I saw that the little man had already turned his horse's head and, by the time I had dropped Nellie and was on my way home, the weary animal was dragging his load up Tennant Road. The little man stepped away from the bridle and signalled me to stop.

'I come with you,' he said, opening the car door. 'I see the way, then I come back to my cart and lead the horse. We stack your wood for you – we make a beautiful stack. All in the price of the wood.'

He was in the car already and I laughed and gave in. At the corner of Hillwood Road I dropped him. 'It's up there – the house with the red roof.'

'Up this road,' he said. 'Tell Master I come.'

Bertie was in his study.

'There's a man determined to sell us a load of wood. Come with me down the road in the car. Then, if you don't like it, we can save his horse a hard pull up the hill.'

At the bottom of the hill Bertie and the little man disputed the value of the load – Bertie with his resentful face, the little man alert, insistent, persuasive. His large dark companion sat dumb on the driver's seat of the cart.

Outside our gates they unloaded some of the wood to make it easier for the horse. They stacked the rest in the garage quick as lightning, dexterous with experience. They fetched the wood at the gate and completed the job – all to the accompaniment of the little man's patter. Every now and again he ran to me to say 'Just ten bob more, lady! See, this wonderful wood! My father will beat me if I go home with only five pounds for wood worth ten pounds.'

'Your father beat you? Your father must be all of eighty!'

He grinned. 'My father is very strong. I'm younger than I look. *Die ou' man is die baas.* You don't want him to beat me, lady?'

I laughed and went into the kitchen to see about our supper because the maids were out. Suddenly Bertie called to me.

'They've done the job and they want candles and a couple of empty bottles.'

The little man's face appeared in the yard outside the kitchen window. In the gloom, with only the beam of the kitchen light shining into the yard, it had a wild ferocious look. *Quite suddenly I found him frightening*. I got some candles, bright green stumps left over from a dinner party.

'There are empty bottles in that box in the corner of the yard,' I told him.

He chose two, and with some extraordinary knack – only too well known to his people – knocked the bottoms neatly out of them. They were glass dumb-bells now with jagged cutting edges, dangerous weapons. Shivers of fear ran over my skin. I followed him to his cart. Deftly he stuck the candles in the necks of the bottles so that they would burn inwards protected from the wind. Then he fitted his home-made lamps, neck down, into sockets on either side of the driving seat.

'Good this way,' he said. 'Otherwise we give our five pounds to the police for travelling without lights.'

The cruel bottles had been rendered harmless and the lights bobbed down the drive as the cart trundled on its homeward way. This time both men rode in it. I was glad to see them go.

The memory of the little man's eyes – wild in his thin face outside the kitchen window – and his experienced speed in breaking the bottles had frightened me. A whole new world had opened up in that one swift glimpse – a world of violence and brutality, of drink and dagga and death in the darkness of the night. It was the 'feel' of a dangerous decade. I had suddenly become acutely aware that the other half of our world lives too – and dimly aware of how it lives.

CHAPTER SEVENTEEN

SUNLIT DAYS

AUTUMN leaves lay thick on the sidewalks and men with little carts and large ponderous horses swept them up and collected them for compost. The first rains had fallen and we could hear the torrents roar down the ravines across the valley. The pines had scattered their cones and our grandchildren came with baskets to gather them for winter fires.

The State of Emergency had not yet been lifted, but on the surface life moved fairly normally once more, except, of course, for the political detainees and their families. Everybody not languishing in gaol – which happily included Amos – had returned 'to the job'. As Sombani put it, 'it is all clean now at Langa and we can go back.' So he no longer occupied his tool-shed armoury but was once again a tenant of the Bachelors' Quarters in the location.

Langa and Nyanga were officially 'all clean', but there had been the usual recrudescence of superstition and sorcery which always goes with African unrest. Prophets had warned the people that on a certain day the sun would fail to rise, a hot wind would blow and the end of the world would come. We gathered that the 'Old Gods' would exert themselves to reprieve the black people, and, this being so, the Bantu bought plentiful supplies of candles in anticipation of the netherworld darkness and plugged their draughty doors and windows against the blast out of hell. The 'day of darkness and hot wind' dawned clear and calm and remained so, and that night a full moon shone alike upon the dwellings of rich and poor. The prophet had vanished and the Bantu saved face. 'What hot wind?' they said. 'We don't know about any hot wind or day of darkness.'

Our gardeners assured us that the police were 'better to the people' and we rejoiced to hear it. I spent a good deal of time at the exhaustive public Inquiry into the Langa riots and incorporated some of it in *The Glass Barrier*, for I was now convinced that no contemporary picture of South Africa, whether fact or fiction, could afford to ignore the racial tension which permeates our lives.

The Referendum to decide whether South Africa should become a Republic or not took place in October. It was a White vote only and the result was a foregone conclusion. The Nationalist Government, after thirteen years in power, was stronger than ever. No Nationalist would put his X against No on the voting paper that asked him whether his country should become a Republic or not, and many people opposed to Government racial policies felt, nevertheless, that the Crown had played its part in South Africa and was now purely symbolic of a sentimental link with the past.

Britain's acknowledged attitude of trimming her sails to

the much vaunted wind of change in Africa had done little to endear her to our White population, no matter what its politics. It was the avowed intention of Dr. Verwoerd to keep South Africa within the Commonwealth, the Democratic Constitution was to remain virtually unaltered and the English and Afrikaans languages would remain equal. So, by and large, most people were inclined to feel that the change to a Republic would make little difference to the home situation and that the old tug-of-war between the two leading political parties – the Nationalist Government and the United Party opposition, whose aims diverged in degree rather than in principle – could continue its monotonous push-and-pull course just as well in a Republic as in a Dominion.

The Yes or No Referendum ballot was to be secret and there was plenty of speculation among friends about the way this or that person was likely to vote. Suddenly we all began to wonder about each other.

'What are you going to do?' somebody asked me. I was amused. She was really interested and rather suspicious.

'It won't make any difference what I do.'

'You must think more positively than that!'

I laughed. Yet it occurred to me that this was how people must feel in occupied countries, where loyalties become confused and every human relationship is tinged with mistrust.

It so happened that the 1960 Annual General Meeting of the Navy League of South Africa was scheduled for October in East London. So my husband and I decided to go up the coast by car, breaking our journey for a few days at Beacon Island in Plettenberg Bay. We left on Referendum Day.

It was a glorious spring morning. We packed up the car and put in the picnic basket and I was moved, as always, by pleasant anticipation of a sunny journey ahead. But first we stopped at the Claremont Civic Centre for me to cast my vote. My husband, who had retained his British nationality, did not have this right.

There were trestle-tables outside the pretty gabled hall and over one was written No and over the other YES. I went to the No table and took a card.

'I can get my card from you and still vote yes?'

'Certainly,' smiled the dispenser of cards. 'Secret ballot!'

It was all very good-tempered. I paused under the oaks to exchange a few words with friends and acquaintances and presently I saw my daughter-in-law with our third grandson, Tony.

'Only one vote!' said the card dispenser, with a playful glance at the small boy.

It was like that in Claremont. Sociable. And apparently that was the mood throughout the country. The non-Europeans divorced themselves from the whole business. As usual, nobody cared what *they* thought or wanted. They therefore ignored the occasion. 'Referendum?' they said. 'What's that? *We* don't know about any Referendum.'

Glen and Tony came to the car to see us off. Piet had voted earlier on his way to work.

'What's in a name?' I said. 'Dominion or Republic – it's the same answer.'

'Only if we stay in the Commonwealth,' Glen answered.

We waved to them and set off on the Garden Route.

We picnicked at our usual outspan on the banks of the Breede river. The first swallows had arrived and skimmed over the brown water, re-discovering old haunts under the bridge. The yellow weaver-birds were busy in the willows and thorn trees on the river's edge. We didn't hurry. The day was so fine and warm, there in the heart of the great Cape grainlands under the blue Swellendam mountains.

When we filled up with petrol after lunch the Referendum results were coming through on the radio. So far they were strongly anti-republic.

The garage proprietor said, 'Man, these are only city results. Hang on for the platteland and you will know how people really feel.'

We knew the country vote would change the picture, and, when we checked in at Beacon Island, there was no longer any doubt about the outcome. The final result, however, was by no means as conclusive as had been generally expected. The Republic was to be. But the margin was 52 to 48 per cent – hardly an overwhelming majority.

I knew that the only remaining member of my mother's generation – her brother, Wilfred Marais, then in his eightieth year – would be overjoyed at the prospect of seeing his country a South African Republic, so I wrote to him at once. I am quoting his reply in full, as it presents a very human slant on the way a true Nationalist feels about his country and her basic problem. My uncle and I do not share all the same opinions, but we respect one another's views, and he and my English husband always found common ground for discussion without acrimony and were genuinely and deeply attached to one another.

October 13th, 1960.

Joy dear,

Thanks for your letter of the 7th written at Beacon Island. It was nice of you to write and I very much appreciated it.

I have no desire whatsoever to gloat about the Republican victory although I have cherished the idea for so many years.

To me our ultimate destiny as an alloyed and completely independent new nation has always seemed to be something natural, inevitable, and desirable. The hardcore of our nation, unlike that of Australia or New Zealand, is not of British stock, saturated with British ideas, British ideals, British blood, culture, loyalty, language and everything else that goes to make up British National character. Our task in South Africa is, in every respect, a much sterner task than that of Australia and New Zealand. We are in the process of hammering together, into a new single nation, two separate peoples who, through pure historical accident and for no good reason whatever, have fought each other for 150 years. The road has been long and the going hard but our progress has been steady and sure. We *must* and we *will* show a united front to the world at large. If not we will perish; for a house divided against itself cannot endure. It is later than we think and we Europeans can afford no more time for stupid sham fighting against each other on fundamental issues. Once together, the task of holding at bay the Black flood that threatens to overwhelm us will be less difficult.

You speak of 'Equality', which has become a very fashionable word in the world of late, but when analysed, it is a word which has no real meaning. A Black man may be equal or superior to a White man in many respects, but he differs from a White man just as a springbok differs from a blesbok. In each case they are a fundamentally different sub-species of the same species. The Creator, in his wisdom, designed things so, and we insignificant humans have not, up to the present, succeeded in improving upon his handiwork by our presumptuous interference. We humans are very clever, and we can even force animals and other living things to interbreed, which were not designed by the Creator to interbreed. Nature so revolts against this interference with her laws that in many cases the offspring of this kind of thing are 'mules', incapable of reproducing their own kind.

This is not always the case, but even where mongrels *can* reproduce, the resultant product is no recommendation for the experiment. If there were not an instinct in us that warns our fundamentally different types of human beings to refrain from interbreeding, the human race would surely long since have fused into a mud-coloured conglomeration of automatons with a long forgotten past of colourful diversity and a dull future of uninteresting similarity.

Dr. Verwoerd is giving the people a few months to digest the result of the Referendum. We can show our worth by making of those months a period of sensible thinking and of mutual and determined good will.

I fully believe that with our great experience behind us, we, in South Africa, will evolve the most feasible method of governing a Multiracial State.

Thank you, Joy, for your letter. The spirit of approach is in the air and I have high hopes for the future of our country, however tough the going may be for some time to come.

Much love,
Wilfred.

Our day's drive from Plettenberg Bay to East London took us through glorious country and I so enjoyed the journey that I was convinced my young heroine of *The Glass Barrier* must have travelled this way with her lover! At one point we turned off the road into the forest to see the famous giant yellowwood tree and I sat scribbling in the note-nook I used for *Glass Barrier* material.

The green gloom and mysterious bird-broken silence of the forest took possession of me. It was eerie and oppressive with its emanations of decaying vegetation and legends of prehistoric beasts and stone-age hunters. The foresters of today might cut paths and clearings but they were intruders. This was the domain of the Stone-Age Bushman with his poisoned arrows, of tiny buck, hooting monkeys, snakes, spiders, exotic birds and the Knysna elephant herd which still roams these hills and forests.

'Let's go,' I said to Bertie. 'This place gives me the creeps.'

'Not enough light or air,' he agreed. 'Too many unseen creatures and the damp smell of mould. Let's get down to the sea.'

We stopped for our noontide picnic in Nature's Valley under trees fringing a half-moon of sandy beach cambered by blue fishing-rocks. The murmur of the open sea mingled with the drowsy hum of bees in the heather, and wild flowers and spring grasses nodded in the sunshine beyond our shady grove.

We had dawdled and it was evening before we reached East London on the border of the Bantu homeland of the Ciskei.

East London is a delightful port and holiday resort among green hills and valleys leading down to the sea. It loves the Navy and the Navy reciprocates its affection. It is considered to be 'very English', and owes its existence to the early British colonists who settled the border with such stubborn determination throughout their long history of kaffir wars, burnt out farms and stolen stock.

Accommodation had been booked for us in a little hotel by Nahoon Beach, where you could eat superbly in an original atmosphere, and stroll through a jungle path to the shore.

Delightful social and civic occasions were combined with the more serious business of the meeting. The Mayor entertained the delegates in the City Hall. He also attended the opening of the Annual General Meeting at which my husband delivered his Presidential address.

As was his principle, my husband took pains to keep the South African Navy in the lime-light and to foster the good will already existing between it and the Royal Navy. Whether South Africa was a Republic or not made no difference. Her long empty coastlines made her vulnerable, and her strategic position between the two great oceans made her important. It was to the mutual advantage of Britain and South Africa to co-operate on a friendly naval basis and it was more than ever necessary to encourage the youth of South Africa to appreciate the importance of the sea around their land and the opportunities of life afloat, either in merchant or fighting ships. He always backed his speech with facts and figures and gave his listeners something to 'chew on'. He had adopted this country and given it his heart, although his loyalty to his own island never wavered, and he was always glad to help and encourage the South African Navy by every means in his power. Perhaps he understood its teething troubles better than most, for, as a very young officer, he had managed to get himself lent to the new-born Australian Navy and had served in her first war-ship the R.A.N.S. *Australia*. He had watched that dominion Navy develop and play a brave part in two wars; he had seen the Canadian Navy grow in importance, and now he considered it high time for the South African Navy to follow suit. He never failed this young navy in friendship. Nor, when the time came, did it fail him.

Our visit to East London was a very happy one and I shall always remember it, because it was the last A.G.M. of the Navy League that my husband was able to address in person.

The shadows had not yet closed in on us and those few days in the pretty holiday port were spent in full sunshine.

CHAPTER EIGHTEEN

THE PACE QUICKENS

NINETEEN SIXTY-ONE and March again – those Ides of March so greatly dreaded by my mother.

The Belgian Congo, given premature independence, was in the grip of inter-tribal warfare. European refugees, witnesses or victims of unspeakable atrocities, poured across the border into the Federation and South Africa, the living proof of the folly of handing over precipitate power to little-trained leaders whose people were, on the whole, closer to barbarism than civilization.

There were revolts against the Portuguese in Angola. Kenya's Jomo Kenyatta, the proven instigator of Mau-Mau, prepared to make his triumphal come-back. The Rhodesian Federation, which should have been the blueprint for a wise multi-racial government, faced constant obstruction from reactionary Whites and power-hungry Blacks. And, finally, at the Prime Minister's Conference in London it was made abundantly and offensively clear to South Africa that her racial policies would not be tolerated within the framework of the British Commonwealth of Nations.

Dr. Verwoerd, now fully recovered from the attempt upon his life, pleaded South Africa's case at this conference. Goaded by the virulent attacks of the respresentatives of newly emerged African States, the South African Prime Minister still managed to keep his temper and to give innumerable interviews without heat or histrionics. He explained separate development at considerable length, and in one statement compared it with Europe, where independent separate states live side by side. They were foreigners to one another but could be good neighbours. South Africa would like to be the good and friendly neighbour to the independent African States already emerged and to those she herself was preparing for gradual emergence. But it is difficult to appear 'friendly' and at the same time insist that your good neighbour only enter your territory by a side-door, and it would be odd to cross the border from one European country into another – Italy into Switzerland, for example – and find on the station or at the airport the public conveniences duplicated and labelled Swiss Only and Foreigners Only or Europeans Only and Non-Europeans.

The great experiment and the wide concept are obscured by these irritations like a cinema screen and a fine picture can be blacked out and ruined by the fanciful hat of the woman in the row ahead of you.

Dr. Verwoerd was well aware of the advantage of remaining within the Commonwealth, but he was left with no dignified option other than to withdraw. The policy of legally enforced discrimination was repugnant to humanity in general and to the Black majority of Prime Ministers in particular. Nothing could alter or disguise that fact.

'So we travel our own road – alone,' I said to Bertie. 'In the opposite direction from world opinion.'

He looked sad. He knew, as I did, that the latest news from London would have far-reaching consequences upon our own family.

When the Prime Minister returned to South Africa he was met by a faithful and enthusiastic crowd at Jan Smuts Airport and given a hero's welcome. South Africa was out of the Commonwealth. Fine! South Africa would go it alone.

Other people's troubles do not lessen our own, but they can act as a counter-irritant and distract our attention from our problems.

About now Sombani complained of peculiar sensations so macabre and distressing that I decided to send him to the Medical Officer at Langa. In my capacity as 'Cressage' Minister for Health the note, with dossier attached, was written by me. A rather fascinating correspondence ensued.

To the Medical Officer in Charge, Langa.

Dear Sir, Our gardener, Sombani, No. 2566718, is in great distress with an ailment so mysterious that he feels he cannot describe it properly and has asked me to write to you.

When he is at rest or in bed the 'thing' appears to be at its worst. He suddenly gets a sort of shock in his upper arms which then passes right through his limbs in a violent tingling sensation 'like a lot of ants'. Sometimes the onset feels like a tight bandage on his arms, or a shuddering, as if he had 'eaten something very sour'. He has suffered from these horrid manifestations since last September when he was home in his country in the Northern Transvaal. He didn't go to a doctor there as he did not want to take Native medicines. When he returned he was much better, but lately the attacks have come on more often and now he is driven frantic by them.

He tells me he does not smoke dagga and we have no reason to think he does, as he is a trustworthy man, and I don't think he is afraid of the 'evil eye'. So it would be a great relief to all of us to know what his trouble is.

Yours truly, Joy Packer.

The Medical Officer promptly passed the buck to the Department of Neurology and Psychiatry at Groote Schuur Hospital. The eminent woman doctor, to whom Sombani's strange case was referred, examined him and gave him a letter to me. During the next two months our gardener was the centre of various investigations and the bearer of a series of notes concerning his health.

Dear Lady Packer,
  I have infinite difficulty in making a diagnosis in this case. He has no abnormality on examination. There is only one possible diagnosis that rings a bell, but it is fairly exotic. I wonder if he could collect all his urine over a period of twenty-four hours (during which period he must not eat any bananas) and deliver it to the hospital. We can then test it. He must report back to this clinic in two weeks time.

A.B.

Dear Doctor,
  Thank you very much for your note about our gardener, Sombani. The case certainly does sound mystifying. We made him stay here twenty-four hours (no bananas) and he presented the specimen to the Sister-in-Charge as directed. I will see that he shows up at Out-Patients on Tuesday according to your instructions.   J.P.

I hate to confess that I am baffled and wonder whether a witch-doctor could not have helped him more than I can! The possibility of the attacks being psychological is strong, but I am impressed by his apparent stability and lack of anxiety symptoms. Anyway, I think we should do a few more tests including skull X-ray and an electro-encephalogram. If these are negative I can get a psychiatric opinion but the language and cultural difficulties make any rapport quite tricky.
  I have given him some tablets and will see him again when the tests are completed.   A.B.

It is most kind of you to take so much trouble over Sombani. We will see that he shows up for his appointment complete with card and clean head.

If these tests show nothing sinister (as I sincerely trust will be the case) may I come and see you? I do know a good deal about the meanderings of Sombani's mind and one or two things that may be still resting on his conscience, but they are a bit too involved to explain by letter! My husband says this would be a waste of your time. If that is so, please forget it. But I know the mind of man is a strange territory and they may have some bearing on his troubles.   J.P.

Sombani's electro-encephalogram is perfectly normal so I feel that a diagnosis of some bizarre form of epilepsy is untenable.

I have asked one of our psychiatrists to see him. Thank you for your letter. I was waiting to see Sombani before replying. I think it would help a great deal if we could meet and discuss him. Does 11.30 on Monday suit you? A.B.
P.S. He is now in the hands of a Jungian analyst!

I went to our big teaching hospital at the appointed time.

It stands on the slopes of Devil's Peak where the buck, wildebeeste and zebras graze in open green pastures or retire into the woods during the heat of the day. Rockeries, blazing with colour, terrace the hospital grounds and refresh the eyes of those who have to wait what must seem an interminable time in and around Out-Patients. I have often read complaints in the press about patients having to wait hours for attention, and their tone never fails to annoy me. The hospital, staffed by dedicated doctors – under-paid and overworked – gives virtually free attention to a multitude of sufferers, and people who must wait do so because neither time nor the human capacity to serve can be stretched beyond a certain limit.

I found the doctor in charge of Sombani's case in the ward she had indicated. She was tall and slight with cool clear eyes, and we talked in a light impersonal office.

The Jungian analysts, she informed me, had their own

methods of overcoming differences in culture, language and background, and Sombani, she was sure, was already much improved. As I was also satisfied that he was better, I suggested that perhaps the treatment might now be discontinued.

'Your interest and your tranquillizers – and, of course, the efforts of the analyst – seem to have given him confidence,' I said. 'But I think really these nervous spasms could be due to the way home-sickness gets him. In waves.'

She agreed. 'They lead such unnatural lives, these people.'

'I've been homesick myself so often,' I said. 'I know it can make people feel physically ill. I've experienced that.'

'And most of these folk are half tribal, half urban, and never sure of anything. Really, you'd expect them all to be psychopaths. Well, tell him to come back to us if he is in trouble. He mustn't feel that we have lost interest in him.'

I thanked her for the immense trouble she had taken and extracted Sombani from the meshes of the health machinery.

A few weeks later he informed my husband that he wanted to go home and find work nearer to his family. His heart was sore to tell us this after seven years. But Cape Town was 'littie bittie far'. It was now the end of summer, he explained, and we would not need him in the winter as we would still have Amos.

'Do you want to come back at the end of the winter?' asked my husband.

'No, master,' he said, rather wistfully. 'I want to stay near my wife and children.'

'If you change your mind after six months it will not be possible to come back.'

'I know, master.'

His voluntary departure was in line with Government policy, which was to repatriate all Bantu in the Western Cape and build up a Coloured labour force to replace them. There was nothing more we could say, except to assure him that we understood his feelings. So we gave him our blessing and a present, and once again – as far as we were concerned, for the last time – Sombani caught his slow train to the north where the great rivers flow, the cattle graze in tall pink grass, and the women brew the best maroela beer in South Africa.

On 31st May the Union of South Africa became the Republic of South Africa – *Die Republiek van Suid-Afrika* – under the active leadership of Dr. Hendrik Verwoerd, the Prime Minister, and the passive figurehead of the erstwhile Governor-General, who now assumed the title of State President.

Tall and grey haired, with fine-drawn features and a distinguished bearing, Charles Robberts Swart is a good choice for State President, an honour which, unlike the Presidency in the United States, carries the glory without the power. Apart from his recent term as Governor-General, he had been Minister for Justice in the Nationalist Cabinet and his manner, though genial, has authority. He looks the part. In his youth he was, for a short time, a movie actor in Hollywood, so no doubt he can play it too! His wife has the quiet simple dignity which characterizes many Afrikaner women called upon to support their husbands in high positions. There is a submissive Victorian deference in their attitude towards their husbands, which should never be taken at its face value, for the Afrikaner woman is a dominant force in the home and always has been. She is the goad as well as the helpmeet of her lord and master. In the early days of the old Cape Colony the women urged their husbands to trek and faced the hardships and dangers of the unknown with stubborn stoicism. Under the broad flap of the sunbonnet was a shrewd intelligence, and a most invincible spirit burned beneath the tight-fitting bodice. The men can buck around as much as they please, but they are the children of a matriarchal people and their women folk don't let them forget it!

That night of Wednesday, 31st May, I made an entry in my writer's note-book.

Today the Republic of South Africa came into being without incident in Pretoria, the birthplace of the old Boer Republic of the Transvaal. It is cold and wintry and rain marred the celebrations. Mrs. Swart the wife of the State President, Charles Robberts Swart, was ill and unable to attend.

To me it all seemed remote and repetitive. Once again a Boer Republic out of step with the pace of modern emancipation has been born.

For the Afrikaners, it is a profoundly moving and sentimental occasion. Many of those gathered in Pretoria from farms and dorps in the veld are seasoned greybeards who, years ago, rode in commando to fight for the Transvaal against the British. Those *oudstryders* – veterans of the Boer War – cannot forget the bitterness of that long ago defeat and the humiliation of seeing their tiny nation conquered and their young hard-won country forced into the British Empire at the point of the bayonet. So naturally, to them and to their descendants this day of May 31st, 1961, is the triumphant culmination of the long struggle for independent nationalism and the beginning of another struggle for survival as an independent power. The solemn intensity of their feeling is reflected in the deeply religious nature of the ceremonial. Once again, to the Afrikaner, God's Will and the *Volkswil* are irrevocably identified with one another.

History is repeating itself and a new Republic is being born which is – after a sixty year gap – the continuation of the last. For, make no mistake, that is what it is – a greater Afrikaans Republic, territorially enriched, highly industrialized, and controlling the destinies of vast multi-racial populations. We must hope that it will not be doomed by the old Boer determination to sit on the hands of the clock, regardless of the time-bomb ticking the seconds away inside it.

My mother would have rejoiced today, as her brother, Wilfred Marais, does. They saw and mourned the conquest of the Boers in my mother's birthplace, the Transvaal. Once I would have felt as Uncle Wilfred does. Now I feel nothing, except a certain apprehensive loneliness. As part of the Commonwealth, world hate directed against us was to some degree diffused. Now it will be concentrated. We are separate, solely responsible for ourselves and our conduct.

We, who do not think exclusively with our fears, emotions and pathological prejudices, are spiritual aliens in our own land – *uitlanders* of the soul. We are not obsessed with the past and with sagas of exodus and national genesis. Nor do we believe that it will be possible to preserve a 'traditional way of life' in perpetuity. If our new Republic will accept the wide laws of human growth, and respect the dignity of man and his right to better himself to the utmost of his ability, the children and grandchildren of White South Africans may still have a chance of growing up in comparative peace and in a country of which they may feel proud.

As from today, High Commission House, two doors away from us, becomes the British Embassy, and very soon South African visitors to Britain will find themselves foreigners in what, for many of them, is the land of their origin.

Subversive elements among the Bantu had organized a three day stay-at-home strike to celebrate the inauguration of the Republic, but, so excellent was police surveillance and so tactfully was it applied, that the strike never materialized and the Bantu went cheerfully to work as usual. When they were asked about it, they laughed gaily. 'What strike? *We* don't know about any strike.'

There was a sense of finality about the birth of the Republic, which was further increased by Dr. Verwoerd's decision to hold a General Election in October of the same year to get a mandate from the country to press on with positive *apartheid*.

As David Beresford Pratt had regarded the Prime Minister as a symbol of *apartheid*, so now many of us felt the Republic to be the last stronghold of the way of life it aimed to perpetuate. With flexibility of outlook and action this Republic might survive and flourish; without such flexibility South Africa was doomed. My husband had always believed in the maxim of being, 'flexible in things immaterial', but our Government has not learned that lesson yet. Nor were the Afrikaners oppressed by the sense of isolation that chilled the English-speaking section of the country. Isolationism is born in them, for they are, naturally, ranchers and not city dwellers. Their history is a saga of trekking from one solitude to the next, of stock and crops, of making their own laws according to God's Will and the immediate necessity, of itinerant teachers for their children, and itinerant pedlars for their women-folk, and of resisting remote authority and ignoring the world beyond their vaguely defined borders. Nothing irked a Boer more than being able to see his neighbour's smoke. He wanted to sit on his stoep and gaze at the far horizon, master of all he surveyed.

The modern Afrikaner is, at heart, little different, although he is entering more and more into the bustling business world. In common with the Bantu, he is adapting himself to the industrial revolution. This South African Republic, like the last, is mainly his and his English-speaking compatriots will have to take it on his terms.

Some, who looked ahead, were not prepared to do so.

Thus, on 28th August, exactly seven years after we had moved into our home, our young family came to bid us farewell.

It was, as my mother had believed, a propitious date for a new enterprise – the anniversary of her wedding day. It was also the anniversary of Glendyr's father's birthday. It is strange how certain dates can pile one event upon another to enhance their importance. Even the season, with all its urgency of early spring and new beginnings, seemed to share the significance of that crisp sunny day.

Like our young people, the grey squirrel with the ragged tail and the white belly was seeking a new home. She found it in the large untidy sparrow abode recently abandoned by Mr. and Mrs. Mossie, who had built themselves a new one. I pointed out the nest in the bignonia to my grandsons. A thin squealing came out of it.

'Listen! Those are squirrel babies!'

The boys listened, intrigued. Ronnie pointed out that squirrels were bigger than baby birds. 'They'll put a strain on the nest.' But presently all appeared to be quiet in Bignonia Alley.

Soon Piet had to say it.

'We must be on our way.'

They were sailing for Australia by the *Dominion Monarch,* and we were not going to the docks to see them off. There had been too much of that in our lives.

We stood in the porch under the sweet-scented mauve wistaria to watch them drive away – the six of them. Hands fluttered out of the open windows of the car as they had so often done before. The sound of the engine faded.

Although the sun still shone it was chilly as we turned silently into the house, not trusting ourselves to speak. We sat by the landscape window and looked out at the loved familiar scene – the lawns, the trees, the valley with bars of amber light sloping across the mountain from the west, gilding the garden and the little stone wall. The doves planed down from the trees for crumbs and bird-seed, greedy as ever, and the mossies flew in excitably, complaining indignantly about the interlopers in Bignonia Alley. They couldn't abide the egg-eating four-legged cuckoo and her brood who had taken possession of their disused nest.

I went and perched on the arm of my husband's big chair, knowing that he shared my sadness. Then, all at once, a thrill of song came through the window, so light and charming that I raised my head to listen.

'A new bird!'

He looked out, past the scarlet trumpets of the bignonia trembling against the glass.

'There,' he said. 'There's your new bird! In the lemon tree.'

'But that's our Mr. Mossie.'

'Similar, but not the same. This fellow is smaller, and a song-bird. Go and get the bird book.'

We identified him quickly. A mountain-canary. He was a little russet fellow with a black head and chest – a rare little jester sent by heaven to make us smile on one sad day. He and Kitty staged an act. The mountain-canary, singing blithely, hopped jauntily along the wall to the seed-table. The cat waited for him to hop on to the platform and then pounced. The mountain-canary squeaked and flew from under her claws. The cat and the canary repeated the performance several times, like quaint decorative clowns. It was charmingly funny. Impossible to believe it might end in tragedy! Nor did it. The canary was too cute.

'He's very tame and trusting,' smiled Bertie. 'Somebody's pet.'

Then, just as we were considering how best to return him to his owners, he got bored with his dangerous game and flew away with a final burst of song.

About an hour later, when I was resting on my bed, I heard a great to-do on the balcony outside my window. There, in the dusk, sat the grey squirrel, her shaggy tail erect along her upright back, every hair electric, her large almond eyes beseeching, her little paws pleadingly upraised. She was chittering desperately, begging for help.

I hurried downstairs and out on to the terrace to inspect the nest she had commandeered from the mossies. The bottom appeared to be tumbling apart and a new-born squirrel lay in the gutter beneath it, a tiny naked hairless creature. The mother fussed above the nest, evidently realizing that it would not bear her weight, and lamented in anguish. I went to hunt for something that would catch the falling nest and returned with an old shoe box, which I fixed strategically in the creeper. But the infant squirrel had vanished and the white cat was licking her lips and washing her face! The squirrel mother ran to and fro along Bignonia Alley crying loudly and grievously. Oh, how I felt for her!

'That's the best I can do, Mrs. Squirrel,' I said.

My husband had come out to join me.

'What a catastrophe!'

He put his arm about my shoulders and we strolled down on to the lawn.

'Poor little thing,' I said. 'So terrible! The bottom fell out of her world. Really it did.'

'Yes,' he said, in his gentle way. 'That makes two of you, doesn't it?'

CHAPTER NINETEEN

TURBULENT SPRING

THAT spring the entries in my note-book were mainly concerned with the garden and its denizens, for these were my solace.

Aug. 29, 1961.
The baby squirrels have vanished from the falling world of the Corner House in Bignonia Alley. So has their mother. And our young family are far out at sea on their way to a new life.

*   *   *

Sept. 23rd. Bertie says this is the official first day of spring. Evidently Mr. Mossie agrees. He has been very abandoned all day. Made love to Mrs. Mossie in the elm and immediately afterwards in the lemon tree! All the doves are behaving lustfully, not nearly as charming and ethereal as the sparrows.

Oct. 17th. Tomorrow is Election Day and our youngest grandson, Willie (in Western Australia), will be two.

I believe the sparrows have fledglings. Mr. Mossie demanded bird-seed quite sharply this evening. He and Mrs. Mossie kept nibbling at it and flying up to the nest in turns to feed the baby birds. The bignonia is at the height of its glory – masses of red trumpet sprays. Too lovely! We are longing to see our new roses in bloom, 'First Love' and 'Exciting'. 'Peace' and 'Queen Elizabeth' are flourishing side by side.

In the charmed spring-time circle of our garden there was this blessing – peace.

But, outside it, the country had been plunged into the turmoil of a General Election.

Once again we had it drummed into our heads that only a strong Nationalist Government could hope to preserve our 'traditional way of life'. And while this cherished idol – this golden Way of Life – was worshipped noisily from the hustings, another way of life, even more unique, was being shaken to its foundations a thousand miles from our western shores.

Tristan de Cunha, one of the loneliest islands in the world, is a British dependency closely related to South Africa by ties of history, geography and economy. That spring the Atlantic Ridge, deep under the rocky island, was shaken by violent tremors, the little huts among the potato patches groaned and shuddered, and sulphurous blow-holes opened up on the once innocent mountain. The rugged islanders looked at one another in alarm. What was happening to their only home?

These people of Tristan knew little of the outside world. It touched them lightly with a lobster canning industry developed by South African Fisheries, and a meteorological station. Their contact with civilization depended upon the two fishing vessels that plied between Tristan and Cape Town at intervals, an occasional visit from some warship of the British or South African Navy, or, more rarely still, a passing liner.

There was no police station because there was no crime, and shopping was done by barter. The islanders wore an odd practical peasant costume and spoke the English of Nelson's sailors. They comprised an inbred community less than three hundred strong, descended from the redoubtable Corporal Glass of the Royal Marines, who, in company with two seamen, elected to remain on Tristan da Cunha when the British garrison stationed there during the Napoleonic wars was disbanded. Wives for Corporal Glass and the seamen were brought from St. Helena by an obliging sea captain. Later an American and an Italian mariner enriched the original stock by two names and a valuable infusion of new blood. Because the first inhabitants were strong and sound the islanders were healthy despite a hundred and fifty years of inbreeding and almost total isolation.

As the tremors increased the growing anxiety of the people on Tristan was allayed by the comforting assurance of their distant guardian, the British Colonial Office, that their extinct volcano was extremely unlikely to erupt. By October, however, fissures had opened in the ground, lava was flowing freely, rock-falls were more and more alarming, and it was evident that the 'dead' volcano was alive and kicking hard!

Fortunately the two fishing vessels were close at hand and a Dutch liner, the *Tjisidane* steamed to the rescue. The British frigate, *Leopard*, fully prepared for earthquake emergencies, set out from Simon's Town and later the South African frigate, *Transvaal*, played her part in the mournful business of winding up a way of life on Tristan. When it was clear that the island was no longer habitable the people sadly said good-bye to the rock home that was all they knew of the world, took to their long-boats, and made for the liner, *Tjisidane*. By some dispensation of providence, the weather, often too stormy for the boats to go to sea, was mercifully calm.

On 16th October, the eve of the General Election that would decide the fate of South Africa, the *Tjisidane* arrived in Table Bay with the Tristan evacuees. The Red Cross office was overwhelmed with offers of help in fitting them out with whatever they might need, and in St. George's Cathedral a service of thanksgiving was held. The people of Cape Town flocked to see the islanders and to pray for them.

They were a strange arresting group with tanned craggy faces as weather-beaten as their island. There was something unreal and dreamlike about the presence of these folk in our midst – a survival come to us out of the past, speaking the language of another century, seeing our modern city with wonder and bewilderment. Sky-scrapers, traffic, telephones, rules, regulations, crowds – black, white, brown and yellow. Go here, go there! Do this, do that! The rugged resigned faces looked at me from the front page of the morning paper – the men simply clad and starkly impressive, the women sturdy in their thick white knitted stockings, their plain skirts, woollen jerseys and head-scarves. A white-bearded veteran, interviewed by the press, summed up their hopes and fears in a paragraph.

'We are one big united family. All we ask is that we are kept together. We feel anxious now that we must learn a new way of life and new laws. But the Lord will protect us wherever we go.'

'So much for a way of life!' I said to Bertie. 'Fate steps in.'

I put the paper aside with the ominous feeling that here was a portent.

'The thing is to recognize when a way of life becomes untenable,' said my husband. 'If you hang on too long you perish.'

'There's a feel of doom in the air,' I said.

He smiled. 'It's the sultry weather.'

The weather was very strange. Hot and oppressive. I could almost believe that Devil's Peak might blow its top and spew forth fiery death. The night was airless too.

In the small hours of the 18th October, election morning, I woke. Our windows were wide open and the curtains were billowing into the room on the breath of a sudden violent gale. It was a hot incalculable wind and, as I closed the window, I thought of the Bantu prophets of Langa who had warned the people of 'the day of the hot wind and the end of the world'. Maybe there was such a day and the prophets had only been wrong about the date. Maybe this was it!

On that hot windy October day the White people of South Africa went to the polls and voted the Nationalists back into power.

It had been a tough fight made more so by a split in the United Party. This massive opposition had been seriously weakened by the break-away of its more liberal element to form the new Progressive Party which advocated a multi-racial state governed by the best brains of all races for all races. The Progressives differed from extreme Liberals in that they rejected any immediate application of the 'one man one vote' principle. Although the Progressive idea appealed to the English-speaking youth of the country, only one representative was returned to Parliament, attractive Helen Suzman of Houghton, Johannesburg. This unproductive breakaway from the United Party was a bitter blow and disillusionment to Sir de Villiers Graaff, the U.P. leader. Lifelong personal friendships were broken on that issue.

De Villiers Graaff, who is still in his forties, is a big robust man who commands the admiration and affection of his followers and many of his opponents. He has a brave war record and boundless energy, enthusiasm and resilience. He has the Afrikaner's friendly approachability, but, like most politicians, he has developed a strong resistance to revolutionary ideas. The policy of his party is moderate and tolerant, but basically it does not differ greatly from that of the Nationalists. It makes many of the human concessions so badly needed in our country, and, instead of autonomous Bantustans, it aims at a federation of races in which each will be given a share in the government of the country. But it insists upon the maintenance of White supremacy.

On the whole the most significant outcome of the election was probably the appointment of Balthazar Johannes Vorster* to ministerial rank in the reconstituted Nationalist cabinet. This 'strong man' in a strong Government has since come to be regarded as the eventual successor of Dr. Verwoerd. Under the recent Sabotage Bill Mr. Vorster, as Minister for Justice, holds the widest powers ever vested in one man in a Democracy. He was born in 1916 at Jamestown on the borders of the Transkei and spoke Xhosa before he spoke English. He qualified at Stellenbosch University and during

* Mr B. J. Vorster became the Premier of the Republic of South Africa after the assassination of Hendrik Verwoerd in 1966 and remains so still.

World War II he was interned by the Smuts Government for campaigning against the war effort. He was at that time a leader of the now defunct *Ossewabrandwag* (ox wagon torch-bearers) an extreme Nationalist organization which Mr. Vorster then defined as follows. 'We stand for Christian Nationalism, which is an ally of National Socialism (Nazism). You can call it anti-democratic dictatorship if you want to. In Italy it is known as Fascism, in Germany it is known as National Socialism, and in South Africa it is known as Christian Nationalism.'

His views, since then, have presumably become more democratic, but he is known to be the toughest and the most implacable protagonist of Government doctrines. Mr. Vorster has every reason to know all the tortuous ramifications of treason and sabotage, and we may be sure he will show no leniency to anyone attempting to undermine the country or the government, either by word or deed. He has a dour reputation for undeviating honesty.

My note-book whisks me once more from important events to the trivialities of our garden.

Oct. 21st. So off we go for another five years of Nationalist rule. The Government's task gets more and more difficult as our privileged way of life becomes more and more untenable. And today, like a warning, the 'big united family' of Tristan da Cunha sails on the mailship for England, sorrowful and lost, shaken out of a humble but precious way of life by earthquakes and volcanic eruptions. Strange how dates keep making themselves important. Today is Trafalgar Day and these people are a survival from Nelson's navy! They came here like weary seabirds, to pause and rest before continuing on their reluctant migration. Even if they return nothing will be quite the same again. They will have touched and been touched by the outside world.

Oct. 28th. Our four baby mossies have left the nest. Evidently they couldn't fly back in and slept out in the bush below the lawn. Mr. and Mrs. Mossie fed them there indefatigably.

*   *   *

Nov. 8th. For a couple of days now they have been eating bird-seed all together on the terrace. Mr. and Mrs. Mossie still beak-feed the children though they are obviously capable of feeding themselves. Their family flights get more and more adventurous and the whole lot squeal with delight as they switch-back through the air, Mr. Mossie in the lead.

Nov. 11th. The babies now feed themselves entirely. One is missing. I suspect Kitty. So now there are always five on and around the terrace – Pa, Ma and three babes. The babes ruffle and shudder their plumage all the time in an itchy sort of way.

Nov. 18th. Pa and Ma Mossie are being beastly to their children! They both keep chasing them away and Mrs. Mossie goes about with feathers in her beak. They don't let the kids sleep with them in the nest. Stacey Skaife (our famous Naturalist and Entomologist) says she wants to start a new family and its only reasonable for her to expect the house to herself.

Nov. 20th. Bertie's heart and the recent recurrence of headaches makes me anxious. He is wonderfully uncomplaining. We go to Hermanus tomorrow. Hope the holiday will do him good.

Hermanus, our annual holiday haunt, was as delightful as ever. But now, for the first time, we did not play our usual morning golf on the pretty course between the mountains and the sea. Instead we walked a few holes in the cool of the evening. Not the hilly ones. The heather was out, and a pair of blue cranes stood statuesque in the rough, where the wild flowers nodded and unwary moles or snakes offered a succulent meal. The crane, at that time, had just been selected as the National Bird of the Republic. There had been some talk of the ostrich, but when the cartoonists depicted this noble bird with its head buried in the sand and its posterior – grotesquely reminiscent of some of our politicians – turned towards world opinion, the idea was rejected. The beautiful emerald bokmakierie was a keen favourite, but the dignified and useful crane won the day and saluted his fellow

South African representative, the springbok. When the weather was about to break we'd hear the sentinel baboon hooting up in the kloof. The swallows skimmed above the grass and we'd speculate on the course of their long journey south to the sun.

In the mornings we'd find some secluded corner in the lovely cliff garden of the hotel. I had begun work on a new non-fiction book and my scribble-book and pen always went with me. Bertie liked to read quietly – heavy books, by my standards, memoirs, biographies, histories of all periods. It was restful and pleasant. When I looked up from my scribbling and away over the grass cliffs down to the sea I'd be amused to observe the flat spit of rock which was the sea-birds' haunt. A colony of white gulls occupied one side of it and the black *duikers*, or cormorants, the other.

'South African birds,' I said. 'Blankes and nie blankes.'

Bertie said. 'That's a favourite theme. Nature knows what's best. No notices required. Only man forgets his place.'

The white birds rose, as if at a signal, and flew in a gleaming irregular skein across the sunny sea. The black ones following untidily, evidently attracted by some shoal invisible to us.

The glistening chestnut kelp boiled and seethed in the rock gullies and cauldrons, snake-like heads rising and falling with the ebb and flow of the tide. Across the bay the white dunes of Die Kelders sprawled in a dazzling swathe between the blue sea and the hills. The long surf-crested rollers crashed upon the cliffs and strands as they had done from time immemorial, tossing their treasures of Venus ears, fans and cowries, into the small sandy coves I had explored so eagerly as a child. They say an ant can fall from any height and never hurt itself because it is so light, and the fragile exquisite shells of the coast are the same, still perfect after the greatest buffetings.

The sun-birds sang their thin quivering song in the palms and shrubs that shaded us as we sat in the garden. My husband tipped his old straw hat forward to protect his eyes from the glare and lost himself in his book, for when he was reading he went into another world the way I do when I am writing. Towards noon we would go down the steps to the sea-pool for a swim, but 'taking it quietly'. 'Don't let him exert himself,' the doctor had told me.

Everything was just the same as it had been on other holidays, yet nothing was the same. We hid our fears from one another.

On our way home from Hermanus we stopped at Somerset West for Sunday lunch with the Syfret family, Miles and Gerda, and their daughters, grown up Caroline and Louise, not yet a teenager. Their black cat had recently had kittens. The Father's indentity was not in any doubt, for half the children took after him and looked like tawny lions. Two of the ginger infants were playing in the study when we arrived – a kitten-dance that made us laugh.

'Don't you want one of them?' asked Louise. 'Surely you do!'

'Our cat's lonely,' I agreed. 'Ever since our little dog was killed she has been lonely.'

'She may not put up with a kitten,' said Bertie. But he was entranced by the playful creatures.

'That one!' I said. 'It's adorable. What is it, boy or girl?'

'All marmalades are Toms,' said Gerda. 'Someone who knows about cats told me that.'

That afternoon, a marmalade kitten with personality and pretty markings rode home with us and was introduced to Kitty to their mutual disgust. Like all redheads, the small one took the offensive immediately, dancing sideways at Kitty, fur and whiskers bristling, yellow eyes blazing, and spitting like fat on a hot stove. Kitty fled. Marmalade then set about consolidating the conquest of the master of the house, and making a firm ally of the cook.

'That's all woman behaviour,' said Bertie. 'Aggressive, cunning, flirtatious, selfseeking and full of charm.'

Marmalade flung him a golden glance from under her long white antennae and purred sweetly. There was a bubble in the purr.

'And when she wants something she cries for it,' I added. 'A soft little needle-cry. Very feminine. I wonder if Gerda has been misinformed.'

Gerda had. Nearly all marmalades are Toms. This one wasn't. Kitty took to the woods with a bad attack of jealous sulks while the new arrival, unconcerned, queened it in the house. She reminded me of the mountain canary who had appeared the day we most needed a jester. She made us laugh with her antics, leaping after the yellow and black butterflies and chasing fallen bougainvillea flowers. She was never far from her humans and when I whistled she came at the double. Not like white Kitty who came at her own pace with plenty of pauses for washing her beautiful fluffy black tail.

On those hot summer evenings, when we sat on the porch, reading or listening to long-playing records, Marmalade danced with the moths or rose-beetles that flew in to the lights. Everything with wings attracted her. Yet she soon learned to leave the birds on the terrace alone.

'She keeps her eye on the ball,' said Bertie, who liked to watch her amusing *pas-de-chats* and her intense concentration.

At sundown, when we strolled round the garden, the cats came with us. There was a truce between them in the sunset hour. They even played catch-catch – 'cats-cats' we called it – and 'paws', a sort of boxing game. Sometimes they did a highly stylized type of wrestling.

'But you couldn't call them friends,' I complained. 'Kitty still has a hate on Marmalade and suddenly goes away.'

'Kitty is lost to us for the time being,' Bertie agreed. 'She's gone for bush.'

On Christmas morning I went to the garden before sunrise to pick fresh flowers for the house. The Peace roses were dramatic, immense blooms on tall strong stems, holding in their hearts all the faint shot pink and gold of the eastern sky. The Karl Drushkys were white as paper and the white cat sat conspicuously under them as she often did – 'for effect' Bertie always insisted. Marmalade, whose speed and protective colouring camouflaged her, appeared suddenly out of the rockery and jumped into my flower-basket, where she sat up and smiled at me. She looked very pert and knowing. Our friend, Beryl Kiernander, who had given us our white cat from the wine farm, Natte Valleij, and who knew about cats and reincarnation and all manner of occult laws, had assured us that Marmalade was highly evolved, as cats go – about three incarnations ahead of Kitty – so I addressed her sensibly.

'Now, be a nice kitten and make friends with the white cat. After all, this is the good will season and it's Christmas Day! Remember, you are the wise one. Even Nanny calls you the wise cat.'

I tipped her out of the basket among the rose bushes. Kitty sat watching. Marmalade played for time while digesting my advice. She washed. Not expertly like Kitty who kept her snowy coat immaculate, but rather sketchily. Then, as usual, she took the initiative and approached Kitty, who surprisingly responded. They went towards each other cautiously, as if ready to spring away. Under the tallest Peace rose they paused, heads craned forward face to face. Very softly they kissed, whiskers brushing lightly.

It was absurd how pleased I felt. The good will season had started well.

CHAPTER TWENTY

THE SILVER SEA

THE winter came and went with its cold north-west winds and torrential storms. We had been eight years in 'Cressage' and our young family had been a year in Perth and loved it. They were settled.

The spears of the silvers glinted in the September sun and the long-tailed sugar-birds showed off among the proteas, but we knew that they would leave us soon for new feeding-grounds. The pin-oak unfurled its green-gold umbrella of lacy baby leaf; the Cape lemons hung like little lanterns amid their hard glossy foliage and stern thorns, and two large black and yellow butterflies hovered perpetually over the fragrant blossom. Fruit and flowers adorn the lemon-tree simultaneously and every year big butterflies come to it. Just two pairs. The petria festooned the porch with its rich blue-bell clusters and a tiny sunbird sang his glittering song as he robbed them of their nectar. The mossies flew about gaily with their latest brood, and the squirrel prepared to give birth in a drainpipe joint under a canopy of bougainvillea. I told Bertie about her.

'If it rains they'll all be drowned!'

'Let nature take its course. She'll make her own arrangements – though I must say they are seldom very satisfactory!'

The heavy bunches of wistaria hung over the arched entrance near the ship's bell and drenched the air with their lovely light perfume; mimosa plumed the woods with chicken-yellow, and the double-flowering peach was a froth of pink.

But my Bertie could no longer enjoy these things. For many months the boundaries of his active world had been shrinking – from holidays abroad to a fortnight somewhere nearer home, from going out to staying in his own house, from strolling in the garden to sitting on the terrace or the porch, till now it was confined to the pale dove-grey walls of our spacious bedroom. Even the few steps from the bed to the armchair by the window had become too great an effort and so, for him, the beautiful view of the mountain, Flats and distant ranges had been reduced to softly stirring tree tops and scudding clouds.

Thus it was I who now made the daily tour of inspection with Amos, using Bertie's long Alpine stock to indicate this or that in need of attention. In the cool of the evening I'd go out and gather my tokens of spring – a spray of mimosa, a sprig of lemon blossom, or the first buds of the new roses. 'Exciting' was a flame with a dark velvet heart and 'First Love' was as charming as her name. I'd put them in a vase and take them to him so that he could see them and know what beauty was unfolding in his beloved garden.

'Your book,' he said. 'You've stopped working on it. You're doing my jobs instead.'

'The book can wait. I've typed your Navy League speech. Shall I send a copy to Johannes? He likes to have it in plenty of time.'

The Navy League Annual General Meeting was to be held in Cape Town the following month. Unknown to him I had already written to inform Colonel Johannes Kreft, the Federal Secretary, that my husband would not be well enough to attend it.

I put the typescript into Bertie's cold hand, and he took it from me, but did not look at it. His eyes were on mine.

'What date is it today?'

'September the fifteenth.'

'And the A.G.M. is on October the eighteenth. Doesn't give me very long to pull myself together, does it?'

He called me back as I turned away, his voice and his smile very gentle.

'Take the mimosa onto the landing, Joy-Joy. It's giving you hay fever.'

I took the vase and went out of the room. Our doctor was coming up the stairs with the specialist physician. They had looked after my husband for five years when necessary, and they were our friends as well as our medical advisers. Their kindness to both of us was unfailing.

'A good night?' asked our doctor, and added, with a shrewd glance at me, 'Not very. You don't have to tell me!'

I gave them my report of the night, and went and waited for them in the study downstairs. Marmalade jumped on to my lap and I felt her small rough tongue on the back of my hand.

'Salt lick, little cat?' Somehow there was comfort in talking to Marmalade and stroking her pretty coat.

Soon after they came down our house-doctor left me alone with the physician. Although it was past seven o'clock he still had other calls to make.

The physician's alert lively face was grave.

'You aren't getting much sleep, are you? Always the broken nights – for months now.'

'That's all right.'

He shook his head. 'Would you consider a nursing-home?'

'Never.'

'Then you must get in a night-nurse.'

'Is it absolutely necessary?'

He explained that it was, and added that he thought he should write to our son.

'I can drop him a line here and now.'

'I'll airmail it with one of my own. I have a letter ready for the post.'

He went to the desk by the window at which my husband always dealt with his correspondence, and wrote to Piet. His back was very straight and decisive like his eyes as he handed me the slip of thin professional notepaper.

'Is the airmail quick – reliable?'

'Irregular. Letters can take two days or ten.'

'How is Piet placed? Has he a partner?'

'He's on his own now.'

'It would be difficult for him to fly home?'

'It would be very difficult for him to leave a new practice.'

He looked distressed. 'It's tough ... it's tough.'

I folded the note rather clumsily and stuck it into the pocket of my cotton dress.

'I won't tell my husband about this – about writing to Piet.'

'No,' he agreed quickly. 'Don't! There's no point.'

After he had gone I went up to Bertie and sat on the bed where he was propped up with pillows.

'We all think you should get more sleep,' he said. 'There's talk of a night-nurse.'

'We could make her very comfortable in your cabin next door. If you needed an injection or something I could pop in and say, "Wakey, wakey, show a leg!" '

He managed a smile.

The Night-Sister was small and wiry with a rope of iron-grey hair round the neat little head under her crisp veil. Her eyes were very frank and understanding.

'Dump your things here,' I said. 'My husband's asleep.'

She looked round the cabin with its porthole and Malta-weave bedspread on the bunk and the seamanlike decorations on the walls. There was a photograph of a battle ensign whipping proudly from the masthead of a warship going into action. Underneath it was printed 'H.M.S. *Manchester*, September 27th, 1940'. My husband had been her Captain then when a British Squadron had put a much larger and faster Italian force to flight. Above the bunk was another photograph, H.M.S. *Warspite*, the Grand Old Lady of the sea, who had broken adrift from her tow to evade the ship-breaker's yard and find her own 'haven, where she would be'. That haven was Prussia Cove on the Cornish coast.

'The *Warspite*?' the Sister asked. 'Your husband's favourite ship.'

'How did you guess?'

'I've read your books. I seem to know you both.'

She was English and she loved the sea. Her eyes rested with interest on a small frame containing a red wax seal imprinted with a hollow-cheeked sensitive profile showing the wig of Nelson's day and the epaulettes of an Admiral.

'It's a direct impression of the fob seal with which Nelson is supposed to have sealed his letters to Lady Hamilton,' I explained. 'And here, beside it, are the words of his last prayer on board the Victory before the Battle of Trafalgar.'

She read them, her lips moving soundlessly.

May the Great God Whom I worship grant to my country, and for the benefit of Europe in general, a great and glorious victory; and may no misconduct in any one tarnish it; and may humanity after victory be the predominant feature in the British Fleet. For myself individually I commit my life to Him that made me, and may His blessing alight on my endeavours for serving my country faithfully. To Him I resign myself and the just cause which is entrusted to me to defend. Amen. Amen. Amen.

October 21st, 1805.

All these things were part of my Admiral and of his faith. You went to meet the enemy, you put the honour of your country before your own safety or interest, you hoisted no flag of surrender, and, lest you should not be destined to fight again, you committed your life to Him that made you.

'I think he's awake,' I said.

She put her cape neatly on the bunk. Then she squared her shoulders and went with me to help another brave sailor fight his last hard battle.

Early on the morning of Sunday, 23rd September, when the bells of St. Saviour's were pealing in Claremont, their chimes floating up the mountainside, the little grey-haired Sister with the understanding eyes took two carnations from the vase in my room and placed them in my husband's folded hands. They were from the 'Tees Lodge' plants that had once bloomed in my mother's garden.

'At peace,' she said, quietly. 'No more suffering or fighting – ever.'

It was my husband's wish and written in his will that, if possible, his ashes should be cast upon the waters from a warship of the South African Navy.

Admiral Hugo Biermann, the South African Chief of the Naval Staff, was away in London and it was Commodore Fougstedt, his Chief of Staff, who made all the arrangements for the Flagship, *Good Hope*, to do honour to the memory of a true friend of South Africa and of her young Navy. As long as I live, I shall remember the kindness and tact shown to me and to our son, Peter, by the South African Naval Officers and by Vice-Admiral Sir Nicholas Copeman, Commander-in-Chief South Atlantic and South America, who was with us on board for that last sad ceremony. There were no reporters present, but the Captains of the South African warships had asked to attend, and the *Good Hope* was escorted by an aircraft of the South African Air Force. Piet had flown from Australia twenty-four hours earlier.

October 2nd was like an English spring day, soft and silvery, all the usual brilliance of the southern sun distilled and muted and Piet drove me to Simon's Town, the little port that held so many poignant memories for me. A police motor-cycle outrider gave us a lead through the main street past the big teak gates of Admiralty House. Here we had met when I was Joy Petersen, a girl of eighteen, and Herbert Annesley Packer was the Gunnery Officer of H.M.S. *Dublin*, and here, as a full Admiral, my husband had served in his last command, flying his flag afloat as Commander-in-Chief South Atlantic. Now Admiralty House was the official residence of Rear-Admiral Biermann, and the British Naval Headquarters had been transferred to Wynberg. We followed the outrider along the familiar curving dockyard wall, past the guard at the gates and down to the berth where the frigate, *Good Hope*, was standing by to put to sea. He saluted us and sped away, stiff as a ramrod on his powerful motor-cycle.

Commodore Fougstedt received us on board. Admiral Copeman was with him and the ship sailed without delay.

It was calm, except for a light swell, and I asked if I might remain on deck. A steward brought me a chair and placed it aft, out of the wind. It was only then that I became aware of the four sailors standing guard with bowed heads, and of the naval ensign flying at half mast. I turned my face into the freshening wind and tasted the tang of it, and watched the strong live flight of the gulls. This was as it had to be – this silver sea that had brought us together, the grey mountains, and the pale sunlight on the white villages at their feet. These, like Simon's Town, were soon lost to sight, and Cape Point Lighthouse on its high rocky cliff came into view, tall, solitary, the saviour of those who go down to the sea in ships.

Somewhere beyond that lonely point the *Good Hope* reduced speed. Swaying quietly to the swell, she hove to. Our son touched my arm and I went with him to where the Padré waited by the table covered with a velvet mourning cloth. His white surplice billowed in the wind as he spoke the simple solemn words that promise life everlasting. The escorting aircraft circled overhead and dipped in salute. The roar of her engines faded and the bugler sounded 'The Last Post'. On land and sea, in home ports and distant outposts I have heard that moving call with its last lingering upward notes that echo on in the heart of the hearer long after they have died away. Thus they echoed now, vibrant and unforgettable, as the silence of the deep and the silver waters of the South Atlantic took unto themselves all that remained of our mortal lives together.

CHAPTER TWENTY-ONE

TRANSVAAL CHRISTMAS

THERE is a gap here. And darkness.

I said good night to my son that night of 2nd October and felt very sad that he must fly back to Australia the next day. I was tired beyond thought. When I closed my eyes I saw that shimmering silver sea, more English than South African. It was beautiful and wonderfully restful.

'Piet,' I said, when I woke. 'Your plane goes today.

'It went four days ago, Mom.'

That was strange. A good many things were strange. Why was he sitting here beside my bed? *And where was my bed?* This wasn't my room. There was a tremendous storm. A door banged somewhere and the wind roared in great gusts and beat against a window with skimpy curtains. Everything rocked. People came in and out – strangers. Nurses in funny little frilly caps, doctors in white coats. But I couldn't see

222

properly. They were figures in a dream. I couldn't speak very well either. My mouth was dry and a nurse gave me a drink of water through a little tube.

'Where am I?'

'Groote Schuur hospital.'

'Why?'

'You've had a sort of break-down. You've been asleep for four days.'

I went to sleep again.

A few days later Piet took me home, terribly shaky, but rested and more or less myself again. Mary and Sybil met me at the car, and it was Nellie's washing day. So she was there too. There were tears in their eyes and I felt as though I had been away for a long time on a dangerous journey. It was very good to be safely home.

The terrific storm of the past week had blown itself out. The waterfalls were foaming down the gorges, the lawn was emerald and the whole garden seemed to scintillate.

As we went into the house I caught my breath in wonder. It had never looked so welcoming. There were flowers everywhere – the formal bowls and decorative urns of the florists, masses of dark red roses, and the simple flowers Sybil had cut from our own garden and arranged in vases the way I liked them best.

My brother, Norman, and his wife, Molly, were there. A hot water bottle was in my bed and the cats came purring up to my room.

'When Piet goes Norman will come down to stay with you while I'm away at Grahamstown,' said Molly. 'I have to go up there for Lucien's half term.'

'Isn't Norman going with you? Half-term at St. Andrew's is a family occasion.'

'No, I'm driving up with another mum.'

It was the beginning of a pattern of help and friendship. It was almost as if people played their parts according to a fixed design. Yet it was not so. Even the flowers that were sent came at different times. As one lot faded another arrived to take its place. There was always some friend who found it convenient to stay with me for a few days. I was never allowed to be in an empty house or to feel alone.

Then there were the letters. They poured in from all over the world – from good friends far and near, from old shipmates of my husband, from people who had read my books and felt they knew me and who wished me well. And there was one from Sombani which touched me very much.

Dear Lady Packer,

I have noted with regret and sympathy the shocking news concerning the death of my Master the late Admiral Packer.

Although I am hundreds of miles away, my heart is there and am very much spiritual depressed.

My heart be so grieved by thinking of the greatest fatherly love which he and his family showed to me on the days of his life, I really cannot find words enough to express my sympathy and to console my Lady with.

I wish the Heavenly Father could extend his hand to the Lady and with his merciful eye look on the Lady and family and take care of them until all the days of their stay on the earth.

Wishing the Lady and family all God's protection,
Yours sincerely,
Sombani.

At first, while I was still weak and off balance, I was alarmed by the sympathetic avalanche. Then one of my friends observed my reaction, and said, with a wave of her hand at the pile of unopened envelopes on Bertie's desk, 'But these are for your comfort! Take your time over them. Nobody expects an answer by return – if at all.'

For my comfort. When she had gone I began to read them quietly and at my leisure. Every person who had taken the trouble to write had sent out a good thought – put it into words and added to its power just as each separate coal placed upon the fire increases its warmth and glow. Nell Melck, a friend in need if ever there was one, came and addressed envelopes for me.

I had a half-written book on my desk at the time and no heart to finish it. But, when it became known that I had been seriously ill, a new batch of letters began to arrive – from the librarians of hospitals, the Red Cross, libraries for the blind. They said, in effect, 'Get well, and go on writing! The sick and the lonely love your books.'

Such messages moved me deeply. They fanned renewed

life into the spark I had believed to be dead. I have always respected the power of thought – good or evil – but now, for the first time in my life, I was conscious of this great power being directed towards me, personally, from many different and unknown directions – a healing force as potent as sunshine.

Piet flew back to Australia and his family, and my friends unobtrusively took over. Nobody hustled me into making decisions. 'You'll know what to do. It will all fall into shape in its own good time. Don't be in a hurry.' Aware of the wisdom of this advice, I drifted.

I spent a fortnight's convalescence at Somerset West with Miles and Gerda Syfret, who had given us the marmalade kitten a year ago. Gerda spoilt me outrageously and so did her small daughter, Louise, who came into my room every morning, bearing Marmalade's Uncle Tim and a tiny Japanese transistor set.

'Tim will keep you company,' she would say, putting him at my feet. 'And you can listen to the news while you have your breakfast in bed.'

After chatting on a good many subjects, she'd skip off to school. She was very interested in my writing, nursing, I fancy, a few literary ambitions herself.

'When are you going to finish another book?' she'd ask.

'One day.'

'Soon?'

'Perhaps.'

Her grown-up sister, Caroline, worked in Cape Town and came home at week-ends, and then Louise was in her element. If she could learn a little about writing from me, she could learn the twist and the cha-cha-cha from Caroline.

I spent idle days in their garden above the sparkling sweep of Gordon's Bay. The roses were in full bloom backed by the breathtaking blue of jacarandas.

Gerda came of a well-known German South African family and had a number of acquaintances in Germany. One of them had sent her copies of a German Sunday paper then serializing *The Glass Barrier*. She showed them to me with keen pleasure.

'My friend says people read your books to get a human picture of South Africa.'

I laughed, recognizing the little push in the right direction. So many little pushes from so many different quarters!

My brother, Fred, and his wife, Cecil, lived nearby in a lovely valley. Their daughter, Yasmin, had come from Italy to stay with her parents, bringing her little Italian sons to meet their South African relatives. The little boys were bursting with life and Italian conversation which nobody understood, and gestures every woman very clearly understood. They endeared themselves to all females by kissing their hands, and the elder, aged five, announced one evening that he was going to marry Caroline. He climbed on to the arm of a chair to make himself tall and looked her passionately in the eye. But, alas, she was already betrothed, and her small swain received his first reverse in the Italian national game of love.

Towards the end of November I went to the Wilderness for three weeks with the friends who had given me the white cat and most of my background material for *Valley of the Vines*.

It was a lazy time, and most mornings I mooched off alone to the beach or the forest or down to the lagoon, or sat in the lovely garden of the hotel, re-reading the first half of the non-fiction book I had left unfinished so many months ago. The fact that I had brought it with me at all pleased my companions, Beryl Kiernander and Betty Frith, though they ignored it and never asked any questions about it.

I had, by then, reached the definite and difficult conclusion that I could not remain at 'Cressage', and had left instructions for the property to be sold. The wire accepting my terms reached me at the Wilderness, followed a few days later by the deed of sale for my signature. The new owners would take occupation at the end of February. I was not being hurried. As I posted the document in the little sea-side post office it seemed to me that this, like so much else, was inevitable and out of my hands.

Marjorie Gilfillan, the intimate friend and companion of my childhood, had written to suggest that I spend Christmas and New Year with her in Johannesburg.

'It won't be a social round,' she wrote. 'Noel and I go to

our farm near Dullstroom right after Christmas. We do some trout fishing and relax. It's right away from everywhere. Just the place for somebody who wants to write. Stay as long as you like.'

When I received her letter I believed that I would never want to write again. Yet, when the time came for me to pack my well-worn air-travel suitcase, I was not so sure. I put in the half-finished non-fiction book called *Home from Sea* and a couple of scribble books. After all, one never knew.

A few days before Christmas I flew north.

When we were airborne the hostess came round with English and Afrikaans magazines. I took a picture paper but it lay unopened on my lap with the Cape Argus which I had brought at D. F. Malan Airport.

Below us spread Somerset West between its peaks and the sea.

They'd be preparing for Christmas down there – Gerda and Caroline trying to keep Christmas gifts hidden from Louise, who had as many eyes as a spider when it came to seeking out Christmas secrets. Cecil and Yasmin would be filling stockings for little Bastiano and Sebastian, and my brother, Fred, would be hunting out his Santa Claus disguise.

In the location cottages on the historic farm of Vergelegen the Coloured children would be all excitement because every year they knew they could expect presents, sweets and paper hats from the generous chatelaine of the old homestead under famous giant camphor trees brought from the Dutch East Indies some three hundred years ago.

The mountains of Stellenbosch and Worcester drew near and the two Pearl Rocks on the summit of Paarl Mountain were rosy in the evening glow. The westering sun still bathed the sleepy Paarl Valley with its vineyards and orchards just about to yield their summer harvest – a scene of plenty. Yet here the peace and goodwill of the Christmas season had been sadly marred, for the little town was the centre of a grim inquiry into the recent cold-blooded killings followed by riots, mob violence and the senseless slaughter of Europeans. The murders were the work of the terrorist organization, Poqo, which aims to 'eliminate all Whites and take over the country by 1963'. Its methods are violence, death and sabotage, its membership is forcibly increased by intimidation, and the members are branded on the forehead and submitted to oath-taking rituals. Those selected for the privilege of killing Whites are specially treated by Poqo witch-doctors.

And already 1962 was on its way out and soon 1963 would be knocking on the door!

The Karoo was bathed in pink light reflected in the mirrors of willow-fringed dams near lonely farm-houses, and then we were flying over the modern garden-towns of the new Free State goldfields, where White and Black work together, each gleaning something of the other's magic.

Within the hour the Reef towns of the Witwatersrand were scattered on the high veld like handfuls of glittering gems, one rich cluster linked to the next by the bright ribbons of well-lighted highways, and just on nine o'clock the richest of them all sprawled in profligate splendour beneath the dwarf Alps of the mine-dumps. What a vast vital golden city Johannesburg is! Its skyscrapers soar upwards while its modern parking-garages probe into earth already excavated by the mines. The heights and the depths are there, whatever way you look at it.

Noel and Marjorie Gilfillan drove me though the warm night to their home on the northern outskirts of the city. Only ten years ago it had been a modest farm 'out in the bundu', now it was a country house with a home-farm – a fine estate of many morgen still in the quiet of the country but with a spreading residential area lapping round its ankles.

As Noel drew up under the trees in front of the house the two Labradors, golden Gunner and black Humphrey, bounded to meet us. Gunner, Noel's dog, was young and muscular, while Marjorie's adoring Humphrey was old and stiff with rheumatism, but active in spite of his disabilities. The night-watchman, a wrinkled Zulu, followed them sedately with his lantern and his *kierie* (staff). The dogs and the old man were responsible for the safety of the house during the hours of darkness.

When Marjorie took me up to my room she opened the curtains so that we looked across the starlit swimming-pool and lawn to a profusion of roses in full bloom. Below them a long sweep of grassland fell away into the distance to meet a wooded ridge where the lights of houses shone through a crest of trees.

'Here, in the Transvaal, trees, like dogs, mean houses and people,' I said.

Marjorie smiled. 'We buy a piece of veld and at once plant trees. It's quite a thought that every tree in Johannesburg has been planted at some time during the past seventy years.'

It is indeed, for Johannesburg is a city of gardens and beautiful homes, of lights and motor-cars, enterprise and industry, of warmhearted generous people, of fantastic fortunes and dire want. It is the most stimulating city in Africa – perhaps in the whole world. It invites and absorbs new ideas and cherishes culture. The theatre, so sadly moribund in Cape Town, flourishes in Johannesburg, which is always a ready patron of art, music and the ballet. Its night-life is exciting and glamorous, while that of my own dear homeport is virtually non-existent.

Cities, like people, have their own personalities. Cape Town lives dreamily in the past and greets the stranger warily. Johannesburg is immediate and intense. It lives for the day and the morrow. The past is soon forgotten, the future is enigmatic and the present is all important. Its economy reflects its resilient temperament and its enthusiasm is redolent of youth. Sometimes, in the comparative stillness of the city's night, there are subterranean tremors and rumbles, as if the honeycombed gold-bearing earth issues a warning. 'Enjoy yourselves! It's later than you know!'

The shopping centres of the outlying districts are superb. If you can find a parking place before Christmas there is nothing you cannot buy. The stores were packed with eager shoppers, the women in fresh printed cotton dresses, no stockings, and an air of casual cheerful smartness. Everybody seemed to know everybody else and Marjorie's shopping activities were punctuated by exchanges of the season's greetings with the assistants in the stores and friends bustling in and out.

At home the all-important farmyard preparations were many. Turkeys, geese, and ducks were being killed and plucked and sent up to the kitchen where old Johannes, who had been with the Gilfillan family since their marriage, cooked them to perfection.

A thunder-storm the night before had cooled the air and Christmas Day was fresh and sunny with a light breeze ruffling the tall jacarandas that a month earlier had been a leafless dream of blue-mauve blossom standing in blue pools of fallen petals.

When I woke I could hear Bantu recruited from the farm, putting chairs on the lawn and a white fence round the pool, so that no little children could fall in before their parents were ready to take them swimming.

The first home celebration of the day took place after the early church service. All the Bantu, who worked in the house or on the farm, assembled on the terrace to receive Christmas gifts for themselves and their families. They showed their appreciation with dignified formality and a Zulu song of praise for a good master – symbolic, I thought, of this last feudal bastion of gracious living, already more deeply undermined than was visible on the surface.

Not long afterwards, the Gilfillan sons and their wives and children arrived, followed by friends and other relations, and when lunch-time came we were twenty strong, including seven small people under eight. The next arrivals were rather startling. A barbaric troupe in furs and feathers unexpectedly appeared on the lawn and performed war-dances, grotesquely painted faces intent and concentrated, horny feet stamping. The Labradors barked furiously and leapt forward to attack the Bantu, but Noel called them off and shut them away before any harm could be done. Midsummer and a war-dance instead of snow and carol-singers! That was South Africa.

Except for the plum-pudding in all its glory of holly sprigs and burning brandy, the Christmas dinner was cold and fully worthy of the French champagne in which we toasted our host and hostess and the health of the new baby grandson born, like his grandfather, in Christmas week.

Afterwards, replete and relaxed, we lounged in the shade round the pool and watched the little ones playing with their new toys under the supervision of an English nanny. Later guests who felt inclined swam in the clear lido-blue water with the children.

Evening fell: the last young families had taken their departure; the torn gaudy wrappings of Christmas parcels had been cleared from the lawn, and the house returned to a semblance of its normal self. Now it was the Bantu's turn. Down at the farm a sheep had been roasted and the beer waited. Everybody was free to join the feast.

Marjorie, Noel and I got our own light supper. When we turned in, content that the day had been blessed by good will and affection, we heard the echoes of song and dance float up the rise from the farm.

I went out on to the balcony adjoining my room. The pool gleamed in the starlight, and the far horizon was veined from time to time with summer lighting.

I wondered if the night-watchman was on duty with the dogs tonight. He had been upset yesterday, complaining of pains because an enemy had laid a spell on him. He had refused European medicine, saying only the witch-doctor could give him *muti* against the spell. Ours is a strange primitive land in which we all interpret the miracles and mysteries of our various beliefs in our own way and according to our lights and our stage of evolution.

I stayed out there in the mild summer night and let memories of other Christmas nights down the happy years float through my mind.

Malta, bright and cold, carillons of church-bells ashore and hymns rising from the decks of warships in the long creeks – my husband a young officer, our son a baby. Portsmouth and Plymouth; the China Station; Athens and the midnight Mass – my husband a Captain, our son a schoolboy. War. The years of separation and fear, Christmas in the blitz and a strange truce to the bombing – my husband in Scapa Flow, Piet at 'Tees Lodge' eagerly waiting to be seventeen and in the war. And, after the war, Simon's Town with all my own folk round me, and the Navy too – my husband Commander-in-Chief, our son a surgeon, already a husband and a father. Then retirement – so short a spell! Christmas at 'Cressage', children on the lawn, shining paper tatters blowing along the terrace as small deft hands launched toy aeroplanes and flimsy kites. It all seemed long ago. Only the memories left. But how good they were!

The roses of the highveld glimmered in the summer night. In Western Australia, they tell me, the roses are the finest ever, bushes fifteen feet high and fabulous blooms.

There, too, it would be summer.

CHAPTER TWENTY-TWO

GREEN HILLS OF HEALING

MARJORIE had said that the farm near Dullstroom was 'away from everywhere. Just the place for somebody who wants to write'.

It was exactly that.

A simple red-roofed house with a high stoep looked across a soft swelling landscape of green hills and vales threaded by the dark winding ribbon of the Dullstroom with its weirs and waterfalls, its lakes and willows. The house — the 'Cabin', they called it — was flanked by pine forests, a grove of acacias, and peach, pear and plum orchards. An avenue of young chestnuts led up to it and a fence of climbing roses enclosed a pretty garden.

Trout fishing was, of course, the main object of the holiday and, on the left of the 'Cabin' door, is a wooden plaque with a fisherman's philosophy burnt into the wood: 'Allah does not deduct from the allotted span of man those hours spent in fishing.' But, as I do not fish, it was for me just a tranquil period of reflection and readjustment. Marjorie's sister, Phillis, and her husband, Cecil Payne, and Bert Evans, completed our party. We each did exactly as we liked. We were sociable but independent. We'd meet for elevenses on the stoep most mornings, the men in waders, jerseys and peaked caps with the sun-flaps to protect the backs of their necks, and Marjorie and her sister with half-Wellingtons over their slacks and rain-proof jackets.

The high escarpment is 6,500 feet above sea level, only a thousand feet higher than Johannesburg, but it has its own climate. It is always cool and fresh and it often rains at night. Sometimes it is stricken by thunder and lightning and the fierce summer hailstorms of the mountains and the high-veld.

I had never been in trout fishing company before, and the fragile rods and delicately fashioned flies enthralled me. Each fly was a work of art, the tiny feathers of birds lending them their flash of colour. Even their names were exciting. Silver Doctor, blue and red; Pink Lady, intricate and tiny; Mallard and Olive, a lovely green; Teal and Yellow, or the speckled red one they most often used – the only one with a horrid name – Walker's Killer. A row-boat took up a good deal of space on the stoep. Noel – an expert carpenter – was fitting it with a swivel-chair, which he had made himself. Presently he would take it down to the lake in the truck.

From the stoep we looked across the valley and the stream to the koppie beyond. Clumps of trees marked the fishing syndicate cottages or an occasional farm. Women with babies strapped to their backs tended the mealie and vegetable crops, the infants lulled by the rock-'n'-roll rhythm of their mothers rising and stooping at their work. Merino sheep grazed on the far slopes. They had recently been shorn and the lambs skipped beside the ewes. It was the season of baby things, the beginning of a new life cycle. Birds, usually in flocks, were pairing off for nest building. Guinea-fowl and red partridges multiplied despite the field-harriers flying low in search of their prey. Clouds of destructive little kwelas rose from the mealie patches, the Piet-m'-vrou uttered his shrill three syllables and kept hidden in the trees, as a cuckoo should. A pair of swallows flew in and out of their nest in the corner of the stoep, regardless of the humans gathered there. For three years running the little couple had come to the corner shelf Noel had placed for them, and raised their chicks before flying off again to some other summer in some other far-off land. A green malachite sunbird, slender and elegant with burnished plumage and a long sharp tail, hovered over the red and yellow cannas. A pair of herons haunted the marshy ground near the stream, and one evening at dusk we were thrilled to see ten European storks. Seven of them were just settling for the night on a dead tree in the valley, and, through Noel's glasses we could see them flap their huge black and white wings as they made themselves comfortable, moving from one bough to another. That tree became their roosting place. Noel and Marjorie knew all the birds and pointed them out to me as if introducing old friends. We were wonderfully 'away from it all'. No newspapers, no letter, no telephone, not even electricity.

Sometimes, if the fishermen were going far afield, I went with them. At others, I took my scribble-book and wandered down one of the veld paths to the stream or the lake. The lake was a favourite fishing place. I enjoyed sitting under a willow to watch one or another of our party play a fish, land it safely in the net, tap it over the head with the metal 'priest' which 'administers the last rites', disengage the hook and weigh the catch. Two and a half to three pounds was common, and what a good lunch that made! The smaller fish were smoked.

The coots always amused me. Suddenly they'd thrash forward on the lake, faster and faster, breasts in air, wings flailing, as if for a take-off which never quite materialized. Or I'd look up to see an Egyptian goose in flight against a sunlit sky laden with fluffy clouds. A colony of cormorants on a rock competed with the fishermen, and weaver-birds contrived their cunning nests in willow branches over-hanging the water, the entrances underneath, safe from snakes greedy for eggs. For this Eden has its snakes.

One morning, while we were at the lake, we suddenly heard a commotion and saw Johannes, the young Bantu who always came with us, hopping about and calling out. 'Slang! 'n slang!'

'He's seen a snake!'

Noel rushed forward with an oar which happened to be lying on the grass, and, sure enough, a slender shining snake was gliding into a clump of grass. Noel, who believed in taking no chances where snakes were concerned, killed it with two well aimed blows, one to break its back and the other to crush its head.

It was only then that Johannes, who had joined eagerly in the chase, sank on to the grass, clinging to his bare foot as he admitted with shame-faced chagrin that 'die slang het my gebyt'. We crowded round him and saw to our horror that he had indeed been bitten. The longish punctures marked the spot about four inches above his heel. In a flash Marjorie had run back to our camp under the willow to fetch her first-aid snake-bite kit. Noel took it from her, bound the tour-niquet quickly round the boy's leg below the knee and drew it tight. Then he made sharp incisions over the punctures, and, when they bled freely, rubbed permanganate into the wound. Johannes flinched and grimaced. 'Ooh, baas!' But he accepted the severity of the operation as a matter of course, and, within minutes, he had been bundled into the back of the truck with the dead snake to be taken to the doctor at Dullstroom village, a few miles away. He registered a few objections. 'It isn't necessary, my baas, you've done what's needed. This is a vlei-snake. He won't make me die.'

'The doctor will decide that,' said Noel firmly.

We watched the truck disappear over the rise. Bert Evans looked at the sky and grinned.

'Three vultures up there!'

The big birds planed round in a circle.

Marjorie laughed. 'Johannes isn't as bad as all that!'

'After Noel's treatment anything can happen. Poor fellow!'

A small flock of hadedas rose from the water's edge with raucous mocking laugher, 'Aha-ha-ha! Ah-ha-ha!' The coots hooted softly, and the weavers among the willow nests squealed noisily in their interminable arguments with intractable mates.

The doctor, unable to identify the snake as harmless, gave Johannes an injection for safety, and by next day the young Bantu had recovered and was back with the fishermen. But had it been the cobra Noel killed a few days later, the story might have had a different ending.

Two other couples, the Trews and le Mees – members of the fishing syndicate – drove over for New Year's Eve dinner, at which the first course was, of course, delicious trout caught the same day.

Tony Trew was then under ordeal by ragging, for he had staggered his friends – and his wife – by suddenly proving himself to be something of a phenomenon. At the ripe age of fifty-five he had written his first novel, *Two Hours to Darkness*, which, though not yet on the book-stalls, was already an international best seller. Trew, the Secretary-General of the Automobile Association of South Africa, had been in the Royal Navy during the war, and had served in a destroyer in the Russian convoys. His own experiences, combined with a factual approach to a thrilling fictional situation, just a step ahead of the immediate present, had combined to create a novel of realistic suspense.

How he turned into an author was a source of amusement to his acquaintances. It was his habit to go to bed early, sleep soundly till two or three in the morning, when he would wake unable to sleep another wink. He consulted a doctor about this tiresome insomnia and was told not to turn in before eleven.

'But I'll never be able to keep my eyes open till eleven,' complained Trew. 'I can read the most exciting book, but I still fall asleep over it.'

'Then write one!' advised the doctor, shortly, 'and see if that keeps you awake!'

So he did. And it did. The result? *Two Hours to Darkness*, the story of a Polaris submarine with a deranged commander. Will he or won't he press the button that could set off World War III? Tony did not merely use his imagination. He acquired and studied every scientific magazine he could lay hands on. One of them – an American paper – described a devastating device that could make an end of the world. The paper in question was later withdrawn from circulation as revealing too much. But, as far as *Two Hours to Darkness* was concerned, it was too late. The device was already installed in the Trew submarine, and the ship was under way.

Tony Trew is slight and white haired, with young alert eyes and a crisp dry brand of humour. He had already completed his second novel and was using his holiday to polish it. Naturally, the polishing was not allowed to interfere with the fishing. He and Basil le Mee kept the rest of the party in gales of laughter. Like Bob Hope and Bing Crosby, they have a hilarious patter of bogus enmity which every now and again gets out of hand, and then their friends are called in to keep the peace.

'I'm dying to retire,' Tony told me, 'so that I can write in the mornings. I can't imagine a better time for writing, can you?'

'It's the best time,' I answered. 'But you'll have to train your wife to insulate you from all interruptions while you write.'

His wife groaned and fidgeted as he said, 'She's the chief interruption herself. That's why I write while she's asleep.'

She uttered another moan and looked at him as if, after many comfortable years, she had discovered an entirely new husband and couldn't quite fathom the metamorphosis. Marriage with a successful novelist was an experience for which she was – with difficulty – preparing herself. Her New Year resolutions must have been interesting and perhaps a little confused.

'What are you writing at present?' he asked me.

'I was more than half way through a book, but I stopped writing it some time ago. I doubt if it'll get much further.'

'You'll go on with it. An author can usually say of his own book, "I couldn't put it down". Writing is an addiction, I find. Once you start you go on, for better for worse.'

There spoke the true author. I wondered how many novels he had flung into the waste-basket before he was 'discovered'.

That night, in the 'Cabin' on the escarpment, talking to a fellow writer about our craft, I felt the long-forgotten urge to tell a tale stir in me once more. Only a few months earlier I had believed that I would never write again. Then one day, just before flying to the Transvaal. I happened to be going through certain papers in my husband's desk when I came across a blue exercise book which he had marked 'Day Book and Commonplace Book' and in which he had written down disconnected thoughts and quotations that had evidently appealed to him. One sprang out at me.

Quote 11. Sir Francis Drake to Sir Francis Walsingham. After Cadiz. 17th May 1587.
'There must be a beginning to any great matter, but the continuing of the same unto the end until it be thoroughly finished yields the true glory.'

For months an unfinished manuscript had been lying on my desk untouched. I had had no heart to work on it. It was not a 'great matter' but it was an undertaking, and the words my husband had written in his angular hand, so full of character and so short of flourishes, seemed to me like an intentional message, not to be ignored. Thus, at the last minute, the scribble-book had been pushed into the suitcase. And now every day I found myself filling more pages with notes and even with a few consecutive attempts at 'the continuing of the same'. In fact, during the past three mornings I had repaired to the solitude of the pine wood behind the Cabin', there to sit alone with pen and paper and yield to the literary addiction, feeling the magic of words making pictures and pictures unfolding in their natural sequence. I think very visually, and that New Year's Eve the screen of my mind suddenly reflected the little stone sundial in Marjorie's rose-garden, and the words round it, 'I count the bright hours only'. A nice New Year resolution! I must learn to count my bright hours only as my mother had always deliberately counted her many blessings and as Nannie, in her small room, re-lived the happy days of her German youth. I was so very rich in bright hours – some almost blinding in their radiance, others quietly satisfying.

Only this afternoon I had gone out and gathered grasses and wild flowers and put them in a vase for the 'Cabin', marvelling at their variety, each one a thing of beauty in itself. Noticing their perfection, I had felt again a piercing pleasure in the small wonders of nature. It had warmed and quickened in me as it did when I watched the swallows dart in under the ceiling of the 'Cabin' stoep to feed their young. They were confident that we were friends and they took no notice of us as they went about their domestic duties. They came alternately with their offerings, first Pa, then Ma, and it seemed to us that each journey found the hungry gaping beaks stretching higher out of the nest, noisier and more insistent. Delight had touched me too in the powerful flight of the storks and the way they settled in the dead tree at sunset – the seven of them – like immense white flowers blooming there, lending the blighted wood the winged splendour of renewed life between dusk and dawn.

There, on the green heights, with friends who understood me and let me be, I gradually began to live again and to steel myself against the ordeal ahead – the final parting with the home we had built so hopefully less than ten years ago. Our first and our last. The ship's bell and the tread-plate of H.M.S. *Warspite* would already be gone by the time I returned, for it had been arranged that these should be removed during my absence. They were, of course, the heritage of our son and of his eldest son who hoped to go to sea one day, like his grandfather.

At midnight Cecil Payne turned on his transistor set.

A peal of bells announced the birth of another year. Noel charged our glasses and we drank to the future. What did it hold – for ourselves, for our country, for all the troubled world? The ten of us clasped hands and we sang Auld Lang

Syne. Glass touched glass, lip touched lip as we wished each other happiness and good fortune, and a moment I had needlessly and greatly dreaded went its way into oblivion.

The sky was overcast and the moon obscured when the guests took their leave, but recent rain had freshened the keen night air and my own mood was deeply attuned to the pastoral peace of this world apart.

Long after the 'Cabin' was in darkness I stood at my window, a prey to haunting memories of the year that was gone and with little interest in the one that lay ahead. It seemed strange that the saddest period in all my life should measure less than the value of one small heartbeat in the waste of eternity. How brief is our human trek through the wilderness of mortal life before we return to the infinite to be, for a spell, one with the past and the future! I closed my eyes to receive a vision of infinity. The void was filled with light – shafts of light and dancing motes, one mote seeking another as 'deep calleth unto deep at the noise of Thy waterspouts: all Thy waves and billows are gone over me.'

Here, in the pure grass-scented night of the empty uplands, mankind seemed no more important than any other living thing. The beasts of the field and the birds of the air mated and bred as he did. They, too, cared for their young, knew pain and fear, death and a sort of mourning. But they asked no questions and made no comments. They accepted their place in the divine scheme, and, guided by timeless instincts, strove only for survival. Tiny birds set out upon their great migrations, unafraid, returning year after year to nest in familiar places and hatch new fledglings to follow in their course. The lambs and calves on the hillside pastures, the pale baby buck up on the koppie, the butterflies hovering over the carmine and yellow cannas, and the fingerlings in the stream were all part of the mighty life cycle which finds its highest and most sacrificial form in the love of a man for his mate and a mother for her child. Or is there a higher love to which we mortals may attain – a love embracing all lesser loves? The majesty of that thought was as vast and remote as the night sky in which the stars now shone.

At dawn I was awakened by those early risers, the hadedas. Their mocking calls passed overhead, harsh and tuneless. What did they care that today was 1st January? They knew nothing of man-made dates and hours. They knew only the weather and the seasons, the day and the night.

The first sunrise of the new year slashed the clouds and poured its golden glory over the escarpment. I looked out at the green healing hills and the dark stream winding between its willows and its vleis where the rushes quiver with little scarlet finches. Wild arums, agapanthus and exotic lilies hugged its banks and the dry bell grasses chimed lightly in the breeze. Already the sheep and cattle were grazing in dewy pastures, the white egrets with them.

The dead tree, leafless and solitary, was etched starkly against the verdant slope. The storks had left their perches of the night and a pair, separating from the flock, winged overhead in the early morning sky. But I knew that the tree had not really lost them yet. They would be back this evening, in the soft bloom of twilight, to bless its barren boughs with life.

Cape of Good Hope, 1963